Longing and Belonging

Longing and Belonging

Parents, Children,
and Consumer Culture

Allison J. Pugh

UNIVERSITY OF CALIFORNIA PRESS

Berkeley   Los Angeles   London

University of California Press, one of the most distinguished university presses in the United States, enriches lives around the world by advancing scholarship in the humanities, social sciences, and natural sciences. Its activities are supported by the UC Press Foundation and by philanthropic contributions from individuals and institutions. For more information, visit www.ucpress.edu.

University of California Press
Berkeley and Los Angeles, California

University of California Press, Ltd.
London, England

Library of Congress Cataloging-in-Publication Data

Pugh, Allison J.
    Longing and belonging : parents, children, and consumer culture / Allison J. Pugh.
        p.   cm.
    Includes bibliographical references and index.
    ISBN 978-0-520-25843-3 (cloth : alk. paper)
    ISBN 978-0-520-25844-0 (pbk. : alk. paper)
    1. Consumer behavior—Social aspects—California—Case studies.   2. Consumption (Economics)—Social aspects—California—Case studies.   3. Child consumers—California—Case studies.   4. Parent and child—California—Case studies.   I. Title.
    HF5415.33.U6C23   2009
    306.309794—dc22   2008037216

Manufactured in the United States of America

17 16 15 14 13 12 11 10
10 9 8 7 6 5 4 3

This book is printed on Natures Book, which contains 50% post-consumer waste and meets the minimum requirements of ANSI/NISO Z39.48–1992 (R 1997) (*Permanence of Paper*).

For Roger Pugh, who always knew I would write
For Joanne Pugh, who taught me how
For Steve, who made it possible

CONTENTS

PREFACE

Ask them straight out, and most upper-income parents will tell you they do not buy much for their children, because they have the "right values." Meanwhile, low-income parents will try to convince you they buy quite a bit, because they are not "in trouble." Go into their children's bedrooms, however, and you will find many of the same objects—the Nintendo or Sony gaming system, the collectible cards, the Hello Kitty pencils.

We are living through a spending boom that is unprecedented, and which is exacting a great price. Childhoods have become ever more commercialized, with hundreds of billions of dollars annually being spent on or by children in the United States alone. In one recent survey, families with children were twice as likely as those without children to report that they did not have enough money to cover their expenses, to worry about whether or not their income was adequate, and to be anxious about the extent of their consumer debt. Parents with income constraints struggle to provide an ever-expanding list of goods that compete with rent, food, clothing, and other basics of life. Families are also concerned that their children have good priorities, that they understand what matters most; to be able to buy more for their children, parents sacrifice things they nonetheless fear might be more important. We might say that the expanding children's market brings with it what feels like a spiritual calamity for affluent families and a financial one for families of lesser means.[1]

What does buying mean to children, and to their parents? Why does buying for children seem to generate so much anxiety and concern? If consumer culture is the "enemy" of good parenting, why do so many parents invite the enemy into their homes?

I started the research that led to this book because questions like these at times defined my daily life, as they do for many parents. With three young children, I found myself continually struggling to find the way toward a more meaningful path, strewn with memories rather than objects. I was surprised that despite the intense cultural scripts surrounding many childhood rituals, families essentially had to invent their own versions of Christmas, Halloween, the Tooth Fairy, allowances, birthdays—each time adopting a particular stance toward the consumer culture that was banging on the door, peering in the windows, and sometimes climbing down the chimney to get in. But even if parents settled on a particular configuration—"one coin under the pillow, but let it be a Sacagawea dollar," say, or "a cheap, slapdash costume, but all-you-can-eat candy for three days"—that felt somehow right within the family, the negotiation was not over. Children, acting in their natural capacity as community journalists, always knew others who did more, who had more, who had the newest or the latest or the best, and then there was consumer culture again, forcing parents to draw a line, to define themselves and their families, to come up with something that was who they were in response to the constant onslaught.

Many parents regard the commercialization of childhood with concern even as they participate in it. Survey researchers report that nearly nine in ten Americans feel that "children today want too many material things," and four out of five parents think America's overly materialistic society produces "over-commercialized children." "All the kids have [gaming systems]. All the parents break like I did," one affluent father told me, his half grin taking back just some of the violence in the word "break," with its connotations of domination, relentless pressure, duress.

"We are roped by these kids, wanting to do something for your kids. Toys are just the worst. It's . . . it's just a waste."[2]

Why do parents engage in the very behavior that they say they deplore? The most common explanations for rampant consumption for children—what we might call "child-rearing consumption"—suggest that children desire, and parents buy, because neither group can help itself, either because of the insidious power of corporate marketing or the heady thrall of instant gratification. In my own experience, in the process of establishing just what we were going to purchase, repeated almost daily and reemphasized by the rituals and holidays punctuating the year, advertising was certainly present, and some materialism, even greed, to be sure. Missing in these popular explanations, however, seemed to be some measure of the social world in which children and their families travel, in which some (but not all) goods and experiences come alive with very particular, local meanings, in which family decisions acquire new emotional salience, and in which children take collective measure of their childhoods.

Let me be clear here. I am *not* arguing that advertising is unimportant in stoking the fires of consumption. Indeed, research on the impact of advertising is crucial, because, like Dorothy in the Land of Oz, such research pulls back the curtain to reveal the corporate sales agenda behind the dazzle of children's media. One very real danger of focusing instead on the social contexts in which things get their meaning for children is that such a project might deflect attention from corporate actors, tactics, and ethics. At worst, such research can reinforce common perceptions of overconsumption as stemming solely from personal choices, or even from individual vice, as opposed to the billions of dollars annually invested in selling things to children. Yet while advertising is undoubtedly a powerful factor in animating children's desires and parents' buying practices, it is surely not the whole of how we come to want things.

Two premises underlie this work, then. The first is that most parents are neither dupes nor hedonists, but rather well-intentioned people trying their best to make do, including to bring up their children to be reasonably healthy, happy adults. The second is that advertising is ubiquitous, and corporate marketing targets children and parents; this book thus assumes a media-rich environment and asks, then what? If we seek to understand the explosion of spending for children, the spread of what we might call the "commodity arms race" in elementary schools far and wide, we would do well to look beyond advertising. We need to focus on how children come to view some things as must-haves and some experiences as must-dos, and how parents respond to these imperatives. After advertising has laid out the menu, how do children's social worlds shape the buying patterns of affluent and low-income families? How is it that Marine World or the Star Wars movies can evoke immediate, intense emotion, and how do Game Boys and Bratz dolls acquire personal, local meanings? What is the impact of such feelings on children's lives?

Some of my questions are contentious ones, ventured in an environment in which practically everyone has an opinion. Low-income buying in particular seems to be a fulcrum of controversy, because privacy of spending is a luxury we grant—and even then begrudgingly—only to the more affluent. Thus before this book even came into print, one reader took issue with the idea that low-income children have consumer desires that they and their parents interpret as psychological needs and go to great lengths to meet. Most low-income parents in the inner-city are concerned simply with their children's safety in a dire environment, this reader argued, writing: "[What children need] in such cases [is] simply not to be shot."

While others may share this view (which is why I raise it here), I could not disagree more (while I am certainly grateful to the reader for articulating it). This book offers evidence to refute the (middle-class) assumption that psychological needs are a luxury the poor cannot afford for their children, by pointing to the moments when they are prioritizing exactly that. We may be full of sympathy for the beleaguered low-income parent plagued by very real urban violence, but we should not also assume that the only or even the best thing low-income families living in dangerous neighborhoods offer their children is survival. The parents in my study—including even those living next to crack houses, yelling at the "perverts watching [their daughters] jump rope"—aspired to something more. For all its sympathy, this assertion—"[poor children just need] not to be shot"—is the flip side of the outrage one white middle-class woman confessed that she felt one day standing behind a family buying expensive prepared foods with their food stamps, exclaiming to me later, "*I* can't even afford that stuff, how can they?" Both views presume to know what low-income families can, or, more exactly, *should*, afford.

Embedded in all discussions of consumption is an implicit measure of what children "need" (not to be shot) versus what they merely "desire" (to hold their heads up at school). But these normative categories are notoriously slippery, and vigorously contested, part of a fusillade in the battle over defining what a child needs, the social contest about moral worth and deserving. This contest does not take place only among scholars or pundits, but also in conversations among children, as well as between children and the adult caregivers in their homes. In essence, this book plumbs those conversations for what they can tell us about how competing definitions of need—among children, between parents and children, among rich families and poor ones—shape the explosion of child-rearing consumption.

This book, then, offers an in-depth look at how children and parents interpret and use consumer culture as they are constructing childhoods. It is a book with many moving parts—children and parents, consumption and inequality, the private and the social—but one that therefore provides a broader vantage point on how the emotional meanings of goods and experiences—in a word, *culture*—twist and turn alongside the structure and shape of people's social worlds. Most important, the book examines and explains the consumption boom that shapes and defines childhood and parenthood today.

The contradictory stories parents offer—as virtuous nonconsumers or as stable providers—signal both the promise and the threat behind child-rearing spending. Children and parents invest great meaning in commodified goods and experiences. Their emotional connections are expressed and felt through the ephemera that corporations sell to them for a profit, and that some families purchase at great sacrifice. Yet the lived experience of inequality makes these connections at once more elusive and more urgent. In this book, I contend these are the real crises of child-rearing consumption.

The costs of consumption make the practices that incur them seem misguided, and the common explanations for consumption on behalf of children make those practices seem inexplicable. And yet the stakes of our misunderstanding are high. If we cannot understand how and why consumer culture permeates the lives and relationships of parents and children, then we cannot address the crises that such consumption engenders.

ACKNOWLEDGMENTS

Books like this one can sound like one long soliloquy, when really they are the product and, ideally, the progenitor of many conversations. As I scan these pages, they are not silent; rather, I can almost hear the voices of the many people who helped to make this book what it is. They stand at the margins, next to the passages that they cared about or the points they wished me to emphasize or omit, their voices rising and falling in encouragement, in argument, in advice, in entreaty. Even though I did not always heed their counsel, I am very grateful for their efforts. Our conversations shaped the contours of this book.

Arlie Hochschild has been an inspiration to me from the beginning, particularly in her ability to practice a sort of "holding sociology," the kind of caring analysis that combines clarity with its infrequent bedfellow, humanity. Barrie Thorne is all that one could hope for in a mentor, with a keen sense of justice and an ethnographer's eye for detail and nuance. Both read this book in its earliest versions, and their commitment to care helps remind me what matters most about social trends for the people who live within them.

I thank Dan Cook, Christine Williams, Diane Wolf, and two anonymous reviewers, who offered detailed and extensive commentary on the manuscript, which benefited enormously from their expertise and criticism. Naomi Schneider at the University of California Press helped to shepherd this project through and was an early believer. I also offer my particular gratitude to Marianne Cooper, who dedicated hours of reading and discussion to making this a better work.

At Berkeley, Claude Fischer, Krista Luker, Christine Carter McLaughlin, Amy Hanser, Manuel Vallée, Nancy Chodorow, Rivka Polatnick, and Sherry Ortner helped frame my thinking at crucial moments, as did Sarah Corse, Milton Vickerman, Jeff Olick, Josipa Roksa, Liz Arkush, Gwen Ottinger, and Denise Walsh at Virginia. Debbie Lewites was an effective, helpful, and opinionated transcriber. Timely and supremely capable research assistance was provided by Jennifer Silva, a young scholar of great gifts at Virginia.

Special thanks go to the families who allowed me into their lives, to come to their birthday parties, to sit in their living rooms, to witness their joy, pain, and striving. I owe them a great debt. I also appreciate the teachers and staff at the schools where I observed, at Arrowhead Academy, Oceanview, and most particularly at Sojourner Truth, for their informed guidance and their dedication to the lives of the children in their care. This project would not have been possible without their participation, and I hope they consider the work that came out of it—even if they do not agree with every word—respectful of their lives and their struggles.

This book was written with the help of a grant from the Alfred P. Sloan Foundation's Workplace, Work Force and Working Families program, for which I am grateful. In addition, this material is based upon work supported by the National Science Foundation under Grant No. 0221499, which helped to provide stipends to families who participated, as well as by the Center for Working Families and the Institute for the Study of Social Change at the University of California, Berkeley. The latter institutions also provided important communities of scholars who heard early versions of my ideas and provided helpful commentary and support, from which this work has benefited.

I want to thank Beth Lorey and Tina Verba for their unwavering support, the kind that you can speed-dial, which has sustained me all these years. Thanks to Taryn and Ray LaRaja, and Barbara and Ethan Canin for such advice, meals, and succor as only fictive kin can give. I am grateful to my family, particularly to Roger and Joanne Pugh, who have been patiently waiting for this moment—cheering each milestone, reading drafts, calling up to kvetch and kvell—with an abiding faithfulness. I hope that Sophie, Lucy, and Hallie come to understand how much each of them contributed to the making of this book, as guide, catalyst, and inspiration. To them, and especially to Steve, thank you for everything.

CHAPTER ONE

Care and Belonging in the Market

It is a few days before Halloween at the Sojourner Truth after-school center in Oakland, California, and I am sitting with some children at a table where they are supposed to be doing their homework. Instead, the children, all of them from low-income families and who attend this center for free or almost no cost, are talking about the upcoming holiday. Aleta, an African-American third grader, is holding forth about her costume.[1]

"I'm going to be a vampire," she announces, gleefully, almost cackling. Already she has the outfit: the teeth, the cape, the shoes. Her mom bought it at Target, she says offhandedly, tossing her head and making the beads in her hair rattle. Simon and Marco, two recent immigrant children about seven years old, are listening closely without smiling, eyeing her like dancers memorizing an audition routine, and occasionally filling in their homework sheets. Thinking to include them in Aleta's fantastic reverie, I ask them what they will be for Halloween, but they find the question difficult.

"I'm not going to be anything," Simon, a recent African immigrant, says flatly, his eyebrows arched high in a disdain he appears to be trying on for size. "I only care about the candy."

Marco, who arrived from Mexico last year, agrees, but then he pauses. "I'm just going to go as me," he says, with a studied casualness.

"The humans were the scariest part of [the horror movie] *Dawn of the Dead.*"

Neither Simon's nor Marco's parents had been in the country more than two years; later, Simon's proud mother tells me Halloween is as meaningless to them as the Tooth Fairy. To Simon's parents, refugees who have been working three jobs to save for a home, a Halloween costume is the height of frivolity, a potent symbol of the children's peer culture to which they, with the bemused confidence born of certainty, turn a deaf ear.

But later on that same day at Sojourner Truth, when another classmate comes up to the table and asks the same question, Simon is prepared, ready to manage the commercial demands of the peer culture in which he has found himself. "I am going as me," I overhear him saying, his high, clear voice piercing the din of children's voices as they get ready for snack. "The humans were the scary ones in *Dawn of the Dead.*"

A few days later, on a quiet, leafy street whose elegant homes seem farther away than the short, seven-minute drive from Sojourner Truth, Judy Berger put her elbows on her teak dining table and sighed when I asked her whether she had ever regretted buying anything for her eight-year-old son Max. A quiet and reflective woman, Judy was nonetheless clearly pained when she described how the popular electronic handheld Game Boy had affected her family's life. They finally bought Max the gaming system for his birthday, after two years of his intense lobbying, in which he pointed out that all of his friends had them, and that "that is what they do for fun, [and] that is what they talk about over lunch and stuff like that," Judy said. The fight had gone on so long he had given up hope that they would buy him one, contenting himself with a magazine featuring Game Boy lore, which he pored over again and again, acquiring a certain Game Boy fluency if not possession. Judy laughed wryly about his absorption, saying, "At least he had something to do on the plane to Australia." When he actually unwrapped the Game Boy on his birthday, Judy recalled, "I have to say I don't think that I have ever seen him so happy before or after that."

But the good feeling didn't last. "It really strained our relationship," she said. "Max was doing it [playing games] every day, every single morning before school we were really fighting about turning it off, and how important—you know, what is more important, finishing this level or going to school on time?" She grimaced at the memory. "So now one of the rules we have is that when it is time to go to school or time to go to violin lesson or camp, when we really have to leave, he just has to turn it off no matter what." After too many arguments about whether or not he could stop in the middle of a game, Judy even called the manufacturer to see if her son was right, was there no way to save his progress, did he have to keep playing until he was past a certain level, could he not just put it down when she wanted him to? When Judy talked about the Game Boy, it was as if she was talking about a teenager's alarming girlfriend, one who distracted her son from making wise choices, one who was outside her control, but also one who, because of her son's intense attachment, could not simply be turned away.

She instituted other rules to control Max's playing. He could play it in the morning only when he had his backpack on, his breakfast eaten, his teeth brushed. He could play for only a half hour a day, and they set a kitchen timer to keep track. He could not play it in the car, even though she knew other families found that convenient. "I am not buying this as a babysitter, you know," she said. "I am buying it for—because I gave in."

Thus when I asked Judy if she regretted a particular purchase, it would not have been surprising if she had named the Game Boy. But she demurred. It is not that she rued buying the Game Boy for Max, she insisted. "I guess I felt almost like it wasn't really, like I couldn't have not bought it, because now we are there in our life," she said, her normally smooth syntax turning convoluted to express her certain ambivalence, the contradictions she was straddling between her distaste for what she considered the Game Boy's addictive, violent, and sedentary properties, and her desire to make Max happy. Most important, the gaming system had so saturated the social lives of eight-year-old boys they knew that she did not think she could relegate Max to that kind of invisibility, that kind of social pathos. "It *is* kind of sad that it feels like it is a given that you will have one," she conceded. "It is too bad that that is where we are." Judy did not regret buying the Game Boy, she regretted *having* to buy it.

THE HIDDEN CRISES
OF CHILDHOOD CONSUMPTION

Commodity consumption for children has exploded, with fully $670 billion annually spent on or by children in the United States by 2004. Many moments of childhood now involve the act of buying, from daily experiences to symbolic rituals, from transportation to lunches to birthdays. As market researcher James McNeal has crowed, "precisely all those activities that we call consumer behavior are performed by millions of . . . children . . . every day in virtually every aspect of life." The U.S. government calculated that the cost of raising a child to age seventeen, adjusted for inflation, climbed by 12.8 percent from 1960 to 2000, but many experts believe even these measures are far too low: a recalculation in an article in the *Wall Street Journal* entitled "The Million-Dollar Kid" *tripled* the most recent government estimates for the richest families. The "commodity frontier" is advancing in child rearing, the sociologist Arlie Hochschild warns, as "companies . . . expand the number of market niches for goods and services covering activities that, in yesteryear, formed part of unpaid 'family life.'"[2]

Many social commentators blame consumer culture for a burgeoning crisis of childhood. Television advertising and overindulgent parents have led to epidemics of children's materialism, depression, hyperactivity, obesity, and other problems, these analysts contend. Books and editorials with titles such as "Parenting, Inc.," *Consuming Kids: The Hostile Takeover of Childhood*, and "Reclaiming Childhood" lament the commodification of children's lives, arguing that childhood in the United States and other advanced economies is in danger of being overrun by the market, with children's lives tethered to the corporate bottom line.[3]

These stories reflect real concerns about children's lives, and how parents and children are responding to new pressures and tensions embedded in the task of growing up. They usefully draw our attention to the billion-dollar industry bent on using whatever works to capture children's attention and allegiance. Yet underlying their critique of corporate capitalism is an acute discomfort with children's desire generally. Is it that children should not be consuming at all (surely next to impossible in this world), or is it rather that children want the wrong things (too adult, too tacky, or just too much), or they want them in the wrong way (too intensely)? Perhaps widespread uneasiness with the often unsubtle, uninhibited nature of children's consumer desire is distracting us from other, more fundamental, concerns: the hidden crises of consumption.[4]

I argue the question we should be asking is this: How is the commercialization of childhood shaping what it means to care, and what it means to belong? An analogy to divorce helps clarify the issue: some family scholars have argued that high divorce rates affect not just the families that break apart, but even those that stay together, through the spread of a "divorce culture" and its weakened assumptions about mutual trust and obligation. In the same way, perhaps rising consumption, by its sheer domination of childhood today, establishes a new cultural environment, with new expectations about what parents should provide, what children should have, and what having, or not having, signifies. The market suffuses childhood today, but it does not do so in the aggregate, like so much liquid poison pouring into one individual child after another, as some critics would have it. Instead, it permeates the relationships in which children are embedded. What role does the market play in these relationships? What meanings do children and parents impart to particular commodities? How does commercial culture thread its way through children's emotional connections, with peers and with parents?[5]

I investigated these questions through an ethnography of childhood consumer culture, involving observations of children at school and with their families, and interviews with parents and other caregivers. I spent three years with the children of Sojourner Truth, and six months with children in more affluent settings, a private school I call Arrowhead, and an elite public school I call Oceanview. I sat at "circle time" with the children, read to them, tied their shoes, knitted with them, threw footballs, jumped rope, and went to birthday parties and on field trips. I listened to their jokes and stories, eavesdropped on their conversations, taped their songs and games, took them shopping, to the car wash, to the library. I also listened to parents from fifty-four families, in interviews generally lasting two to four hours, sometimes over several visits. I talked to teachers and other school staff and attended neighborhood meetings, award ceremonies, fundraisers, and festivals. (Chapter 2 offers more details about the methods of this research.) Through these efforts, I immersed myself in the childhoods and parenthoods of people grappling every day with the exigencies of consuming for children, its practices and meanings. I found that the hidden crises of consumption for children lurk in the convergence of inequality, care, and the market, which enables consumer culture to saturate children's emotional connections to others.

THE ECONOMY OF DIGNITY

I argue that the key to children's consumer culture, to the explosion of parent buying and the question of what things mean to children, lies in social experiences much like the incidents described at the beginning of this chapter, the exchange about costumes and movies among Simon, Marco, and Aleta at the Sojourner Truth center, and Max's lunch-table discussions about Game Boys as recounted by his mother, Judy. I observed similar conversations among affluent and poor children alike, in private schools and public, on playgrounds, at birthday parties—wherever children gathered. Everywhere children claim, contest, and exchange among themselves the terms of their social belonging, or just what it would take to be able to participate among their peers. I came to call this system of social meanings the "economy of dignity."

The "economy of dignity" echoes a phrase coined by Arlie Hochschild, who dubbed the exchange of recognition between spouses— for gifts of time, work, or feeling—the "economy of gratitude." Couples negotiating who would do the laundry or make dinner owed or banked gratitude, depending on how their behavior measured up against their sometimes unstable bargain about who should be responsible for what. Similarly, I argue, children collect or confer dignity among themselves, according to their (shifting) consensus about what sort of objects or experiences are supposed to count for it.[6]

The dictionary defines *dignity* as "the quality or state of being worthy," but we might reasonably ask, worthy of what? I suggest that for children a vital answer is "worthy of belonging." I use "dignity" to mean the most basic sense of children's participation in their social world, what the Nobel Prize–winning economist Amartya Sen called an "absolute capability . . . to take part in the life of the community." With dignity, children are visible to their peers, and granted the aural space, the very right to speak in their own community's conversation.[7]

By focusing on dignity, I am not talking about a particularly common view of why people buy: competitive status-seeking behavior. Buyers buy, according to this tradition, in order to establish themselves as better than those to whom they compare themselves, to "gain the esteem and envy of one's fellow-men," as Veblen put it more than a hundred years ago. While inducing jealousy is certainly part of the emotional landscape of consumption, my use of "dignity" refers less to "envy" than to the "esteem" of others, the goal of joining the circle rather than one of bettering it. Through claiming that their own bodies were part of the costume, Simon and Marco were not so much seeking honor, demanding respect, or even striving for status, I argue, but rather they sought, with a measure of bravado masking their momentary desperation, to join in.[8]

Children together shape their own economies of dignity, which in turn transform particular goods and experiences into a form of scrip, tokens of value suddenly fraught with meaning. Children's lives can traverse several different economies of dignity—at school, at their after-school program, and in the neighborhood, for example—where different tokens can become salient in the peer culture resident there. And when children—even affluent ones—find themselves without what they need to join the conversation, they perform what I termed "facework" to make up for the omission.[9]

Simon and Marco, for example, knew that Halloween was the official children's holiday in American culture (and as a safely secular holiday it was one that was fully celebrated by their public school, which—not unusually—arranged for costume display, candy distribution, and parades during school time). These boys' facework was to interpret their total nonparticipation—at their young age still problematic—not as their families' choice to opt out but as a different sort of costume, an innovation on the cultural imperative of being scary that had even greater cachet by referring to a popular movie. With this discursive move, they demonstrated their cultural bilingualism, translating their own lives into what would make sense—even more, make dignity—in the social world of the after-school program.[10]

The reach of the economy of dignity does not stop at the schoolhouse door, however. Like Max Berger and his fight for the Game Boy, children bring their consumer emergencies home to their parents, who largely control what their children have and how much it matches what they need. What makes some parents more or less attuned to their children's social milieu and the role particular objects or experiences play in it? How do parents handle their children's consumer desire?

I found that when children came home with their desires turned into needs by the alchemy of dignity, most of the time parents heard them and responded, while only very occasionally parents ignored, resisted, or denied their children's desires. Like Judy Berger, who, as we saw, bought Max his Game Boy despite her extreme reluctance, responsive parents prioritize their children's social belonging. This practice has a long history in American culture, as exemplified by Sinclair Lewis's 1920s antihero George Babbitt. In one telling episode in Lewis's classic novel, Babbitt's wife cautions him against disciplining their son's teenage friends at a party, because "we wouldn't want Ted left out of things, would we?" In reply, however, although "Babbit announced he would be enchanted to have Ted left out of things," he then "hurried in to be polite, lest Ted be left out of things." Babbitt, and Judy Berger, are not alone. In one national survey, about half of parents with children under age thirteen confessed: "While it's often against my better judgment, I sometimes buy my children clothing and things they want because I don't want them to feel different from other kids."[11]

The prospect of feeling "different from other kids" animated many parents' buying practices, but I found parents and children watched for three specific forms of difference, each with varying impact: interactional, personal, and social. Interactional difference includes the momentary variations that arise in conversations, such as whether or not someone has gone skiing, can do a handstand, or owns a set of Heelys, the popular sneakers with wheels built into the sole. Personal difference refers to enduring characteristics adhering to the person, such as facts about his or her family, or individual traits, such as being shy or gifted in music. Social difference stems from social categories such as race, gender, class, sexuality, nationality, and the like. The child's unique configuration of difference, coupled with family resources, shaped how much parents bought, in order to shield, cure, or cultivate. In addition, parents were motivated not just by the prospect of the child's difference from others, but also by their own emotional memories—often their anxious recall—of their experiences of being different as a child. These motivations combined to create parents' relative sensitivity to their child's belonging, leading to which desires parents could ignore and which they could not.[12]

Both affluent and low-income parents were responsive to children's wants, but this did not mean these groups bought in the same way. I found that parents aimed their buying to accomplish different symbolic goals depending on where the parents were on the income ladder. Affluent parents practiced a form of "symbolic deprivation," pointing to particularly meaningful goods or experiences that their child did *not* have as evidence of their own moral restraint and worthiness as parents. Affluent parents often disparaged aloud the need to belong as a form of conformity, and children's desires often contradicted the stated goals of adults, some of whom explicitly sought not just to "keep up with the

Joneses" but to be "different from the Joneses." Symbolic deprivation was how affluent parents resolved the contradiction between their normative beliefs and their practices, between their ideals and their material plenty.[13]

On the other end of the class spectrum, most low-income parents implemented a form of "symbolic indulgence," making sure (sometimes at considerable sacrifice) to buy particular goods or experiences for their children, those items or events sure to have the most significant symbolic value for the children's social world. For many low-income parents, symbolic indulgence was the best they could do within their resource constraints, even though their personal experience of the pain of difference often led them to prioritize children's belonging above almost all else. These consumer practices thus comprised the way low-income parents demonstrated their own moral worth and value as parents.[14]

PERSONAL VICE OR SOCIAL ILL? WHAT WE TALK ABOUT WHEN WE TALK ABOUT BUYING

Many of the more popular current explanations of the children's spending boom focus on corporate marketers or personal vices and thus feel less like understanding than judgment. While they portray part of the consumption story, they omit the conceptual tools we need to comprehend Judy Berger's regret that "it is a given you will have a Game Boy," or Simon and Marco's discursive facework to invent a new Halloween costume.

Some commentators explain the consumption boom by looking first to the children, whose consumer desires seem to arouse considerable adult anxiety. Children are often portrayed as "agents of materialism," to use Robert Wuthnow's term, conduits for the commercial culture that Americans regard with mixed feelings. Bloggers by the thousands decry children's seeming addiction to video games, collectibles like Yu-Gi-Oh! cards, or Air Jordans, while in works with titles like *Born to Buy* scholars issue warnings depicting the psychological costs of consumerism. Waggish terms such as "the nag factor" or "pester power" capture the notion of parents subjected to children who know no appropriate limits. Media portrayals feature children as either unwitting dupes to corporate marketing, or avaricious and amoral; in one editorial pledging a series on "how much of parenting has been reduced to fending off requests from children for commercial products," a national newspaper opined that childhood "has been transformed into consumerhood."[15]

Yet, as media critic David Buckingham wrote, there is "at least a degree of irony in adults accusing children of 'consumerism' when their power to consume at all is almost entirely in the hands of adults themselves." Some writers point out that commercialized children surely learn from their materialistic parents, those who enact their own status concerns through their children's toys and wardrobes. On a more fundamental level, a number of scholars have recently argued we should hardly be surprised by the spread of children's consumption, because children's culture mirrors that of adults generally. Widespread concerns about the intensity and extent of children's marketized desires, these analysts contend, reflect more about our misguided need to consider childhood as it never was—a time and place apart from the cares, woes, and temptations of adult life. As childhood expert Daniel Cook has argued, consumption is not separate from childhood, as the profane is distinct from the sacred; children are "always, already embedded in market relations," and the market is "indispensable and unavoidable" in constructing childhoods. Perhaps childhood has turned into consumerhood, then, because adulthood has, too.[16]

Stories about greed, whether in children or adults, certainly have their magnetic appeal—witness the annual journalistic exercise in charting spending excess during the holiday season, leading to articles with headlines like "18 Shopping Bags and 3 Empty Wallets, One Family's Ritual: Daylong Orgy of Buying Christmas Gifts." Yet charges of materialism, with its underlying image of uncontrolled vice and unrestrained desire—as in the hedonism captured by the headline's term "orgy"—seem less to offer answers than to raise questions. Who are those people who just cannot seem to get their spending under control? Why are they driven by desire for the latest doll fad or video game to stand outside stores before dawn, name their children after favorite brands, or go to extreme measures to buy?[17]

WHOSE NEEDS? WHOSE LUXURIES?
SPENDING AND INEQUALITY

The morality tales of spending are part of a cultural contest of who can buy and how much. Whether consumers are depicted as the poor and minority "combat consumers," as Elizabeth Chin argued, willing to rob to buy Timberland boots, or the luxury-obsessed wealthy, intent upon owning the largest yacht or the most diverting East Hampton castle, popular representations of materialism or greed are most often portrayals of the vice of Others, mostly for the benefit of an assumed white, middle-class audience.[18]

In families' daily lives, however, inequality and consumption are deeply, mutually implicated, albeit in complex, sometimes counterintuitive ways. Poor families are *not*, as one analyst recently asserted against much evidence, somehow "relatively insulated by their poverty from the consequences if not the temptations of consumer marketing." Indeed, until recently, most research has shown that low-income families spend disproportionately *more* on their children than do wealthier families, suggesting that in times of budget constraints, in many homes children's needs are more fixed, more compelling than those of adults. Marketers have dubbed the children's market "bulletproof," meaning that it is practically impervious to economic dislocations, because parents report being unable to take pride in cutting back on children's expenses.[19]

Talk of spending immediately raises questions of need versus luxury. But even the economist Adam Smith understood that needs are fungible, relative, based on cultural standards. Lauded by free-market celebrants, Smith is less well known for his passages recognizing the primacy of dignity. "By necessaries," he wrote, "I understand not only the commodities which are indispensably necessary for the support of life, but whatever the customs of the country renders it indecent for creditable people, even of the lowest order to do without."[20]

Thus we might say that a family's relative means to spend (inequality), and what a family spends to mean (consumption), are intricately, intimately connected, although not in a simple, linear way. As one shifts and changes, so does the other—and not merely with the stiff formality of figures and numbers, but in the warp and bend of human feeling. Inexorably, inevitably perhaps, the standards of childhood change, with "needs" chased by children and adults from marbles and bicycles to Nintendo Wii and iPods. These shifting standards are met by shifting emotions, the despair of the parent working two jobs to cover what used to be the basics, the dread of the middle-class parent trying to stave off the addictive appeal of the latest fad, the triumph of the taxi driver's daughter when she uses her own money to buy her own PlayStation. While greed or materialism might fuel some of their actions, their intense emotions hint at a deeper mystery, of the meaning of things, of care, and of belonging.

NOT-SO-HIDDEN PERSUADERS

Some researchers have argued that the meaning of things, and hence the urge to buy, stem from the powerful reach of particularly effective corporate marketing. Corporate marketing is so insidious and potent that it can make children desire, and parents desire for their children. There is certainly plenty of solid research into the impact of advertising, demonstrating that corporate marketing is increasingly sophisticated and unfettered, and that children are particularly vulnerable to marketing tactics, as children are believed to be unaware of the advertisers' persuasive intent until about the age of seven. Much of this research is conducted by psychologists, who fabricate "strange situations" involving individual children exposed to ads and then asked about products, and there is a plethora of studies showing children do indeed respond to corporate efforts to convince. A number of scholars have also documented the expansion of campaigns to plumb the psyches of children, the weakening of advertising regulation, and the development of new and even more powerful market tactics to lure buyers, such as the thinly disguised market research among "tweens" involving staged and sponsored "sleepovers" where girls talk about products. Corporate marketing, this research demonstrates, is targeting children with a gimlet eye.[21]

Given the soaring and pervasive rates of children's media exposure, the attention these scholars pay to corporate actors is undoubtedly warranted: American youth spend more time with media per week (6.4 hours) than they do with their parents (2.3 hours), with friends (2.3 hours), or in school (on an annual basis). We may not yet have reached the moment predicted more than a half century ago by E. B. White in a science-fiction story, when "children early formed the habit of gaining all their images at second hand, by looking at a screen, [and] only what had been touched by electronics was valid and real." At the very least, however, children's lives are increasingly beginning to approach the atomistic existence modeled by the psychology experiments, as more and more they watch TV alone in their rooms.[22]

Yet these arguments rely on a rather weak notion of human behavior, in which people have all the substance of tissue paper, blown this way and that by nothing more than the airwaves, or by their individual vices. Either the corporations are too powerful to resist or parents are too weak to set limits or delay gratification; the answer to exploding consumption is thus either more corporate regulation or more parental responsibility. While these perspectives are commonly argued against one another, they share a common perception: parents *buy* merely because they (or their children) have been successfully *sold*.[23]

CONSUMPTION AS CARE

Other scholars argue that consumption is a social practice, one in which people are communicating meaning to each other through goods, although these experts disagree about just what kind of meaning consumption conveys. Some researchers contend buying for children is driven by parents' efforts to establish their children's socioeconomic status—or, more subtly, to shape their children's class-specific tastes—through their purchases; by parents enacting their class status in the practices they employ to make purchases; or by parents' recognition of the role that consumption plays in signaling the full citizenship available only to those with means. More recently, scholars have explored the intersections of the market and intimacy, arguing that consumption forges "connected lives," in the words of Viviana Zelizer. These researchers expand our notion of why buyers buy beyond the obsession with status, arguing that consumption acts as a symbolic language through which buyers make connections to others. As the British anthropologist Daniel Miller contended, shopping for others can be considered a devotional rite, and commodities "the material culture of love." In this vein, parents buy for children to strengthen emotional bonds that are fraying due to increasing work hours, cultural prescriptions encouraging children's defiance, the high incidence of divorce, or the strains of poverty, among other factors. These scholars contribute a critical observation: the importance of feeling in motivating action, in shaping cultural meaning, in spurring consumption. As the sociologist Sharon Zukin observed, "the things we need to buy are framed by our love for the significant others we buy for."[24]

Yet in focusing on the bridging of consumption, analysts sometimes seem to gloss over how consumption can separate as well, and downplay the very real inequalities embedded in the sheer capacity to spend. In addition, even though people may use commodities as a tool to express their connections, the very system of commodification exerts its own influence on the relationships it mediates, much as a set of tires will drive a car forward or back but not up, say, or sideways. We need not "presume that the realm of commodities debases the realm of sentiment," sociologist Eva Illouz cautioned, but "the vocabulary of emotions is now more exclusively dictated by the market."[25]

Families adjust to new circumstances, and evidence suggests they are indeed adjusting to the commodification of childhood. Arlie Hochschild has analyzed some of the strategies parents use to handle the pressures of overwork and what she calls the "commercialization of intimate life." She points to people using goods to represent their ideal selves ("we'll go camping someday"), to engage in "caring consumption" to avoid family conflict, to revisit the question of just what aspects of family life—birthday parties? photo albums?—are and are not appropriate to pay someone else to do. As Hochschild reports, however, these adaptations have their own impact, just as someone favoring a bad knee can start to feel a twinge in the good one, too. Relationships—between men and women, between parents and children—suffer from the sacrifice of our time, energy, and focus on the twin altars of cultural capitalism: work and shopping. Hochschild warns that such practices serve "to push men and women further into the worlds of workplace and the mall," to decenter family life as the focus of collective rituals, and finally, to "materialize love."[26]

BEYOND THE FAMILY: THINKING ABOUT CHILDREN'S CULTURE

Consumption has thus evolved into a kind of care, of how adults form connections with children, albeit in service to the market. Yet market culture does not just connect lives vertically, as between adults and children, but also horizontally, among children themselves. Zelizer urges us to view consumption as a set of economic processes laden with "continuously negotiated meaning-drenched social relations"—in other words, with culture. In answer to this call, this book sets out to consider the specific meanings, and the social relations, behind children's consumption. How does consumption figure in childhood culture?[27]

Sociologists have an important contribution to make here. Culture scholars have demonstrated that people create and experience meaning in groups via particular rituals, interactions, and institutions, which serve to shape and communicate norms and expectations. The personal, local interpretations of commodities and events that comprise contemporary childhoods are not simply idiosyncratic, but rather grounded in social locations and fraught with social implications. "Tastes," observed Oxford's Douglas Holt, "are never innocent of social consequences." In an influential work on how tastes develop, Pierre Bourdieu argued that parents socialize children into having "good" taste, through at times unconscious cultural practices of investing certain goods—or a certain approach to goods, such as a knowing connoisseurship—with the power to establish group boundaries. Yet much of this research considers children as if they lived only in families, and not in communities of their own, with cultures of their own. As media researcher Ellen Seiter has noted, children's desires can infuriate parents who consider them "kitschy" or "distasteful," because children are often oblivious to the class dimensions of taste as opposed to those expressing age or gender. Thus while analysts like Bourdieu have argued goods and experiences have variable meanings *across* households, it is important to note that the meanings of goods and experiences can conflict *within* households as well. The process of parents socializing children to the "right" cultural capital, then, is perhaps not quite as seamless as some researchers might suggest, because of the dynamic influence of children's own cultural imperatives.[28]

As Patricia and Peter Adler wrote in their work on preadolescents, children do not "perceive, interpret, form opinions about, or act on the world as unconnected individuals. Rather, they do all these things in concert with their peers, as they collectively experience the world." Yet unlike advertising, the influence of peers or peer communities on children's consumer desires has not been extensively studied. Clearly, as one psychologist declared, "more research on peer influence, especially with younger children, would be welcome." A British study echoed this observation, pointing out that "much work on children's consumption . . . focuses on the relationship between the market and children, to the neglect of other pertinent social relationships," and arguing that "any investigation [must evaluate] the influence of other . . . child actors within the networks that make up their daily life."[29]

Studies of the impact of peers on children's consumer preferences have mostly focused on adolescents and have largely demonstrated that consumer goods provide for a certain status. Only a few projects have gone further, observing that items such as clothes or food not only confer status but evoke a crucial sense of belonging, painful in its absence. "The experience of being present in a chosen group but being unable to exhibit membership rites was a particularly agonizing one," observed a team of British researchers. Their study of teenagers and advertising reported many incidences in which teenagers "described the experience of being 'left out,' 'talked around,' or 'blanked' when they were unable to participate in a particular exchange because they had not experienced the ad in question." In another study, on Chinese children's food consumption, a student reported: "I have to try new things. Otherwise when classmates are chatting, if everyone has tried something and you have not tried it, then you have nothing to say."[30]

Having "nothing to say" is akin to not belonging, to a sort of unwelcome invisibility. This study takes as its central focus the social interactions that put children in the position of "having something to say" or not, that thereby give particular meaning to the products, services, or commodified experiences children may have heard about elsewhere. My purpose here is not to ascertain exactly where the influence of advertising stops and where that of peers begins, but rather to explore how children's social lives shape what children consider important, and how that affects parent spending. Children's concerns about fitting in are only part of the story, however. Why would these anxieties matter so much now that they act as an engine moving the commercialization of childhood forward? To obtain an answer to this question, we must step back from the microlevel study of children's social worlds to examine the broader picture of the revolution of childhood that has taken place in the last thirty years.

CHILDHOOD IN PRIVATE AND IN PUBLIC

At the beginning and end of every episode of *Teletubbies*, the toddlers' television series on PBS, a large baby's head appears as the sun, smiling down on the brilliant colors and curious shapes that mark Teletubby land. We hear the baby's voice, cooing and squealing, as the narrator greets and bids farewell to the bright, pear-shaped Teletubby characters who stand and wave. The baby's head is giant, luminous, drawing the viewer's attention to the heat and joy of childhood pleasure, dwarfing the miniature Teletubby world.

In the manner of cultural images everywhere, the giant-baby-as-sun captures some truths and reworks others. In some ways, like the television baby, children are ever larger in their worlds, their joys and pleasures reverberating, their needs and predilections even at times dominating their environments. In many families—not just middle-class ones—this image holds true inside the domestic sphere, with important implications for childhood, parenting, and consumption. To be sure, some children are still neglected, abused, or oppressed, the perpetrators protected by the privacy of the home. Yet in many other families, children's symbolic presence has swelled to new dimensions. Like the enormous baby smiling down on the scene below, children's desires are magnified within the home; as in the television program, children's desires are then met through the market, if not with endearingly dumpy little characters, then by Pottery Barn Kids or Toys"R"Us.

Yet the sun is the apotheosis of the free and the public, and children are giant-sized only in the private sphere. In public, children's role has shrunk to the size of tiny glass figurines, brittle, silent, and unable to command significant public support, attention, or presence. As the historian Steven Mintz observed, "kids have more space than ever inside their homes, but less space outside to call their own." It is this twin paradox—of children as private giant and as public figurine—that has fueled the development of what the sociologist Barrie Thorne called "the privatization of childhood."[31]

In the private sphere, demographic and cultural patterns involving children have expanded their importance in American families. First, children's footsteps echo in the lonely halls of their homes. When men left the family farm in the nineteenth century to join the paid workforce, people felt considerable concern and confusion about just what a family was without Father there all day. In response, scholars have argued, they made holy the image of Mother as "homemaker" and invented rituals—birthdays, Thanksgiving—that persist today, resonant in their ability to recall what historian John Gillis termed "the family we live by." More than a hundred years later, similar anxiety coalesces around women's increasing turn to full-time work, and about family instability due to divorce. As mothers' work lives look more and more like fathers', who but the child is left to sacralize as the vessel of all that is dear about domesticity? As the percentage of single parent households maintains itself at historically high levels, who but the child is left to symbolize family devotion? As community bonds wither, who but the child is left to embody parents' emotional connections?[32]

This confluence of trends suggests children loom larger in families than they ever have, and their desires may thus loom larger as well, as soaring advertising budgets targeting children attest. On a practical level, children's increasing participation in family and personal shopping affords them greater opportunity to enact their own priorities and goals in the market. Yet children's symbolic impact could be even greater; parents may have been better able to ignore or defer children's desires when they didn't form the acknowledged center of the family's emotional life. When children are all that is left of family, the urge to cherish them as the last vestige of intimacy is strong indeed. As the essayist Adam Gopnik observed, "the romance of your child's childhood may be the last romance you can give up."[33]

Changing notions of childhood and motherhood accompany these demographic trends. Sociologist Annette Lareau found that middle-class parents pursued a strategy of concerted cultivation, in which their children's individual talents were coaxed and channeled through organized activities, and through which their children acquired "a robust sense of entitlement." These practices relied upon new ideas of children, who went from being economic contributors to the household to priceless individuals defined as not-yet-adults, whose primary task was their own development. In tandem evolved what Sharon Hays has dubbed "the ideology of intensive motherhood," a brand of parenting she identified as focused, dedicated, child-centered, self-sacrificing, and, not coincidentally, expensive. While these trends centered in the middle class, they established standards that found their way into the homes of working-class families, at the very least through institutional practices and assumptions they faced. For parents, what was at one time a whim or pleasure to buy for their children had turned into a mandate.[34]

For all their increased private power, however, children comprise an ever smaller share of the public. Falling birthrates mean children now form a smaller proportion of the population in the United States than they have for the past several hundred years. Yet although such demographic trends might lead us to expect for them decreased competition for resources, say, and thus improved well-being, instead children's poverty has risen dramatically in the last thirty years, in comparison with that of the ever-increasing ranks of the elderly. While the "feminization of poverty" has been widely recognized, the less visible trend has been a "juvenilization of poverty." "Why have children lost ground vis-à-vis the elderly?" asks demographer Suzanne Bianchi. "Sources of public transfers differ greatly for the two groups, with those going to children less generous and declining over time and those going to the elderly more generous and much less susceptible, at least politically, to erosion over the past two decades."[35]

Most government spending for children is delivered by states aided by federal block-grant money and is subject to political and economic fluctuations, researchers have found. "States—the main source of social welfare spending for children—have faced sizeable budget deficits and have attempted to shore up their bottom lines by reducing spending," one study reported. On the federal level, while per capita social-welfare spending on children grew overall from 1980 to 2000, these gains were largely in Medicare and food-stamp allocations. Other areas of federal social-welfare spending on children declined in real dollars.[36]

The geographer Cindi Katz links this disinvestment to the abandonment of poor and working-class children, by both global capital, which finds them no longer economically useful, and the middle class, who increasingly turn to private markets for solutions to child-rearing problems and thus withdraw from lobbying for quality public services for all children. Property tax revolts that swept the nation in the late 1970s, such as Proposition 13 in California, were fundamentally a protest against social spending for children, most often poor and minority, who attended the schools these taxes underwrote. Writing about youth in Harlem witnessing the government's shrinking of the "social wage," including the lopsided provision of education, Katz observed: "Large fractions of those coming of age were butting up against the limitations produced by these broad-scale political economic shifts and their local fallout. For growing numbers . . . all bets for the future were off."[37]

As the public provisioning has receded, the distance between families in the United States becomes even more meaningful—in freezing the structure of opportunities, to be sure, but also in raising the stakes of "making it," and communicating to others that you have. The gap between rich and poor yawns wider than ever; by 1998, the wealthiest one-fifth of families had an average net worth of $1.1 million, while the bottom two-fifths were worth $1,000. Over the past three decades, such earnings inequality and a host of other factors—including changing family structures, the shifting nature of work, increased racial and ethnic diversity across American families, and new antipoverty policies—made resources less equitably distributed across American families. Children have not escaped this trend; in fact, they are at its leading edge, as children are twice as likely to be poor as adults. While one in five children lived in poverty in 1994, more than half of all children lived in homes of relative prosperity. Over the last decades of the twentieth century, the difference between the two groups grew ever wider, as family income from 1969 to 1989 declined among the poorest children while increasing (by nearly 20 percent) among the richest children.[38]

These developments—the emptying out of the home and the sacralization of the domestic child, the withdrawal of the state and the expansion of the market, and the rise in inequality—form the backdrop to the explosion of spending on children. New interpretations of children's needs (and new attention paid to them), new standards of meeting them through the marketplace, new stakes of failing to do so—all combine to make child-rearing consumption urgent, prevalent, and fraught with emotional meaning.

MAKING MEANING: CULTURE AS PROCESS

The realm of emotional meaning, wherein neutral objects and events are transformed into things and experiences that matter to people, is the realm of culture. Culture is often defined as a system of meanings, in the words of Sharon Hays "a social, durable, layered pattern of cognitive and normative systems." Yet perhaps this description makes culture sound a little more ossified, more finished, than people experience. We do not invent culture out of whole cloth, of course, but we do work with what we receive, albeit often unconsciously. We mix and blend meanings across social realms and experiences, bringing one to another in a daily project of individual and collective creativity that nonetheless often serves to reproduce understandings and relationships. As my research focuses on how children and parents make meaning out of things, I emphasize here the movement, the dynamism of culture, by proposing that we think of it as a process.[39]

What is the process of making meaning? Meaning comes from a sort of emotional thinking, so that the way we feel about commodities and experiences colors the way we perceive them. We might conceive of culture, then, as a patterned, collective process by which people attach personal, emotional significance to their world, indeed, as a sort of dynamic, two-way bridge between the social and the psychological. Much of that process is captured in interactions that serve as occasions to reconfirm, and occasionally to reshape, the powerful social asymmetries that order our experience.[40]

In this work, I argue that certain shared cultural notions—powerful ideas about what parents owe their children, about the challenge posed by difference, about the primacy of belonging—make it near-impossible for most American-born parents of varied class and race backgrounds to ignore children's yearnings. To be sure, our trajectories and choices are profoundly shaped by the "organization of human existence," the social institutions, categories, and resources that frame and produce social life. But what makes children yearn, and parents buy, is also in part a cultural story of what we value and what we fear, ideas that are continually made concrete in interactions, rituals, and daily experiences. Taking into account the institutional backdrop, this book tells that cultural story, exploring how consumption expresses care and belonging for children and parents, how social inequality and intolerance can make care and belonging feel scarce or plentiful, and how such feelings shape contemporary childhood.[41]

The organization of this book reflects one of its central themes: the similarities and differences across families of widely varying backgrounds in their experience of children's consumer culture. In chapter 2, I describe in greater detail the disparate communities of this study, and how their sharp contrasts shaped the kind of ethnographic work I did there, while making the similarities across sites even more intriguing. Chapter 3 immerses the reader in the worlds of children, both rich and poor, where I explore the economy of dignity, its tokens of value, and children's facework strategies for navigating it. Then, chapters 4–6 consider what happens when children bring their consumer desires home: chapters 4 and 5 exploring the circumstances in which affluent and low-income parents respond to children's entreaties while deploying symbolic means to frame those responses as honorable, and chapter 6 weighing the circumstances in which parents say no. Chapter 7 evaluates the implications of the privatization of childhood for another kind of consumption, that which shapes children's future—the "pathway consumption" of children's contexts, like the neighborhoods, schools, and other spaces where childhood takes place. In chapter 8, I conclude by considering the ties between children's consumer culture and that of adults, weighing the implications of this new math—the equation of belonging with possession and care with provisioning—and offering ways in which interested adults can mediate the drive to belong, neutralize the power of difference, and make dignity more available to all. Parents looking for advice on how to shop and what to buy for their children will not find those answers here, then, but they *will* gain a deeper appreciation of the consequences of their choices.

CONCLUSION

At the center of the word *belonging* is a synonym for *desire*, as one contemporary novelist recently observed, and these twin ideas explain the particular magic of children's consumer yearnings. In service to these yearnings, I argue, spending on children has exploded, and this trend has been costly for American families. Compared to families of decades ago with or without children, today's families with children work more hours, accumulate more debt, and declare bankruptcy more often. Affluent families lament the sheer quantity of children's stuff but can also mourn the degree to which parent-child relations are mediated through consumer goods. The cost is no less significant for low-income families; research documents the great lengths to which low-income families go to equip their children. Low-income parents take on extra jobs over Christmas, plan birthday gifts and seasonal clothing purchases long in advance, juggle creditors to be able to float expenses, and otherwise strive to meet children's designated needs, protecting their place in the family budget.[42]

There are also other costs to this spending race, beyond the impact on individual children and their families, that we all bear. On a society-wide level, the trend promotes a culture of spending that redefines care and belonging as mediated through the market. Those who want to opt out find it difficult to do so. The cost of raising a child increases, and the impact of income inequality on the distribution of opportunity is intensified. Furthermore, poor children—attending high-poverty schools with an economy of dignity that can contrast sharply with that of some of the more affluent schools—are perhaps enduring what we might call an unequal distribution of sentiment, one in which differences are subject to intense peer discipline of scorn or invisibility. Not only, then, are the opportunities afforded by different contexts for children highly unequal, but so too might be their emotional allowances, suggesting perhaps another cost of commodified childhood: the stratification of feeling. We might consider collectively these expenses of modern spending practices as an invisible tax, a tax that no one collects but one that we all pay, adding to the $300 price tag for the Nintendo Wii, the $90 American Girl doll, or the $165 pair of Air Jordans.[43]

But perhaps most important, the commodification of childhood turns the child into a pipeline of commercial culture, the cause of the ratcheting up of standards, the target of cultural animosity about the costs of rising inequality even as he or she is its primary victim. Who bears the emotional fallout for these trends? Furthermore, who takes on the burden when parents do the "right" thing, eschew consumer culture, ignore their children's entreaties? A hint, perhaps, lies in the identity of who often shoulders the blame for what are really the residual effects of materialism, greed, and the effectiveness of advertising: children. Calling children the conduit of commercial culture is a bit like faulting fish for the water in which they swim.[44]

Children's emotional experience records the impact of consumer capitalism on all of us—the expansion of work time, the expression of love through things, the pressure of increasing inequality, and the diminution of public provisioning, which has withered like a raisin. Could adults' anxiety swirling around children reflect instead worries about our own materialistic culture, our own inability to stem desire, our own failure to connect with others? We could be relegating to children what we fear for ourselves, while all along they just want to belong.

CHAPTER TWO

Differences in Common

Studying Inequality

I set out to study how families of different income levels experienced the constant ratcheting up of standards for a "good-enough" childhood. I wanted to see how children of all kinds of households construed the meanings behind the events and equipment that seemed to matter most to them. I sought to investigate how low-income families managed the consumer treadmill with constrained resources, how affluent families handled the steady drumbeat of children's consumer culture, and how the relationships of parents and children up and down the income ladder reflected and shaped the market for children's goods. I conducted this research in Oakland, California, where class, race, and other categories of difference diverge and converge in ways that allow for some reckoning of the shifting nuances of difference and belonging.

RAISING CHILDREN IN OAKLAND

Rising from the San Francisco Bay to the eastern rolling hills, Oakland is the third largest city in California, and a fairly unequal city for its size, ranked by one study tenth in the nation for income inequality. In 2000, Oakland was more unequal than its surrounding county, the state of California, and the nation as a whole (entities that all include suburbs, however, which are normally a more homogeneous area). The economic boom of the 1990s contributed to this gap, as workers with a bachelor's degree or more saw a 5 percent increase in wages, while the wages of workers with a high-school diploma or less decreased by 5 percent. Class and race and geography intersect and overlap in Oakland, so that affluent whites, Asian-Americans, and some African-Americans living in the hills compete for city resources with poor African-Americans, Latinos, and some Asian-Americans living in the flats.[1]

Oakland is more unequal than many American cities, but its experience—of the decline of stable low-skilled jobs, the stagnation of low-skilled men's wages, the draining pressure of suburbanization, and the unintended consequences of federal community redevelopment policies—is not atypical of the urban trajectory in the United States in the late twentieth century. One historian argued that "Oakland embodied the seeming contradictions of the postwar American metropolis. It was characterized by poverty amidst wealth; racial apartheid at the heart of liberalism; and high unemployment in periods of economic growth."[2]

As do their peers nationwide, most of Oakland's children experience this poverty even more acutely than do the city's adults; in 1999, one in three children in Oakland lived in poverty, while only one in five adults did. One can see the breadth of the need presented by Oakland's children in a few telling facts: more than a third of children in Oakland's public schools are classified as English language "learners"; more than half of the city's children (56 percent) live in families where no adult had full-time year-round employment; and more than three-quarters of children enrolled in Oakland Unified were eligible for "compensatory education," an aid category designated for low-achieving children from low-income households. Just as the history of Oakland tells a story of urban inequity analogous to that of the nation's other cities, the lives of Oakland's children today reflect those of their low-income urban peers across the nation.[3]

In Oakland, schools draw only from their surrounding neighborhoods, and thus they are embedded in this pervasive inequality. Under this arrangement, a handful of hills schools have mostly wealthy white and Asian students, whose families raise hundreds of thousands of dollars in extra monies for their schools. In the flatlands, however, elementary students attend what the Harvard Civil Rights Project called "apartheid schools," where mostly African-American, Latino, and Southeast Asian poor children congregate and fail. About fifty private schools serve area families who decline to send their kids to public school at all.[4]

While I selected Oakland in part for its typicality as a fairly unequal city in a nation of unequal cities, I sampled for variation in choosing the school sites within Oakland where I did my fieldwork, as well as in selecting the participating families whose children attended those schools. I settled on my sites based on three principal criteria: proximity to each other, to accentuate the same and different worlds that the families inhabited; high contrast in household income, which meant selecting public schools with very low and very high percentages of children eligible for free and reduced-price lunch; and language composition, specifically excluding schools with a large percentage of children with limited English proficiency, so as to ensure I would understand their playground interactions without an interpreter. I further narrowed down the field of public schools based on contacts in the UC Berkeley School of Education, where teachers gave me names of people in various schools to get permission to conduct research. See table 1 for a summary of demographic and other characteristics of the school sites.

One of my first decisions was the age of the children on whom I would focus. In presentations of this research, inevitably someone in the audience talks about how intense these issues are for older children, such as those in middle or high school. I chose, however, to include children aged five–nine, because I hoped to study children young enough that parents made most of the decisions about what the children had and where they were, but old enough that they could have opinions and make them known. Some of the children were eleven or twelve by the end of the study, and others had older siblings that parents talked about as well, but for the most part my findings are based on children in what

Table 1. *Characteristics of School Sites*

	Sojourner Truth (Bryant Elementary)	Arrowhead	Oceanview	Oakland Unified Elementary Schools
Racial/ethnic composition (%)				
White	5	60	67	6
Nonwhite	95	40	34	94
African-American	70	n.d.	14	42
Asian-American	6	n.d.	8	15
Latino	17	n.d.	4	34
Other	2	n.d.	8	3
Economic indicators				
Students w/ free/ reduced-price lunch (%)	78	n.a.	1	68
Students w/ financial aid (%)	n.a.	25	n.a.	n.a.
Tuition	n.a.	$13,450	n.a.	n.a.
School facts				
Enrollment	367	224	282	26,439
Grades offered	K-5	K-6	K-8	K-5
Student/teacher ratio	20 to 1	16 to 1	19 to 1	20 to 1
Teachers w/ credential (%)	78	n.d.	94	87
Annual fund-raising	$1,000	$488,000	$150,000	n.d.

SOURCES: Sources for Arrowhead data include annual reports, admissions materials, and the school Web site. For the two public schools and for Oakland schools in general, sources include Ed-Data (the Education Data Partnership), the *Oakland Tribune*, and the U.S. Census.

NOTE: The abbreviation *n.a.* means "not applicable," and *n.d.* means "no data available."

is known as "middle childhood." I also intentionally adopted a community sampling strategy, in which my informants knew each other from the schools and to some extent lived in the same social world. This choice stands in sharp contrast to the more common method of interviewing many individuals who are not acquainted or connected, the "unrelated talking heads" that predominate in social science research. Most important, this research design had profound effects on my findings by enabling me to see how meanings are constructed as a social process, in interactions from the playground to pick-up time, in relationships from neighbors to friends. In addition, however, this research design posed unusual challenges for maintaining people's confidentiality; thus I sometimes resorted to unusually elaborate methods to alter people's identifying characteristics without unduly changing the meaning or context of the stories they had to tell.[5]

A TALE OF THREE COMMUNITIES

The three schools where I conducted my fieldwork could not have differed from each other more dramatically, and the dry facts that underlay their stark differences became vividly apparent the very first day I approached the various school authorities for permission. At Bryant Elementary, the principal, an African-American woman with a long history at the school, listened patiently to my long, tentative, rather nervous description of my project, and then said she'd think about it. A few days later, she stepped aside with me in the school yard and politely but firmly declined to let the school participate. No matter how well intentioned I was, she said, "the people who read your study" might criticize the consumption habits of the poor families whose children attended Bryant, and she did not want to expose those families to such (white, middle-class?) judgment. "What will they think of all the money they spend on pictures?" she asked, referring to the school photographs that students' families bought voraciously, for sharing with kin and friends.

In contrast, when I showed Neal McCabe, the director of the private school Arrowhead, the letter I used to recruit parents to participate, he made a correction to the sentence that indicated where interested parents should return the form. "Let's have them put it in the envelope outside the office," he said, easily. "That way it can fit right into what they are used to doing." "An academic studying the kids"—the introduction McCabe used for me as we passed various teachers and staff—was such a commonplace around Arrowhead that the school even had a customary way of handling sample recruitment letters. My reception at the upper-income public school Oceanview was similar. The principal there offered to put me with Ms. Sullivan's classroom—whom she described as a "real pro"– and Ms. Sullivan practically rubbed her hands together with glee, saying, "I know just where I'm going to put you."

The differences between these communities' reactions stemmed not only from their varying exposure to research, or familiarity with inquiring academics. The principals also reflected the differences in social position of the families whose children attended their institutions. McCabe and the Oceanview principal were relaxed, even enthusiastic, about receiving help from another pair of trustworthy hands, because their parents were not normally subject to widespread social censure. In contrast, the Bryant principal's fears were not unfounded. As we have seen, the buying habits of low-income parents are apparently considered fair game for commentary and criticism by anyone from bloggers to politicians. In addition, the social censure low-income families experienced had "teeth," posing certain risks. While I was conducting the study, for example, a local district attorney initiated a new program to prosecute parents for their children's school truancy, treating it "in every way possible as a criminal case." Many of the study's low-income families either had lost their own children to the authorities or knew someone who had. The intervention of others based on decontextualized knowledge—"however well-intentioned"—was no idle threat.[6]

Nonetheless, part of the general opprobrium surely stems from a lack of understanding about low-income spending. Convinced that more light and less heat on the issue would generate more positive cultural conversations and policies, I was determined to press on. Instead of observing at Bryant, then, I secured access to the Sojourner Truth after-school center across the street, which if anything heightened the contrast in family resources across the study sites. Sojourner Truth served only those children who went to Bryant and whose families made little enough money to qualify, but also whose parents had the initiative to apply. Other Bryant children had different arrangements—some went to the local YMCA, others were cared for by a relative, while some, if they were old enough to be released from the school without a grown-up, wandered the streets aimlessly, rather loosely following their parents' instructions, which were often to go directly home and call their parents when they got there. Some of the latter group were graduates of Sojourner Truth, which served children only through the third grade; often fourth graders would stroll through the after-school center a little forlornly, jump rope for a while, join in conversations about the planned festivities for Black History Month or Halloween, or "help" keep order or pass out snack before heading home.

The sharp differences among the schools were also evident in their physical space and the bodies of those who inhabited it. At Sojourner Truth, a long, low cement building was flanked by two asphalt playgrounds. The gate to the left playground stood ajar, and parents, older siblings, and babysitters would often leave cars curbside, sometimes idling, to go through it unchallenged, reemerging with a littler one in tow. In the playground, kids played basketball, using a space between two of the monkey bars as a hoop; they sometimes swung an old telephone wire for a double-dutch jump rope; they kicked dead balls from one end of the yard to the other, running to retrieve them as they landed and stayed put. All but a few of the children were African-American, most lived with their single mothers, and almost all received a tuition subsidy to attend. The self-reported incomes of the families I interviewed from this group were on average $18,600, well below the constructed "minimum necessary" to make it in the region and only $200 higher than the federal poverty line for a family of four.[7]

Although the driving distance from Sojourner Truth to Oceanview was but a seven-minute dash, the symbolic distance was far greater. Oceanview Elementary sat nestled in the gentle hills of Oakland, the quiet interrupted by the sound of the school bell or the droning buzz of construction from frequent house renovation in the pricey area. A three-bedroom home on less than a quarter-acre of land in the surrounding neighborhood was worth more than $1 million and such houses often sold in a week, even in a national housing downturn, sometimes for hundreds of thousands of dollars over the asking price. One of the draws in the neighborhood was the school, considered among the best public elementary schools in Oakland; Oceanview accepts only a few transfers, as it fills its halls with children from the local intake zone. Three-quarters of Oceanview's students are white or Asian, while those groups make up only one-fifth of the district's overall student population. Even more telling, just 3 children out of the school's 279 participate in the free and reduced-price lunch program, a standard poverty measure, compared to 62.8 percent districtwide. The average income of my Oceanview informants was $166,600, and most of them were white, although one-third were affluent African-Americans.

Finally, at the private school Arrowhead, a series of buildings lined the perimeter of an open space about the area of half a city block, in which many trees both low and sweeping dotted the terrain. One tree was dubbed the Fairy Tree; the children would leave small treasures in its curved and gnarled arms and tell stories about its inhabitants. Over in the corner of the open space was a new Astroturf lawn, where some children would turn somersaults and throw Frisbees, while in the center was a large area filled with sand, where a few children would sit on long swings hung from heavy chains, tracing invisible pendulums. Off to one side was a large rectangular garden, with many homemade signs. Sprinkled throughout were some climbing structures, monkey bars, basketball hoops, and picnic tables. With its large space broken up into many small, contained areas, including hiding places and spaces for fantasy play and sports, this school felt like it was designed by and for children.

What lay outside the school campus was also telling. All around the perimeter were tall steel fences; Arrowhead parents had to punch the code word "love" into the mechanical lockbox to get in. Outside of all that love, on the other side of the fences, was the sketchy Oakland neighborhood in which Arrowhead found itself, including a large public school with 93.4 percent students of color, more than half of whom were eligible for free lunch. Meanwhile, in 2004, families paid Arrowhead Academy an annual tuition of more than $13,500. Arrowhead was a progressive school with many gay/lesbian, adoptive, and scholarship families, making it more diverse in racial/ethnic and other terms than the hills public school. Among my sampled families, the average reported income was $186,000, although no family earned less than $60,000, and several "lived off their investments" or earned more than $600,000 annually.

ETHNOGRAPHY IN THE MAKING

I spent three years observing and participating at Sojourner Truth, and six months each at Oceanview and Arrowhead; at each site, I was officially a "volunteer," with undefined duties that in practice ranged from tying shoes to reading to children to making huge vats of pasta salad to throwing footballs. An abiding maxim in qualitative research stipulates that the researcher should continue on until no longer surprised by what she observes, and to some degree, I stopped when my developing concepts seemed to apply well not just to the people I had already met, but to those I was meeting. Yet the tenet has always struck me as a somewhat deadening assumption about ethnography; an assiduous observer is in some ways continually surprised, as most thinking, living people we observe are not predictable except in the broadest terms.

I also stayed at Sojourner Truth the longest because it took years for me to gain access to enough parents to interview, another seemingly simple difference among the sites that was actually revealing of more complex truths. At Sojourner Truth, with a few exceptions, most parents were not connected to each other, grounding their social networks instead in kin and near-kin relationships rather than the school. They did not participate in e-mail communities, exchange group phone lists, or establish phone trees for emergencies or field trips. As Annette Lareau has documented among low-income families, Sojourner Truth children did not generally have "playdates" with school friends unless they were close neighbors, too, and their birthday parties at home, if they had them, were usually family affairs. In addition, and not coincidentally, parents were disinclined to join the study unless they knew me personally. For this reason, I had to approach most Sojourner Truth interviewees individually and in person, often after getting to know their child well, sometimes after the parent had heard about me for months at home from the child. What this also meant, however, was that every person at Sojourner Truth whom I asked to participate, agreed to do so. When in the second year I finally caught up to Aleta's mother to ask her to participate, for example, I first introduced myself, to which she replied, with a smile: "Oh, yeah. Aleta won't let me forget it."

This rather drawn-out individualized procedure stood in marked contrast to the more impersonal efficiency of recruiting volunteers at Oceanview and Arrowhead, where both parent communities were extensively linked by e-mail and phone lists, as well as being socially integrated. "Would you like someone who has recently left the school?" asked one Arrowhead parent, thumbing through her school-issued phone book. "How about someone who spends a lot?" Only at these schools did some parents decline to participate, however, saying they were wary of being involved in a study or were too busy to schedule the time. After I worked in the schools for a while, I distributed among the parents a letter eliciting their participation in interviews; only at Arrowhead and Oceanview did these letters draw wide response. I also supplemented these groups to achieve racial/ethnic, class, and other variations, recruiting particular families described to me in interviews or known through their children at school.

Thus it was as if Sojourner Truth was an aggregate of many individual families whose social centers were elsewhere, while Oceanview and

Arrowhead served as community centers for their mobile professional parent bodies, their links forged by virtual connections. In addition to shaping the contours of my research, these differences were also suggestive for these families' experience of the economy of dignity. Affluent parents might have been more aware than low-income parents of all that their children wanted, because they were integrated in the same community as their children, and thus bore witness to the same comparisons. In contrast, most low-income parents relied on their children to tell them about particular forms of scrip; the intensity of their desire to buy seemed to stem from their relationships with their children, and less from their independent observation of the economy of dignity at school.

In many ways, the children were different, too. At Sojourner Truth, the children were generally interested in and excited to see me. "Oooh, it's Ms. Allison, Ms. Allison," the chorus of whispers would travel around the room when I walked in. Rasheed found himself caught in a bind when he insisted to the head teacher Ms. Graham that he needed my help with homework, but then proceeded to tell me how he knew everything already. "Why do you need her help then?" Ms. Graham demanded, and then, upon his stutter, she waved him off with an "Oh, just go out there already." The children saved seats for me on the bus on field trips, drew pictures of and for me, played Mancala and football with me, vied for the chance to hold my hand, and on one afternoon tried in vain to teach me how to jump rope double-dutch style. The often stern Ms. Graham seemed to loosen some of the rules around me—when the children read with me they were allowed to skip sitting for the sometimes interminable "circle time," for example—and often when I came in, the atmosphere was at first quite gleeful and free, as it was during birthday parties or field trips, before settling down to a more normal emotional level. As one pair of ethnographers put it, I "became a playmate and a toy" whom the children sometimes "saw they could put . . . to use to achieve some personal goal," such as going outside before it was "time" or avoiding having to sit in the circle.[8]

At the more affluent schools Arrowhead and Oceanview, in contrast, while the children were certainly friendly, knitting with me, drawing for me, calling on me to watch while they scrambled around the monkey bars, I was less important in their social world, and rarely marked as a new or interesting person. As at Sojourner Truth, they would sometimes treat me as a toy—two Arrowhead girls once spent the better part of an afternoon trying to convince me that they were sisters—but I seemed to be less exciting overall for them. The varying levels of emotional energy that surrounded me at the different sites reflected an important distinction about these different contexts. In the intensity of the Sojourner Truth children, for example, we can discern some features of their environment: the rarity of white people in the after-school program, the exuberance celebrated in the African-American community, the normally strict confines of Ms. Graham's very tight ship.[9]

Despite the exciting aura around my Sojourner Truth entrances, however, I quickly became as boring for the children there as I was for the Oceanview and Arrowhead children. I actively encouraged this reaction, generally by receding into the background more, watching them tear around the playground, or reading to them if they asked, always responding with warmth, but usually not initiating play. Much social science advocates a low-key role for the ethnographer. In studies with children in particular, writers counsel researchers to eschew explicit displays of authority or adulthood, and to reach instead for what one author has called "the least adult role." In this research, I was careful to avoid claims of authority—at Oceanview, Ms. Sullivan snorted when she heard me introduce myself and say "I can't get you in trouble"; I accepted responsibility only in a few isolated cases at Sojourner Truth when the teachers needed me to cover for them and I did not feel comfortable saying no. In this way, I strove to be there for the children without imposing the censure of an adult presence upon them.[10]

INTERVIEWS

In addition to the observation component, the research involved interviews with fifty-four family members. I interviewed fifteen families from each site, as well as a small subsample of middle-class families in an out-lying area. I attempted to capture the variation in experiences within the schools themselves—by race/ethnicity, family structure, income, and other criteria (see table 2). For most families, I interviewed only the mother, although in a handful of cases, I interviewed both parents or just the father. Generally, I asked to interview the primary caregiver, and let the family decide who that was. On occasion the children were also at the interview; I experimented with ways to make them feel more at ease, for one family (Margaret Roa and her daughter Theresa) even sitting in their living room putting on nail polish together. I also interviewed a handful of children before deciding that interviewing, which required forming a narrative of self and thinking abstractly, was a method better suited to adults; I found I had more success in understanding children's experiences of consumption and inequality from informal conversations and fieldwork observations.[11]

While my primary informants came from three communities in the expensive Bay Area, they largely fell into two groups differentiated by socioeconomic status, or class. "Class" is not a term about whose definition there is much consensus in social science. For my purposes here, I consider education, income, and occupation as determinants of class; while I refer most of the time to my informants' income status, the two rather starkly different groups of informants differed with regard to the other measures as well. None of my low-income participants had a four-year college degree, although a few had some postsecondary education; and if they were employed, they had jobs like "nurse's assistant" and "retail clerk." In contrast, almost all of my upper-income group had bachelor's degrees, and if they were employed, most had jobs like "headhunter," "lawyer," "doctor," and "researcher."[12]

Interviews were semistructured, focusing in part on what Arlie Hochschild has called the "magnified moments" of social ritual, and the adult interviews were in-depth, lasting mostly between two and four hours. I interviewed several of the adults twice, which I found helped to confirm impressions, rectify errors, and, most important, develop trust.

Table 2. *Characteristics of Families Sampled for Interviews, by site*

	Sojourner Truth	Arrowhead	Oceanview
Racial/ethnic composition (%)			
White	0	57	67
Nonwhite	100	43	33
African-American	82	29	26
Asian-American	9	14	7
Latino	9	0	0
Economic indicators (%)			
Students receiving free/ reduced-price lunch	90	n.a.	1
Students receiving financial aid	n.a.	29	n.a.

SOURCE: Self-reported data from parent interviews.

NOTE: The abbreviation *n.a.* means "not applicable."

Interviews covered themes from how the family handled such events as birthdays, children's teeth falling out, and Halloween to feelings about school choice, community investment, and the politics of race and class. All participating families were paid $50.

Most participants said they enjoyed the experience, with some commenting about how it almost felt like a therapy session, how the experience of thinking deeply about these matters made them view them in new light, or how they enjoyed the time to reflect. "We're having fun talking," said Carrie, from Oceanview. "I feel like you're just a new friend!" Or, as Paulette offered: "That was good for me. I needed to talk! It worked both ways!" One low-income couple, interviewed together, mentioned they rarely had time to be with one another, and so the interview was like a gift to them. That said, however, most Sojourner Truth families still seemed to view me as something alien—albeit sympathetic—to their own experience. Malcolm Clarke said that while *he* enjoyed the interview, he couldn't speak for everybody. "They might think you're . . . you're trying to be funny, you're trying to do research about me?" he said, perhaps giving voice to some of his own discomfort with the process, despite his protestations to the contrary.

To some degree, it was useful when parents perceived me as more distant from their own experiences, as when low-income informants would verbalize taken-for-granted assumptions about what the state welfare system CalWORKs made them go through, or how dangerous their neighborhood was. "Girl, this drug-infested area!" Erika exclaimed. Still, this distance likely made some of their references more cryptic, especially when these informants were apparently talking about the illegal economy, as when Sandra Perkins discussed her neighbors: one who "spends a lot of money on clothes for her kids [but] don't have no job" and another who "doesn't buy their kids clothes at all, [but if] they stop spending their money on other stuff [said meaningfully], they could afford it."

In addition to the interviews and observations, I also accompanied some of my sampled families shopping, following the anthropologist Elizabeth Chin, who took inner-city children to the store with $20 and recorded their purchases, which she found were aimed more at forging relationships than gaining status. I did not pay for what my informants bought, but I paid close attention to how they approached the task at hand, the acquisition skills they demonstrated, and the "devotional love" they enacted through shopping for others. Like the differences among schools and families, differences in the shopping episodes illuminated some of the contextual differences shaping my informants' lives, such as the extent to which middle-class informants allowed children to buy with their own money, or the easy familiarity of some low-income informants with retail store clerks, who exchanged personal gossip and information about what store was hiring.[13]

THE MAKING OF THE ETHNOGRAPHER

Most people who met me in this research saw a middle-class white woman, an older graduate student with jeans and short hair, an apparent mother who talked about children's movies and head lice and other parent concerns; for most people that perception informed their responses. Based on this view, some found the fact that I sought to do research "across class" problematic, even irritating. One early advisor even asked, her arms folded and her eyebrows raised, "And why is it you think they [the low-income parents] would want to talk to you?"

To be sure, in the beginning they probably did not. At Sojourner Truth, while the staff allowed me to volunteer and recruit families for participation in the study, I was at first largely viewed as an oddity, a white lady in a sea of black faces. Babysitters would come to pick up children and assume I was in charge, or substitutes would see me and ask if I were a therapist, since practically the only white people who came to Sojourner Truth were counselors seeing troubled children. In the first year of my research, Sojourner Truth staff could be quite reserved around me, offering guarded approval when they saw me work with the children. "It's nice to see different people taking an interest," one teacher of the preschool-aged children said, her bland reference to "different people" clearly referring, really, to "white people."

Later, however, Ms. Graham and others came to take me for granted, enough to ask me to watch the children while they went off to do errands, to drive the children on field trips, to demand souvenirs from vacations, to chat about daytime dramas, or tease me about my hair or the disordered state of my car. Ms. Graham occasionally seemed to rely on me as a witness—of demanding parents, unsympathetic administrators, or unruly children. "You've been here a long time, you know how Loretta gets," she said, recounting to me one particularly volatile incident. "You know how she explodes. Because I am supposed to protect the other children, I can't just let her go and be wild like that."

At Oceanview and Arrowhead, in contrast, I was never an anomaly, blending in with other parents at field trips or volunteers on site. At Arrowhead, for example, parents picking up their children from the after-school program had to sign them out on a hanging clipboard;

occasionally there was a small line of parents waiting to do so. One evening, after one parent had signed out, I took the clipboard, intending to hand it to another, acting in my role as helpful volunteer. To another waiting mother, however, I must have looked instead like a parent who had just jumped the queue, and so she reminded me rather emphatically that there was, after all, a line. On field trips at Oceanview, parents asked me which classroom my child was in, or whether I was new. In addition, I knew several families with children who attended both schools, and "met" several interviewees through mutual friends— at a Christmas fete, at a child's birthday party, at a college reunion. These were experience-near contexts for me.

The ethnographer's characteristics are not just important in how they shape others' perceptions of her, however, but also in how they shape her perceptions of others. And in this regard, as is the case for many others to whom we summarily apply these social categories, my own background is a bit more complex, a mélange of keen immigrant ambition and landed gentry that informs my own interest in inequality, particularly class inequality. One of my grandfathers was the child of a construction worker and his contract bride, who emigrated from her Italian village with $7 in her pocket. The other grandfather once invited us all to Thanksgiving dinner at the haughty country club to which he belonged, but not before writing my family a letter describing in great detail what we children were supposed to wear and how we were supposed to act—surely demonstrating his deep suspicion that we were not being brought up to know either. The sense of not quite belonging in either world, familiar to children of all kinds of mixed marriages, was my inheritance. This backdrop, though invisible to unknowing others, shaped my own perceptions and certainly made particular features of social life seem vitally important—the significance of class inequality in shaping people's trajectories, the awareness of difference and how it wends through children's social worlds, the reading of child-rearing and other behaviors as class practice.

CHOOSING THE STORY TO TELL

My analysis of the data from this research involved an interactive dance of observation, analysis, and reflection punctuated by constant checking and rechecking of the evolving story and conclusions with informants back in the field. Coding and analysis followed a process by which I identified several "themes," or observations about repeated concepts, and the larger issues to which these concepts appeared to be linked. Themes included such repeated topics as "possession," "the American dream," "electronics," and "connection to community." I gathered instances of these themes to develop into analytic memos, which subsequently guided my evaluation of those themes that were most pivotal in structuring this book. This analytic process included exploring several themes, returning to the interviews and fieldnotes to test the salience of these identified themes, and using that back-and-forth of exploration and testing to siphon out a sense of which themes are more present, more apt, or more explanatory than others.[14]

Qualitative researchers across the social sciences, informed by critiques from feminist and postcolonial studies, have written extensively about the dilemmas posed by studying others, particularly the practice of doing research on poor or marginalized subgroups. These dilemmas include ethical charges of benefiting from inherent inequalities, and epistemological ones about the stance of the researcher and her claims to knowledge. Some have tried to avoid charges of exoticizing or exploiting the Other by conducting research on their own communities, or "studying up" instead of "studying down." In considering these powerful critiques, I reach for a certain reflective pragmatism. I recognize this work replicates what Julie Bettie called "the colonizing aspect" of ethnography, in talking "about subjects who are not empowered to talk back," the children subordinated by their age, and many of the adults, by income, by racial/ethnic inequalities, by their status as single mothers—in short, by the multiple ways in which they were silenced and sidelined by categories that are real in their social consequences. I put my informants' stories to work, in service to a narrative that is necessarily partial, that reflects my own positionality and politics, that they may not agree with, or that may not reflect their perspective. Nor do I pretend that my informants and I derived equal benefit from this endeavor; my personal and professional rewards surely dwarf what I have to offer those who participated.[15]

Yet I believe these critiques are best used to inform our research, rather than to paralyze it; to modify our practices, rather than to stultify them. "It is our capacity, largely developed in fieldwork, to take the perspective of the folks on the shore, that allows us to learn anything at all—even in our own culture—beyond what we already know," Ortner noted. "Further, it is our location 'on the ground' that puts us in a position to see people not simply as passive reactors and enactors of some system, but as active agents and subjects in their own history." Thus, in the conduct of this research, I sought to honor the various perspectives of my informants while recognizing the impact of my own, to demonstrate my appreciation for their participation, and to take seriously their capacities for action within their social constraints as I constructed my best account of their obstacles and how they navigated their way around them.[16]

GIVING BACK

It is my hope that this book will change the way many people conceive of parent spending and children's consumer desire, for both low-income and affluent families. In addition, however, I sought to give back to the communities who welcomed me. Ironically, although I wanted very much to demonstrate my appreciation to the Sojourner Truth families, some of whom overcame deep-rooted suspicion to invite me into their homes, my efforts to do so often went awry. For example, I sought to recruit some of the Sojourner Truth children to a summer camp for gifted children run by the University of California at Berkeley. The camp's abbreviated hours, its unfamiliarity, its location in a town twenty minutes away, and the extensive application it required, which was intimidating to parents without college degrees—all meant my fairly laborious efforts were completely in vain. I arranged for an outside organization to pay for the children to see the a cappella group Sweet Honey in the Rock perform; while most appeared to enjoy the performance, it paled in comparison to another field trip arranged as a surprise for them a few days before: attendance at a Golden State Warriors basketball game set up by the Police Athletic League. I tried to bring something small to eat or drink to each interview, but even this led to a few mishaps—bringing soda because that is what the children liked, even though my family does not drink any, felt somehow patronizing, while homemade lemonade, which my family does drink, was greeted by the children with some silent nose-wrinkling. Far from erasing the built-in oppositions of researcher and researched, of author and "informant," these efforts were instead further evidence of the cultural chasms between us, even as our common concerns as parents—about popular movies or toys, about educational opportunities and equity, about children's culture—served as points of convergence. In the end, easier for each community to accept were my small contributions of time and money, and, I hope, the light this book sheds on the passions and power of child-rearing consumption.

CONCLUSION

The schools and communities in which I did my research could not have been more different, in the racial and class characteristics of families, in the resources at their disposal, in their emotional landscape, and in their reception of me as a white, middle-class woman and academic. Yet while the differences were surely visible, even glaring, the comparison offered up a more subtle and complex story. Everywhere children had or talked about many of the same commodities and experiences—whether others had seen the latest Star Wars movie, what kind of lunch box they liked, or if they had played the new Xbox game. Everywhere parents were struggling with children's desire, saying yes more than they wanted to, saying no whenever they could. As I shuttled back and forth from one world to its opposite to its opposite yet again, the ways in which parents and children in each site engaged in consumer culture came into relief, and while the differences were surely crucial, the similarities—across the great divide of Oakland—offered up their own powerful significance. It is to these stories, and their meaning, that we now turn.

CHAPTER THREE

Making Do

Children and the Economy of Dignity

It is a chilly afternoon in northern California, and the Arrowhead children are roaming the school's expansive play yard at dismissal time, selling puffballs. Made from loops of yarn secured with a knot at the center and then cut into fringe, puffballs are soft colored spheres, but as far as I can tell, the children do not use them in any games or stories, preferring only to make and sell them to each other and any willing adults. The going rate is a penny a puffball. Claire, a first grader, pudgy and earnest, walks by slowly, calling like a street peddler: "Puffballs for sale! Puffballs for sale!"

Francesca, another first grader, with a blond Afro that frames her wide eyes like a lion's mane, asks me to help her count her money. We discover she has collected twenty cents, and I ask her what she is going to do with her take. "I'm going to give it to my parents so they can buy a house," says the six year old, whose parents I know are a prosecutor and a high-tech entrepreneur. "My dad really wants to move, but all the houses we're looking at are too expensive." Francesca runs off to tell Claire about her new, higher total but comes back dejected. "I tried to tell her, and she didn't want to hear it!" she exclaims in disappointment.

Some of the Arrowhead children seek refuge from the damp cold in a one-room portable building they call the Addition, where the private school's after-school program hosts the knitting club and other activities. A handful of second-grade girls and one or two boys sprawl on the carpet, turning yarn into puffballs. Two first-grade boys build with Legos in the corner, and another group of four plays a board game. The atmosphere is calm, with a low hum of chatter among the children, occasionally punctuated by comments from the two women staff members who help the knitters start and end their projects. We learn one of the teachers just recently cut her hair, donating two feet of it to a wig charity for children.

The conversation turns to birthday parties. Tamsin, a second grader with curly brown hair, talks at length to her friends about her upcoming slumber party, her proud, happy voice hovering over the heads of other children (boys, as well as younger and older girls) presumably not invited. Her mother always has a treasure hunt throughout her house, she announces with anticipation. Every year she thinks up little rhymes as clues, and each girl gets to solve one clue that leads to the location of the next clue, as well as to a small present. "What kind of a present?" a friend asks, leaning in with curiosity. Tamsin says that last year the present was Sticky Feet, a small toy that they threw on the ceiling, and she laughed as she described the air thick with flying Sticky Feet. The year before, the presents were Slinky toys. "I have two dogs that are new since the last party," Tamsin said. "I hope they don't eat up all the clues."

Francesca sits on the floor, knitting with her own yarn, a soft skein of magenta. She is making a scarf for her mother, as is Margaret, a third grader nearby. Francesca is focused on her project and doesn't pay much mind to Tamsin's soliloquy. She is proud of her scarf. "Knitting is better than buying," she announces to the group. Next to her, Claire bends over her puffballs and pipes up about her own birthday party a few weeks ago. "It was at the Bladium," she announces, referring to an indoor soccer stadium in nearby Alameda that offers birthday parties starting at $300. The boys playing the board game argue softly about where the game piece landed. The knitters listen to Claire while they lean in to pick out new yarn colors, or hold up their work to fix a difficult puffball knot.

Claire had fifteen guests at the Bladium, helping her celebrate turning seven years old. "I was the worst goalie," she said, smiling ruefully.

Children talk. They assert, they mumble, they brag, they beg, they encourage, they sympathize, they argue. Through talk, children, like adults, mold and shape the relationships that form their environment. Children use talk to establish, if only momentarily, who is part of their world; their conversations are like a country pond into which they dive—sometimes entering with nary a splash, other times grabbing both ankles and launching themselves in a "cannonball." They make connections to each other through the common water swirling about them, through talk about the things important to their lives, about puffballs or movies, sneakers or school.

Though the Addition hums with puffball manufacturing like an unusually cozy factory, the children there are not wholly obsessed with money or material goods, at one point Francesca even issuing the pronouncement that "knitting is better than buying." Nor does mainstream popular culture or rational evaluations of what is "useful" define all that is worth their attention, as the fad for the homemade puffballs of uncertain play value would attest. Tamsin's pleasure in describing the treasure hunt created for her party stems from more than just the particular small toys it involves each year.

Yet if we pause to analyze the talk that surrounded the Arrowhead children that day, we can see how market culture permeates their environment, framing their efforts to participate in the ongoing activity. The thriving informal trade in puffballs floats along, buoyed by an ambiance of measure and barter. Francesca knew that her family could not quite afford the houses her father wanted to move into, the children were aware that donated hair made it possible for poor kids with cancer to get wigs, Tamsin understood that her mother bought the little gifts that her friends ended up with at her party.

Moreover, market culture circles the children's discussions like a moat around a fortress. In order to join in the birthday party conversation, for example, the norms of children's talk meant that only children with celebrations somehow equal in stature—in elaborate preparations, in rarity, in superior fun—could leap in to share. Children who celebrated their birthday in the park with pizza and a cake, then, could not speak up, since ordinary parties were not in the same category, not really as worthy of mention as those in which particularly time-consuming and careful arrangements were made. Princeton scholar Randall Collins has suggested that such talk is a kind of ritual, observing that "rituals mark boundaries of inclusion and exclusion."[1]

If most children were excluded from chiming in, then who could enter the discussion? Claire volunteers her story about the Bladium, on some level "matching" the treasure hunt despite involving in all likelihood little more planning than a soccer practice with dessert. What makes the Bladium "count" enough to warrant mention? Claire does not give details of someone's extensive set-up, excellent food, or even terrific play, as downplayed by her appealingly modest "I was the worst goalie." But a party at the Bladium is unusual, even for these privileged children, and furthermore, it has the added sheen of a commodified experience, "enchanted" by the privatized lure of all a commercial venue can provide—which includes, although Claire does not say it out loud, a professional party coordinator, a sports café, and a game arcade for party guests insufficiently occupied by the 2.5 acres of available sports arena.[2]

Such conversations form the crux of what I have termed the "economy of dignity," the system by which children make themselves audible, and therefore present, therefore mattering to their peers. Even for children, consumption is a language, a symbolic medium that communicates a message—an insight with a long pedigree, from Veblen to Bourdieu to Baudrillard. As Harvard sociologist Michele Lamont reported, her informants considered "consumption . . . a criterion for cultural membership, equating money with 'belonging.'"[3]

While the word "economy" usually pertains to the realm of material life and its orchestration, including motivations, production, distribution, and consumption, an "economy of dignity" emphasizes the dynamics of symbolic life. Like those of adults, children's social worlds are the shared ground for symbolic life, where cultural meaning is made, and the tenets of dignity established. Each such social world features its own economy of dignity, most closely resembling a black-market economy, one children conduct on the margins of an order established by adults, its features often reflecting the negative space where adult rules are not felt. These economies have their own scrip, or meaningful tokens, their own norms about managing children's conversations, and their own processes of negotiating value. Children used different scrip in their social milieu, employing them to transform themselves into citizens of their public sphere. Children effect that magic by engaging in facework—the impression management that involves the presentation of an honorable self—in order to gather dignity in public.[4]

The sociologist Erving Goffman first coined the term "facework" to signify how someone gamely participates in the social regime, particularly in ginning up expected feelings in front of an audience, as when mourners demonstrate sadness at a funeral. A trenchant observer of the "expressive order," Goffman focused on the unspoken rules by which people maintained "social life [as] an uncluttered, orderly thing," emphasizing the sometimes perverse mutuality of sustaining each other's face, under which people labor for the good of politesse. Because of his famous and unique interest in "not . . . men and their moments [but] moments and their men," however, Goffman relied on a rather anemic view of the person. He paid little attention to why people would try to enter a conversation in the first place, except, as he put it, to advance a "line," a rather tautological concept of their own "view of the situation." In addition, Goffman's actors seem to have a confusing relationship with their own feelings—on the one hand, they deploy them strategically to save face; on the other hand, feelings are like the earth's magma, bubbling up from within, as when a particular line "feels" inauthentic. Most important, Goffman's version of "face" reflected his rather knowing, winking view of human behavior, in which all the world's a game, to be played to varying levels of success. But even if everyday culture is a constellation of games, these are best considered "serious games," as the anthropologist Sherry Ortner has argued, with high stakes in an asymmetrical world, "played with intensity and sometimes deadly earnestness."[5]

I rely on Goffman's concept of facework, then, as the evocation of the presentation work people do in front of interested others, but my use of the term differs substantially here, because I anchor it within the *person* using facework, rather than in the *conversation* whose norms the facework preserves. Children are less concerned about satisfying expectations they already sense, I would argue, than about gaining the standing to take part in their social world. In the economy of dignity, children do facework not just to "*save* face," to rescue the social citizenship that enables their sense of belonging in a group, but also to establish it in the first place, and through varied and creative means. As Goffman himself observed:

> What the person protects and defends and invests his feelings in is an idea about himself, and ideas are vulnerable not to facts and things but to communications. Communications belong to a less punitive scheme than do facts, for communications can be bypassed, withdrawn from, disbelieved, conveniently misunderstood and tactfully conveyed.[6]

As I use it here, "facework" is an umbrella term referring to a number of different processes that do such cultural work, as we see below in both low-income and affluent settings. Children employed facework most often to manage their interactional, personal, and social difference from others, sometimes downplaying them, other times highlighting them. Through such efforts, children constructed and contested the salience of commodified goods and events in signifying belonging and care.[7]

"I'M THANKFUL FOR MY ANCESTORS": SCRIP AND SYMBOLIC VALUE

One afternoon, the children at Sojourner Truth were making Thanksgiving posters about things for which they were thankful. They undertook these projects in the same way they did their homework, quickly, with a lot of oppositional chatter back and forth between the desks ("You used too much glitter." "Was I talking to you, Janelle?" "At least I'm not an egghead."). But while their attitudes were anything but reverent, their posters read like prayers. "Thank you for my clothes, my toys, thank you for the roof over my head, thank you for taking care of me," read one. "Thank you for my mother and my sisters," read another.

Marco, the son of recent Latino immigrants whom we saw in the first chapter inventing a new Halloween costume, was having trouble creating his poster. He scribbled a few words under a scrawled picture and brought it up to Ms. Graham, who looked at it and turned him back, saying: "You did this too quickly, go back and work on this some more." Obediently, he trudged back to his table, observed by Loretta, a reckless, rather unpredictable African-American second grader who never could resist getting involved, a bit like a thrill-seeking, slightly untrustworthy test pilot running for city council.

Loretta and her sister Yvette had lived not so long ago in foster care, and though their mother had once been drug addicted, even homeless, the mother had regaled me with stories of how they celebrated with feasting and presents when she got the children back—"Girl, we was just buying everything—shoes, clothes, pictures, food," she recalled. In contrast, Marco's family had come to America from Mexico within the last two years, and they had bought very little for the children in the interim, except essentials like food and clothing, and for the family, a large television.

When Loretta saw Marco sitting at his desk, seemingly stumped as he contemplated the assignment of rendering what he was thankful for, she made a suggestion, leaning in to point at his paper. "Thankful for what you *have*," she directed him, in a half whisper. Marco just looked at her, his sturdy body unmoved. Then, suddenly roused, he flung out, "I am thankful for my *ancestors*."

In this exchange, the two children were invoking perhaps the most meaningful and effective tokens of value at their disposal. "What you have" was highly symbolic for Loretta, recalling family togetherness and hope, the day she and Yvette got to come back home to their mother. On the other hand, Marco's response was forceful, pulling out his own alternative: a sense of family history and, perhaps, past sacrifices. In all likelihood Loretta was as thankful for her family as Marco was, yet by countering her formulation with an explicit reference to family, Marco implicitly suggests "what you have" is spiritually empty, materialistic, the very opposite of "my ancestors." This negotiation about what to be thankful for reveals for us the counterframing that Marco attempts as an alternative to the consumer culture that predominates, in a discursive move that creates space for someone who has little to claim by way of possessions.

It was rare for children's interactions to feature such a direct exchange about what might be valued as scrip in their world. More commonly, children tossed out news of their possessions or experiences like fishing lines that never crossed, much as we saw in the birthday party conversation in the Addition, where the Sticky Feet description floated there right alongside the reference to the Bladium, without direct comparison. Indeed, this seeming avoidance of comparison was part of what led me to seek out another explanation for children's conversations about goods and experiences, beyond simple consumer competition. If what was sought was merely victory in a status contest, we might see children engaging each other directly about the merits of this or that item more often. "Oh yeah," Claire might have declared to Tamsin. "Well, the Bladium is better because you get to play soccer," rather than her more understated description of her own party. By adding their own experience alongside that of their peers, rather than forcing a win-or-lose challenge, children seem to be less striving to triumph than forging a community around particular valuable tokens, such as for Claire, "those of us with fun birthday parties."

What makes something count as a form of scrip? In an important sense, such tokens are whatever works to gain the child entry into the ongoing conversation among his or her peers. At each field site, what worked as scrip was a fluid and dynamic list; I observed children constantly lobbing new gambits by trial and error to create symbolic chits in the conversational air.[8]

Marco's ability to innovate notwithstanding, however, most of the time what counted as scrip fell into discernible patterns. Children made the most symbolic value out of claiming access to popular culture—from actually owning or using to merely knowing about electronic game systems, the cards and toys marketers promote as "collectibles," dolls, and clothing, as well as particular movies, music, or destinations. One day at Sojourner Truth,

> Thelma takes out her Game Boy Advance. "Whose is that?" I ask. "Mine," she says. "My mother gave it to me. I'm getting some new games for Christmas." "I have a Game Boy," said Curtis. "I have a Game Boy," said Lamont. Marlaine didn't say anything.

Declaring themselves to their communities when they could, children launched their efforts to claim and own symbolic value like fireworks sputtering into the sky.[9]

Discussion about destinations, or outings to special places, often commercial ones, was also particularly salient. Low-income children, and their parents, frequently referred to Marine World, a Bay Area theme park with animals and water shows located about a forty-five-minute drive from Sojourner Truth. One day with the Sojourner Truth children, I rode the bus on a field trip, sitting next to two petite friends—Jasmine, a happy African-American second grader, and Alisa, a shy Latina first grader.

> Jasmine wears a t-shirt that says "Princess." "You are your mother's princess," Ms. Graham says, grinning. Jasmine announces, "It's my birthday tomorrow." "What are you doing for your birthday?" I ask. She says, "I'm going to Marine World." Alisa says, "I am going to go to Marine World and SeaWorld." Jasmine says, "I am going to Marine World and SeaWorld."

While Jasmine's family may well have been taking her to Marine World for her birthday, a tandem visit to SeaWorld (a twelve-hour drive away in San Diego) is less credible. But in the moment when children are engaging in facework, the game of meeting and matching the scrip claims of others can generate its own logic.

In general, the destinations and possessions that numbered among the tokens of value were heavily advertised, and the children's awareness and use of them as cultural proxies for belonging reflected the reach and power of corporate marketing to children. Children relied on these prepackaged symbols to establish their claims to the community based on such shared values as being cool, savvy, popular, older than their years (but not an adult), and not poor; this list captured some of the primary social anxieties of these children, who were working hard not to be mistaken for being unaware, awkward, or unable to afford what others had. Yet the purported value and meaning of these commercial goods and events were not always assured, and the rooms of Sojourner Truth rang with the efforts of children to establish a sense of shared values.[10]

The children did not always have the means to participate in these declarative riffs on possessions or destinations. Like Marco, some then improvised with noncommercial tokens to counter or meet dignity claims based on consumption. These alternative forms of scrip—such as particular knowledge about or competence in playing with (someone else's) Yu-Gi-Oh! cards, for example, or Marco's trope of family— worked best on those occasions when children recognized their meanings as also valid within the constraints of their economy of dignity.

One day, for example, a first-grade boy, Derrick, took out some Magic cards, a popular collectible item. Derrick was very large for his age, almost the size of a third grader, but he was not very quick and bore an air of oafish geniality—"He's like Baby Huey, that old cartoon, he just has no idea how big he is," Ms. Graham observed. I was not sure where he got his cards; his mother, a janitor supporting four children, had told me how hard it was to get food on the table toward the end of some months. Three older boys in the class, Simon, Rion, and Curtis, were drawn to the cards instantly, and as Derrick held them up high in the air, they followed him to the corner for a game as if he were the leader of a marching band. My fieldnotes recorded how a conflict revealed the boys' perspective on the symbolic tokens of possession and skill.

> Derrick makes a fairly big deal about dealing a deck to Simon, who keeps trying to look at the cards as if they were a hand he was being dealt. But apparently Derrick has already given Rion, not Simon, the hand they are going to play with, so Derrick thinks Simon should not be looking at the cards. Derrick doesn't explain this misunderstanding, however. Rather he just keeps yelling at Simon not to look, and then when Simon does look, Derrick takes the cards back and re-deals, talking about hiding "the dark star."
>
> Simon says to Derrick: "Why you doing this? It's like playing with someone in kindergarten." "We'll whup him [Derrick] anyway," Rion says to Simon. Later, Derrick is crestfallen. "They won't play with me anymore," he tells me, while Curtis circles him chanting, in a sort of Sesame Street cadence: "Cheat-ing, cheating, say it with me! Cheat-ing, cheating!"

Derrick waged his own social effort here, securing the attention of older boys with his cards, trying to hold on to the moment of his triumph by leading them to the corner, then dealing. Meanwhile, Simon, like Marco, was the son of recent immigrants who scoffed at the vestiges of children's consumer culture that seeped into even their home; the boy's attempt to surmount this disadvantage was the facework that opened chapter 1. I had been to Simon's house and seen for myself: the sum total of Simon's toys was a bicycle, a Connect Four game, and a plastic McDonald's giveaway. Yet somehow he mustered the technical competence to claim mastery of the Magic card game, to deliver the ultimate insult to a first grader ("it's like playing with a kindergartner"), and to rally the other boys to his defense.

In these types of cases, the children demonstrated another feature of scrip tokens: the tension they embody between the popular and the distinctive. Like fashion, forms of scrip call upon collective understandings of symbolic value borne out of shared experience, but those commonalities also enable individuals to set themselves apart, as Malcolm, a third grader, demonstrated on another day shortly before Martin Luther King Day. Ms. Graham was leading a discussion with the children in a circle around her.

> They were all on the rug, and Ms. Graham was deeply involved in a discussion of things that slaves didn't have and that the kids had today—e.g., refrigerators, washing machines, microwaves. "I have two microwaves," Fia announces. Volunteers Malcolm, "My great-great-great-grandfather was a slave."

In another setting, one could conceive of the information that your great-great-great-grandfather was a slave as something one would not necessarily announce proudly. But Malcolm, a widely admired child with one earring and a half-regal, half-insolent carriage, used his knowledge of ancestry as a bit of scrip, right on the heels of Fia's two microwaves. What made dignity here was that Malcolm knew who his great-great-great-grandfather was, which lent his family the gravity and sense of history not common among the children. Paradoxically, the distinctiveness of some forms of scrip—which arises only in relation to others—also establishes their users as members of the same community. Lamont saw fit to announce that he owned a Game Boy because everyone did, while at the same time Malcolm's pronouncement had social value because knowing one's family history was unusual; both boys trafficked in the variable tokens of dignity.

Thus differences varied in their meaning and value. Interactional difference, or the momentary kind, based on whether or not you are "thankful for what you have" or have seen the latest Eddie Murphy movie, was critical for establishing belonging, and such differences seemed to pose urgent challenges for children. Differences that were more personal (of character, knowledge, or body) and social (such as race or class) were more mixed—some, like your knowledge of family history, were worth cultivating, while others were important to hide. Sometimes children countered one kind of difference with another—for example, Simon made up for his lack of Magic cards, an interactional difference, with his skill in playing, a personal difference.

Furthermore, the three types of difference are of course intimately related; whether or not a child had been to Tahoe or knew how to play the piano certainly depended at least in part on his family's class status. Social differences often seemed to lurk behind interactional differences, as if the latter were signaling the former, as Julie Bettie discovered in her analysis of "style" differences in a California high school. In some environments, certain social differences carried more stigma than others. Thus while interactional differences were crucial for children everywhere, the importance and worth of other kinds of differences varied from context to context.[11]

SCRIP AND THE SOCIAL CONTEXTS OF CLASS

At the private school Arrowhead, Game Boys were prohibited at school except during "holiday camp," when Arrowhead provided child care during vacation. One day, Noah, a white affluent boy, was unable to bring one in, and thus had to overcome what was a momentary disadvantage with facework. Generally the task of those who perceived they had something to prove, facework most often comprised the strategies of children without certain goods, skills, or destinations to talk about—even under the graceful redwoods of Arrowhead.

> Noah and two other boys sat on the couch in the Addition playing games on their Game Boys, apparently all Game Boy Advance SP—the latest ones for sale at the time—with the background tinny wail of the Game Boy music. Among the three boys on the couch there were only two Game Boys, with Noah in the middle, sitting close to one and then the other, looking over their shoulders.
> "Do you have one too?" I asked. He nodded. "Where is it?" "My parents don't let me bring it," he said, mumbling. Sitting between the players, Noah kept up a low whine with a lot of "Please, can I play, let me play, I just want to play this one and 19 and 20." I asked some questions about the games—"How many levels are there? How hard is it to move up?"—and Noah answered while watching the other ones over their shoulders.

Then a third Game Boy came, delivered by a teacher to a chubby second grader on the floor; it looked a little different than the others. "It came from my mom," he announced. All three players sat there, without moving, the little tinny music playing on, punctuated by "Oh, a golden capsule" or "Ow!" or "Why does it say 'no one hurt'?" or "I love level 23, it's so easy." Finally one of the fourth graders handed his Game Boy over to Noah before coming down to play with Legos on the floor.

Certainly in this vignette Noah did not have a lot of dignity as it is conventionally understood. Nonetheless, he was knowledgeable about his peers' activity, aware even of how to ask for just a limited favor ("just this one and 19 and 20"), included in their circle, and rewarded by the fourth grader's eventual capitulation. He attempted to overcome his temporary disadvantage through claims on friendship and demonstrations of technical competence. While it is likely that the parents who prohibited Noah from bringing the device to school thought that he would be outside biking, instead he was inside, manufacturing his own belonging.

Earlier, we observed children wrestling with social belonging at Sojourner Truth, where students were from households with incomes under the federal poverty line, who might be expected to have anxiety about proving themselves as "not poorer than others around them." What about more affluent children like Noah? Were their dignity needs different? What did their forms of scrip reflect about their preoccupations or social anxiety? What kind of meaning did they attach to things?

Most children at Arrowhead, as well as at Oceanview Elementary, the elite public school perched in the hills overlooking San Francisco Bay, came from families with extensive resources of time, money, education, and networks, compared to the families of Sojourner Truth children. Yet with a few exceptions their symbolic tokens were highly similar, differing more in scale than in kind.

Surprisingly, the particular possessions that enabled children to take part in social conversations among their peers were largely familiar across communities that in other respects differed dramatically. Children at all three field sites talked about collectible cards, although at Sojourner Truth, despite Derrick's episode, Yu-Gi-Oh! cards dominated play among certain sets of boys, while at Arrowhead, Magic cards were more in fashion, and more girls played with them. Game Boys were highly coveted, valued, and discussed at all three sites, again mostly by boys. Girls discussed clothes, music, and dolls at all three locations, although the kind of clothes, music, and some of the dolls varied, from Bratz dolls (about $20) at Sojourner Truth to American Girl dolls (about $90) at Oceanview and Arrowhead, for example.

Affluent and low-income children alike talked about special destinations, but these destinations differed in scope; affluent children called upon other, pricier venues than Marine World or SeaWorld, such as Guatemala or Chile. "Going to the snow" appeared to be particularly symbolic for these northern California residents. One day at Oceanview, for example, the teacher handed out a permission slip for a field trip that Friday, when Rachel announced to the group that she would not be able to go because she was going to Tahoe. Later, the class was reviewing their "favorite things" for self-introductions they would be making on videotape.

> Several said "snowboarding" or "skiing at Tahoe." Turner, an eager African-American boy, said his favorite thing was playing with Sam, but Sam, an Asian-American boy who spoke next, said he liked best "snowboarding at Tahoe."

One day at Arrowhead, before the school's spring break, I watched a mother picking up her child from the after-school program. As she waited for him to hoist his backpack on his shoulder, he asked: "Can we go to Mexico, Mom?" She laughed, meeting my eyes, and I said to her, "What can you say to that?' "Okay," she said, her hands in an open gesture, rather enigmatically, I thought. Adventures—to the snow or around the globe—earned Oceanview and Arrowhead children the sense of belonging, the ability to participate in the daily conversation surrounding them—high stakes that then shaped children's desires.

Despite these surface differences between forms of scrip for lower-income and affluent childen, through which they (and their parents) enacted their class identities, the underlying symbolic meanings were broadly similar. Popular culture, travel, and other talk in each of the field sites often touched on the same themes—of being cool enough, old enough, and wealthy enough to be socially visible.

While scrip tokens were broadly similar across affluent and low-income milieus, there were a few thematic differences. When affluent children contested the commercial meanings of others with their own counterframings, for example, in doing so they sometimes suggested they knew better ways to spend their money. As an example, one day at Arrowhead two white boys played with Pokémon cards. "How many do you have?" asked one. The other one hazarded a guess. "600? I don't know," he said. "I just bought them, a lot of packs, new, there are two decks. My grandmother gave me $500 for my birthday, now I have $40." The other little boy playing with him stopped and looked at him for a moment. "I'm saving my money for college," he said.

How do you match someone who says he has almost $500 in Pokémon cards? By contesting the notion that that is a good use of money in the first place. Faced with the towering magnitude of one boy's Pokémon consumption, his playmate implicitly posited a competing value system. But instead of saying "I spend time with my family" or another possibility such as might have been used at Sojourner Truth, the money saver suggested that his friend was a "flawed consumer," and offered an alternative that symbolized responsibility for one's self and commitment to a future. Rarely, affluent children also sounded antimaterialistic themes—such as Francesca's "Knitting is better than buying"—through which they also tried on alternative belief systems.[12]

WHAT SCRIP SIGNIFIES: THE CLAIM TO CARE

It is perhaps unsurprising that children's forms of scrip relied on particular symbolic markers to claim positive qualities for themselves, such as talent, wealth, skill, or long family pedigrees. But children's tokens of value also established the bona fides of another claim, one that struck at the core of children's identity as worthwhile, one that traversed income inequality: that of the child as "cared-for." Ultimately, part of the deeper appeal of possessions, destinations, and other mediated claims—in which the children used particular objects or events to represent good qualities about themselves—was in their ability to imbue the children with the aura of those who received the care, time, and attention of others. And just as children's anxieties about being poor, uncool, or unaware were revealed by the strenuous work they performed to deny that with symbolic goods, so too did children's efforts to show themselves as cared-for suggest that at bottom they feared they might not be.

By this logic, then, children who had possessions were more than deserving or lucky; they were cared-for. Poignant examples abounded at Sojourner Truth.

> Shakeira comes over to me and sits down. "Hello seven year old," I say, [referring to her recent birthday]. I ask if she had a good time, and she says: "Yes. My mom works at Toys"R"Us, and I have a whole bag of balls, and I have a ball and what's that thing you hit it with?—a racquet—I have two of those."

In numerous examples, the children seemed to equate care with provisioning, as in the plaintive voices captured in the Mother's Day cards the children created one day. "My mom is special to me because she keeps me warm, she buys me clothes, she buys me toys and food, walks with me, reads to me, pays for the house. That's why I think my mother is special," read one card. But being cared-for was also its own source of pride, which extended beyond money or consumption. Jacquette was very proud of attention she got from her father, even though he had many children by women who were not her mother, and was currently incarcerated:

> Jacquette takes out a card with a letter from her father inside it. It spells out her name on top in kind of a gothic calligraphy. At the bottom it says "I (heart) you." In the middle, it has a cartoonlike figure

in raised plastic. "He's not around, he's in jail," Jacquette explains. "He's in the big house," pipes in Theresa, her best friend, sitting next to her. Jacquette reads us the letter, which says: "Hey momma, I think of you every day, I hope you are still doing well in school, because if you keep on getting good grades then you will stay out of trouble. I love you and think of you all the time, Sincerely, Juron."

Jacquette treated the card from her father as if it were a sacred relic, as well it might be—a piece of ritualistic testimony to the fact that she was known and cared-for, even if the caregiver was "in the big house."

The complex relationship between owning possessions and being cared-for was demonstrated at Sojourner Truth one day when David wanted more nachos from Aleta. David, a diminutive Chinese-American first grader, had a sister Jenny with whom Aleta wanted to play, as my fieldnotes recorded.

> Aleta was eating her nachos and complained to me that David had told his sister Jenny not to be her friend because Aleta didn't give him enough nachos. Aleta told me she had "given him plenty of nachos, and candy the other day." David announced, "My mother says I can't have any candy from anybody, any friend." I ask him, "You've never had candy?" He says, "I can have it if my mother or my father gives it to me, but no one else." He added, "And I'm going to McDonald's on Friday."

Here David does a complicated discursive dance. The seeming non sequitors of his announcements start to cohere, however, when we see them as part and parcel of the same gambits for dignity. On the one hand, he acknowledges the power of possession and tries to wrest control over the nachos from Aleta, by rationing Aleta's access to his sister. When Aleta brings up candy, however, David announces that he cannot have candy, a confession that would be perplexing if we viewed possession as the only good here. Instead, however, David is asserting his mother's prohibition as evidence of her caring protectiveness. Going to McDonald's, then, is right on topic—his mother cares about him enough to shield him from the implied danger in others' candy, *and* to indulge him in commercialized pleasure.

Were these pointed demonstrations of care (and its underlying anxiety) limited to low-income children? Children in more affluent locales seemed also to work hard to convey that they were cared-for, suggesting that to some extent they shared the same anxieties as low-income children, despite their contexts of plenty. They often seemed to be intentionally portraying themselves as somebody's focal point. The difference was that affluent children used a wider variety of tactics to do so, as we saw in Tamsin's birthday-party description at the beginning of the chapter. Tamsin used the elaborate preparation her mother undertakes to represent her own centrality as the object of somebody's extensive caring. Other children talked about their extracurricular lessons in the same way, as if the "concerted cultivation" of their individual talents and skills was evidence they were cared-for.

> A fourth grader talks to the group (about four–five children, two after-school teachers, and me) about how she takes math and Chinese and guitar after school, and how grueling that outside schedule is. She is taking Chinese at "a lady's house" because she is going to southern China next year for two years with her parents. She is taking math because "Arrowhead is bad at math, and in China they are ahead in math, like doing sixth- or seventh-grade work in fifth grade. But also Arrowhead is bad in math," she adds confidently.

Implicit in this girl's soliloquy was the notion that someone cared enough about her academic progress to notice that Arrowhead is "bad at math" (a fact she was announcing to other Arrowhead students), and to arrange for her to get some supplementary tutoring. Annette Lareau observed that through such middle-class cultivation "children learn they are special." Data from my fieldwork suggest they also learned to equate that kind of parental scrutiny with what it means to be cared-for.[13]

DIGNITY PROCESSES

In addition to finding that particular items or experiences served as scrip, I also identified four kinds of facework strategies used at the different field sites, through which children navigated the economy of dignity. Children engaged in bridging labor, claiming, concealing, and patrolling. Like scrip, facework strategies were remarkably similar across class, differing more in detail than in kind.

Bridging Labor

Bridging labor, as Simon and Marco demonstrated in navigating Halloween at Sojourner Truth, was the strategy of those who did not have as much as others, who had to work to be included. At Arrowhead, for example, Desirée, an African-American third grader, faced the problem of reinterpreting her father's blue-collar occupation amid her peers, affluent children of parents with mostly professional jobs, as fieldnotes demonstrated:

> Her dad puts in driveways, she said, followed quickly by "which is really cool, you know why? He's been to all sorts of famous people's houses, like he and my uncle worked on a driveway for [popular musician] Alicia Keys, and for the Shaq [basketball player Shaquille O'Neill]."

Desirée used the aura of celebrities and popular culture to transform a perceived lack into something admirable, a token of family background. Through bridging labor, children used their discursive agility to surmount a deficit in coveted goods, in destination, in skill or activity, working to portray that deficit as an asset.

Claiming

Children in both poor and affluent sites also engaged in claiming, or suggesting outright that they owned what they did not. One day, for example, I asked the Sojourner Truth children to draw "a picture of their world":

> Most drew their houses and neighborhoods, but a small group drew their rooms. Aleta included such details as a bed, dresser, and a

"DivaStar rug," which featured the face and body of a favorite character. When her mother came later to pick her up, she smiled as she looked the picture over. "The DivaStar rug is a wanting item," she said. "Everything's in there but that rug."

Aleta narrated her drawing while she was sketching the fictitious rug, but did not let on that the rug was not actually part of her bedroom. In this way, her facework borrowed from fantasy, one of the ways that children engage with the consumer world, as the anthropologist Elizabeth Chin has described, by "wanting an item and not just possessing it; by knowing lyrics to commercial jingles without ever laying eyes or hands on the object itself."[14]

Children also claimed rights to beg, borrow, or steal particular items they coveted. At Arrowhead, class differences among children became more marked during "holiday camp," when the children were allowed to bring not only their Game Boys but also their bicycles from home. One girl, Sharla, an African-American child who lived with her single mother in subsidized housing, didn't have a bicycle. A dynamic personality, Sharla convinced her white, middle-class classmate Erin to lend her one, but the instructors, worried that Sharla was taking advantage of Erin, thought to establish rules about when it was "sharing time" and when it was "not-sharing time":

> [The instructor] tells them: "No, it's time for Erin to ride it now, you come in here, Sharla, and help me with these masks." As Sharla hands over the helmet, she says to Erin: "Okay, you can have it for now, but later it will be my turn again. You can have it for now though."

Here Sharla acted as though she owned the bike—"You can have it for now"—in an example of claiming, cultural work that makes up for a perceived lack of something. In so doing, she asserted her right to borrow the bicycle, indeed even to pretend it was her own without explicitly taking on the borrower's supplicant position.

Patrolling

Children do not always let their friends claim ownership they don't have. Another process in the economy of dignity is what we might call "patrolling," when children evaluate, challenge, or affirm others' dignity claims. Children monitored others' claims for fantasy and for whether or not they were obeying children's rules. One day as the Sojourner Truth children were walking to a field trip, for example, two boys were talking about a new gaming system.

> Rasheed says something about having a particular PlayStation or other module, and then explains to me, "It's $600." The boy he's with says, "No, you don't have one, Rasheed," and Rasheed does not protest.

Here Rasheed's claiming—his attempt to engage in facework based on fantasy—is reined in by his classmate, who is patrolling for accuracy.

Concealing

Just as children conducted facework to render certain characteristics visible, such as Malcolm's knowledge of his slave ancestors, they also worked to make other features invisible, in particular working to conceal differences from their peers that they perceived as negative. Children almost always worked to hide interactional difference, through bridging labor and other efforts. But they also concealed those personal and social differences that carried a stigma, although which differences those were varied from context to context.

Poverty is a social difference, and through observation of low-income children and adults in her mixed-income field site, Barrie Thorne has called efforts to obscure signs of poverty "shame work." At Sojourner Truth, a homogeneously poor setting, children were fairly matter-of-fact about signs of their poverty. One day I observed the head teacher, Ms. Graham, preparing to take the kids on a field trip.

At one point Ms. Graham asks, "Who didn't bring a lunch?" There are kids who brought a bag lunch; those who didn't do so get a plastic bag containing a sandwich on white bread, a nectarine, and a drink. It looks like she is putting together about ten (out of twenty) bags, but it is hard to tell how many because even kids who brought their lunch used a plastic bag to do so.

Ms. Graham's question, in the context of American schools, is a charged one, in that she is asking who among the children qualifies for free lunch, a well-known poverty measure. In other settings, children regard actions that make them look like they might qualify for free lunch with shame or fear—one of my informants refused to let her parents even fill out the form. But none of the kids at Sojourner Truth reacted to Ms. Graham's inquiry either by hiding their own response or by craning their necks to notice who responded. Thomas Scheff has argued that shame is a social emotion, stemming from "threats to the social bond"; at Sojourner Truth, the acknowledgment of poverty seemed to pose little threat to the children's social bond.[15]

Nonetheless, Sojourner Truth children purposefully hid evidence of more unusual family characteristics because they feared a stigma would inhibit their ability to feel included in the group—a kind of preemptive shame work with strategic ends. They tried to conceal second languages spoken at home as signs they were just recently arrived in the country, or court-ordered therapy appointments as signs they or their family were "in trouble." One day, when Loretta was absent, I asked her sister Yvette where she was. Yvette did not answer, but Fia, who was nearby, took up the question, only with a jeering tone. "Yeah, where?" she said, and Yvette said, "Shut up, you," as if Fia knew better and was harassing her. Fia may indeed have been, for Yvette then told me, clearly embarrassed, "She went to therapy."

Affluent children tried to conceal their own perceived sources of shame, which despite their comfortable backgrounds included income and class status. One little boy at Oceanview showed some distress, for example, because his mother paid for his milk money with a check at the office, instead of sending him with the money every day. "He was embarrassed because he thought that kids were going to think he was stealing his milk because he didn't have to pay money," said Carrie, the school secretary. "So you do see these funny things, just because of the peer pressure or whatever."

For other affluent children, the problem was of a more rarefied kind. One garrulous white Arrowhead father said his sons Dean and Max played on a travel soccer team with many Latinos from more constrained backgrounds.

> [My kids] play soccer; it's the one place where we just sort of splurge and buy them expensive shoes. Dean said to me the other day—because they play soccer and they play year-round and they are on their feet all the time!—and this is so typical of him, Dean said to me: "You know, Dad, next time I get soccer shoes, I don't want to get an expensive pair of shoes. I just want to get a basic pair of shoes." You know they play with a lot of kids from socio-economic-disadvantaged backgrounds, and they don't have a lot of that stuff.

When Dean asked his father not to "splurge" on expensive soccer shoes, as was his wont, his father interpreted the request as Dean's laudable effort to avoid making his teammates feel bad, which was certainly possible. At the same time, however, sometimes having the perfect equipment looked foolish, overprepared, coddled, snobbish, or perhaps most important, different in some way. At Arrowhead, a progressive, diverse school, an affluent lesbian adult told one teacher that she felt more uncomfortable at Arrowhead because she was rich than because she was a lesbian, picking up discomfiting feelings from people coming to get their children from playdates at her opulent house in the hills. Similarly, some children engaged in their own sort of "shame work" to conceal from disapproving others, even when what they were hiding was their affluence.

"I WANT YOUR TOOTH FAIRY": THE CONTEXT OF COMMUNITIES

Affluent and low-income children alike adopted certain strategies to make their own dignity and establish their bona fides as members of their communities. Yet children's economies of dignity did not arise out of a vacuum, dependent merely upon the personalities involved or even the socioeconomic resources at their disposal. The sociologists Nina Eliasoph and Paul Lichterman have outlined how members of local groups shape culture for each other by obliging people to express certain emotions, "preserving members' sense of humanity—in a way that that society or subgroup defines it." They argued a "group style" acts as a funnel to shape those emotions in particular ways, through "culture-in-interaction." My data indicate similarly that children's communities of shared experience, and the institutions in which they were embedded, also shaped the particular tokens of value that developed and the processes that were deployed.[16]

At Sojourner Truth, children's personal experiences of poverty—specifically their intimate knowledge of material hardship and its attendant stressors, such as unstable home lives, parents busy or absent at work, and anxious overburdened caregivers—shaped much of their meaning-making. Emotions swirled, for example, around the topics of fathers (their presence or absence, their involvement), bodies (who was fat, and for boys, who was strong), and academics (being smart, being dumb, and being too interested), but most of all, around issues of property and ownership, such as possession and stealing. Each of these topics was salient because of the emotional charge lent them by external social inequalities—fathers were interesting, for example, because their unstable employment patterns and their periodic incarceration meant they weren't predictable the way mothers were. For matters of consumption, as we have seen, evidence of poverty was not that interesting, precisely because having little was so routine, but claims of ownership were important and exciting because of its unusual nature. For example, one day Loretta was talking about her upcoming birthday party.

When Aleta's mother came to pick her up, Loretta came bounding
up excitedly and spoke directly to her, not to Aleta: "I am going to
have a party, and I want Aleta to come. We're going to get our nails
done. Can Aleta get her nails done?" Aleta's mother smiles and holds
onto Loretta's hand, which is splayed out: "Well, you aren't going to
have nail polish, right, just clear stuff, right?" Then Loretta added
that her mother had said she had enough money to pay for Loretta
on her birthday but not for the other girls, so could Aleta come and
get her nails done with them, and could Aleta's mother pay for that?
Aleta's mother did not respond with distaste, disappointment, or
even surprise but instead said, "Okay." Loretta leaped up to Aleta
and said: "You can get the clear stuff, just not the color."

In another setting, asking birthday party guests to pay for themselves
would be perhaps embarrassing, not something you would blithely
announce as you invite friends. But instead Loretta doesn't hesitate,
Aleta's mother isn't surprised, and the girls who are watching don't offer
any censure.

It was precisely the relative homogeneity of the poverty at Sojourner
Truth—itself an outgrowth of the larger structural inequality of income
and opportunities in Oakland—that contributed to its particular emotional landscape. All the children there were poor, and their parents all
had the unpredictable access to money that led to what I have termed
elsewhere "windfall childrearing," making a difference in whether or
not they could get an "icey" or go to Marine World. It was not as if one
group of people were always poor, always unable to see movies or have
Game Boys, while another group of people were always rich, showing
off sneakers or talking about adventures. The very parity among them,
coupled with the random-seeming nature of their good fortune, made
possessions seem scarce and unpredictable and made their dispensation
the source of great emotional force.[17]

In addition, practices by the Sojourner Truth teaching staff amounted
to a laissez-faire approach to children's culture, in which teachers inter-
vened only when intense emotions or physical fighting erupted from the
daily scrum. This is not to say that the teachers did not care about the

children or what they learned from the formal or informal curriculum. Married to a local preacher, the head teacher, Ms. Graham, personified the community "othermother" described by the sociologist Patricia Hill Collins, frequently offering the children her deeply caring counsel in stentorian tones. She clearly saw as her mission to lift them up by straightening them out about the right goals and the right way to achieve them, a self-perceived mandate particularly evident one day when the children asked about jewelry. Speaking without pause for breath, with characteristically stern humor, she responded: "No, that's something you all care about because of MTV and the rappers, but that is not important . . . what is important is that you learn to read and write and think for yourselves so that you can take care of yourselves when you are an adult." She also sometimes willingly played a role in the children's peer culture, as when Jasmine's mother let slip that "one girl" had gotten $5 from the Tooth Fairy. Ms. Graham greeted the news with a long "Whoooooeee," as Jasmine announced to the group of children seated on the rug, "That was me." "That was you?" Ms. Graham asked. "Whoooeee. I want your tooth fairy." As Jasmine smiled from ear to ear, Ms. Graham's allegiance to the children, and their perspective, was indisputable.[18]

Ms. Graham's policy of nonintervention in most children's disputes, however, meant that an economy of dignity established by the children reigned supreme—emphasizing popular culture, the effervescence of possession, and the high risks of most kinds of difference. Thus children's culture-in-interaction at Sojourner Truth was linked to structural inequalities outside of the classroom, which made certain topics interesting; fostered by a laissez-faire attitude from staff, their group style then shaped the kind of meaning—competitive, aggressive, where even the right to participate was at stake—to be made from such topics.[19]

For affluent children, the two field sites offered a window into two economies of dignity that differed quite dramatically. The extent to which affluent children engaged in concealing, for example, depended less on their vulnerability to charges of poverty than it did on the cultures of dif-

ference at their schools. At Oceanview, as at Sojourner Truth, school offi-
cials refrained from getting involved in children's culture, interceding
only in the rare instance of physical violence or prolonged emotional dis-
turbance—in short, when an incident interfered with academic learning.
For the most part, peer culture at Oceanview was a high-pressure system,
in which the stakes of appearing different were significant. Katerina, an
Oceanview mother, explained how her daughter Marina refused to go to
school one day:

> They criticized her food, which is apparently different than others'.
> Because we don't usually have a sandwich. I don't send sandwiches to
> school. You know, kids—they made fun of her. And Marina one
> day—this had never happened, I mean Marina is a very strong little
> girl. She said she didn't want to go to school. One day she said,
> "Please don't make me go." [I asked,] "What is wrong?" My kids
> [are the kind who] run out the door! [They usually say,] "Bye!
> Maybe we'll see you later!" [But] she was truly mortified. They had
> laughed at her. I said, "What happened?" She said: "Mom, they . . . I
> hid my face in the lunchbox, and I just wished I wasn't there."

Children cried, bit their nails, cornered each other in the school yard,
ignored some, ganged up against others, and otherwise inhabited an
emotional landscape that sometimes seemed to resemble the oppressive
regime of a storied British tuition-based school like that described by
George Orwell. In this classroom at Oceanview, as at Sojourner Truth,
the cost of not belonging was sometimes not just invisibility, but falling
victim to social discipline.[20]

In contrast, at Arrowhead, a progressive school, what happened in
the school yard was seen as as much a part of the curriculum as English
or science. As one teacher reported:

> There are days when the kids come in from recess, and I was plan-
> ning to teach math, and they'll come in and say, "Hey, Jimmy said
> this or that to me, called me a name" or whatever, and then I'll think
> to myself, "Whoops, well, there goes math." At Arrowhead they deal
> with these things as a classroom.

Adults at Arrowhead implemented a program that tackled children's culture-in-interaction head-on, through circle time, group role-plays, and an explicit social curriculum to help children handle conflict. The ensuing warm emotional landscape meant that most social difference—particularly in sexual orientation, racial/ethnic background, or family structure, but not necessarily class—was celebrated rather than shunned, as one parent reported:

> I just remember Cameron standing up. She got on the stool to get something out of the cabinet. She went like this [she raises her arm in a salute], and she goes, "I am an ally to gay and lesbian people!" You know, here is this kid! It made me laugh.

Children's peer culture was mediated and shaped by interested adults, who explicitly addressed the value of social difference in a number of arenas.

For the most part, however, adults at Arrowhead left moments of interactional difference alone, although there was an incipient movement to change this practice. One teacher had recently sent home a letter asking parents to have a conversation with their children about being sensitive about how they talk about vacations. Her own son had come home from school, the teacher told me, asking, "What is your favorite island in Hawaii?" The same teacher also sparked a furor when she asked a child who had gotten on a travel soccer team not to discuss it at recess, since there were other children who had not made the team. That night, she heard from the child's father. "Please don't tell my son what he can and cannot say about his soccer. That is not school business, that is not a classroom or school matter," the teacher reported being told. After checking in with Neal McCabe, however, the teacher wrote back, defending her action as part of the school's caring ethos. As Layla, another parent involved in the school, mused: "There are so many subtle moments at school that happen with kids who come with expensive shoes or an electronic device or talk about holidays—where you go for your holidays." The school was starting an affinity group of parents and teachers who could come together to talk about these issues, and plan the school's response, she said.

> I heard stories about a birthday party where everybody was supposed to bring an American Girl doll. Well, they are very expensive evidently. And just asking the question—what is in the purview of the school? And what is beyond our kind of . . . areas. And how far can we infiltrate or push into the family life? And what is right? And what is our role? Do we just get people thinking? Do we change policy? Do we . . . I don't know how that would all sort out.

This is not to say that children's culture at Arrowhead was entirely created by adults; to be sure, children had moments of limited resistance in which they effectively used the constraints established by adults to attain social goals contrary to adult intentions (as when one savvy girl called after a retreating boy's back: "If you don't want us to chase you, you can just say that to us. . ."). The extent and kind of adult participation largely served to shape the emotional landscape of the school, however, and thus apparently how it felt to be a child there.

The implications of these institutional factors for facework, and for children's attendant consumer desires, were mixed. Children's economies of dignity in these three sites varied in intensity, in the variety of their forms of scrip, and in the goals of their processes. The topography of feeling at Oceanview, particularly the high stakes of shame, made the economy of dignity there, and children's desires to master it, more intense than at Arrowhead. Oceanview children patrolled for violations of norms related to gender, class, academics, and many other realms; they punished deviants in anything, from what they brought for lunch to what they wore. At Arrowhead, meanwhile, peer punishment for social differences—while not unheard-of—was rare, and difficult to see firsthand, although isolated instances were reported to me by parents in interviews. Desirée's mother told me her daughter was asked by the only other African-American girl in her class, an affluent child, if she lived in a house or an apartment. "What is that all about?" Desirée's mother asked me rhetorically, her voice flat, her eyes rolling in distaste. But as a rule, Arrowhead was not a place where children had free rein to punish others for social difference, as at Oceanview and Sojourner Truth. Arrowhead children sometimes did experience conflict, but generally it was not organized along that particular axis of difference.

At the same time, Arrowhead and Oceanview (and, for that matter, Sojourner Truth) shared a peer culture that valued money, goods, and destinations, in which interactional sameness held sway. Indeed, consumer goods both real and discursive seemed to be more of a presence among children at Arrowhead than at Oceanview, a sense corroborated by parents I interviewed who had experience with both schools. Part of the reason for this was the more restrictive environment at Oceanview. What children brought to Oceanview was more strictly controlled—"If you bring anything to school, it gets confiscated," one mother explained—whereas at Arrowhead, one parent observed that "the net effect of giving kids free choice" was to invite children's consumer culture in.

Additionally, the children at Oceanview had many axes of difference along which it was crucially important to align themselves, so perhaps while they cared very much where they fell on a particular axis, the intensity of their desires did not focus specifically on interactional differences to the exclusion of social or personal ones. In contrast, at Arrowhead, there was essentially one axis of difference around which children could make inequality, since others were largely reshaped by classroom meetings and themed discussions. Perhaps in some sense, consumption was all the children had left with which to separate themselves in their economy of dignity. As Ellen Seiter has persuasively argued to explain children's "kitschy" tastes in opposition to adult notions of refinement and class, perhaps Arrowhead children talked more about money, goods, and experiences because the topic was still theirs, one in which they could wrest their own identities and meanings from adults.[21]

Children respond to different kinds of difference differently. Everywhere interactional difference, based on whether or not you are able to be "thankful for what you have" or to talk about snowboarding like the rest, was critical for establishing belonging, and such differences seemed to pose urgent challenges for children. Personal differences were more mixed—some, like your knowledge of family history, were worth cultivating, while others, like the psychological problems that induced you to go to therapy, were important to hide. Social differences like race or class varied in whether or not they were perceived as stigmas, and in the intensity with which they resonated. At Sojourner Truth, for example, children gathered around to point and say "Ewww" at a newspaper picture of two lesbians who had recently been married at City Hall, while at Arrowhead, one girl mentioned casually to another that she herself was a lesbian, a comment greeted without great surprise or interest, although a boy nearby asked her, "Why?" (She shrugged in reply.) As we have seen, sometimes children countered one kind of difference with another—Simon and Noah, for example, both adopted the strategy of compensating for their momentary lack of possession with their skill and knowledge about playing.

As the examples of Sojourner Truth, Oceanview, and Arrowhead suggest, different contexts may feature varied economies of dignity, in which different rules apply—in one context, children may claim dignity based upon the presence and involvement of fathers, for example, while in another, upon particular prowess in electronic games. Dignity may be scarce, as in a zero-sum society, in which assaults on others' dignity increase one's own store, or it may be more abundant, with less explicit anxiety about its distribution. Within these economies, the tokens of dignity can be hoarded, shared, negotiated, and otherwise exchanged as children make their own worlds amid the constraints in which they find themselves. While all sorts of groups might evince an economy of dignity, the contours of that set of patterned interactions differ from group to group, and these differences are linked to features of the group—the homogeneity of the group and its institutional context, as well as the social locations of its members according to class, race/ethnicity, and other social categories.

CHILDREN AND THE FEELINGS
OF CONSUMPTION

In the classic children's book *The Hundred Dresses*, Wanda, a recent Polish immigrant girl who "didn't have any friends" and whose "faded blue dress . . . didn't hang right," approaches a group of popular girls exclaiming over a new dress, and ventures hesitantly that she herself has a hundred dresses at home. Maddie, another girl who had popular friends but was poor herself, thought: "Maybe [Wanda] figured all she'd have to do was say something and she'd really be one of the girls. And this would be an easy thing to do because all they were doing was talking about dresses." But the girls round on Wanda for "lying," teasing her daily about it, and it is not until Wanda moves away that they discover she has made a hundred beautiful pictures of dresses, with "dazzling colors and brilliant lavish designs." The story is about Wanda but also about Maddie, who remains haunted by her weakness in not stopping the torment.[22]

Though her claim of a hundred dresses was extreme, Wanda was not trying to best the group of popular girls, to achieve a higher status, but rather to connect to them in a search for belonging, as Maddie observed. But her facework strategy of "claiming" to own the dresses failed because of its outlandishness, and she fell subject instead to the patrolling taunts of the very girls she sought to join. The simple poignancy of her effort, and of Maddie's social awakening, makes the book still powerful, more than sixty years after it was written.

As depicted in *The Hundred Dresses*, children's lived experience of a particular economy of dignity can be intense and painful at all socioeconomic levels, and the charged emotions that ensue serve as a powerful conduit for cultural meaning to be affixed to goods. The book also delivers a potent message about where most of these intense emotions come from: not the parents, but the peers who own the child's heart. As the writer Judith Harris observed, "a child's goal is not to become a successful adult, any more than a prisoner's goal is to become a successful guard.

A child's goal is to become a successful child." Children perform cultural work to accomplish this goal, using facework processes such as bridging labor, claiming, concealing, and patrolling, most often to surmount some sort of perceived lack. Commodified goods and experiences thus wend their way through children's connections to others—to peers as the fabric of belonging, and to parents as the symbol of their care.[23]

Parents of young children establish the contexts of their social worlds—the neighborhoods, the schools, and the after-school activities—and do so through a range of strategies—market, civic, and familial. Parents and other caregivers also equip children with the lunch boxes, toys, clothes, and other commodities that together constitute material childhoods. But it is the children themselves who live at the nexus of these decisions: they reside in neighborhoods, attend schools, and go to after-school care in places chosen by others, and do so with or without the right "stuff," which is deemed worthy of social honor by the peer culture at large in these contexts. The cultural innovations, the discursive feints and sleights of hand, that children undertake are all the more affecting for children's fundamental inability to establish the facts of their own lives.[24]

At bottom, the children in this study suggest by their talk that dignity involves recognition by one's self and others that one is a full-fledged person. The conversations may seem casual, their topics—who has a GameBoy, where was your birthday party—as inconsequential as a laundry list. Yet for the children, the mundane inscribes their shame and their triumph every day.

Emotions, however, are rarely captured best by single words, as the novelist Jeffrey Eugenides has noted. "I don't believe in 'sadness,' 'joy,' or 'regret,'" his lead character observes almost whimsically in the Pulitzer Prize–winning work *Middlesex*. "I'd like to have at my disposal complicated hybrid emotions, Germanic train-car constructions like, say, 'the happiness that attends disaster.'" Similarly, while we might use the word *dignity* as a certain shorthand, the hybrid emotions it stands for include a mélange of pride, anxiety, relief—the pride that shores up any claim for visibility, as well as the anxiety experienced by anyone who is not sure he or she is already visible, and the relief of establishing the connection that was before uncertain. Add to this any combination of warmth, indignation, desperation, and jealousy, depending upon how one evaluates the social environment and one's standing within it—am I connecting to friends, to people who should know better, to peers who never expect too much from me, to others who are always competing?— and dignity is a complex state of being indeed.[25]

Children's culture-in-interaction makes meaning and inequality out of consumption, for upper-income as well as lower-income children, but the various contexts shape the meaning that gets made. Institutions establish the overall emotional landscape through which children must travel, so that school feels unpredictable, even threatening, for example, or "safe and fun," as Arrowhead's school Web site claims. Nonetheless, all of the children involved in this study, no matter where they went to school, talked about consumer goods and experiences, whether they were buying, using, or fantasizing about them. Economies of dignity studied here varied in how they feel—intense or muted, conflict-ridden or smooth—but there was surprisingly little variation in the forms of scrip, processes, or strategies of the children who inhabited them.

This chapter has outlined the processes by which children come to imbue certain possessions and events with a powerful personal meaning. What happens when they bring these meanings home? How do parents respond when they are faced with the consumer emergencies the economy of dignity engenders? The next set of chapters considers children's consumer culture from the point of view of the parents, who act both as its moat and as its drawbridge.

CHAPTER FOUR

Ambivalence and Allowances

Affluent Parents Respond

Like many affluent parents, Katerina Simon both welcomes and deplores her family's experience with consumer culture, her ambivalence pulling her mothering this way and that like a toddler in a toy store. An immigrant from Greece, she married an American she met in college. They managed to catch the coattails of the high-tech economy as it went fluttering by, and for fifteen years lived and worked together in the Bay Area, buying a house in the Oceanview neighborhood and having two children along the way. On the one hand, Katerina thinks "wanting things is good," such as when her seven-year-old daughter Marina wants more clothes and accessories for her American Girl doll. "You need to have motivations in life," Katerina says. "It's good, if it gets you to do things, and I think it's healthy." On the other hand, she tries to teach her children that they cannot just "ask and get whatever they see," by limiting their gifts, and even using little tricks in stores to distract them from their desires. "Which is a hard thing in America. They say, 'I want that. I want it now.' And I say, 'Well, you have to wait for a reason to get it.' Why would you buy something otherwise?"

While Katerina is serious about limits, the Simon family does celebrate not only Christmas, Easter, and birthdays with gifts and sometimes feasting, but also individual "name days" (the holidays for one's patron saint), as well as the Catholic festival of the "Three Kings" twelve days after Christmas, which "you try to make as fantastic as you can," she says, opening a photo album to show me the extraordinary display of unwrapped gifts around an extensive Nativity scene. Add to this list the day the children were promoted to a new skiing level and when they lose a tooth—clearly, the Simons' year is sprinkled with "reasons to get it." Yet Katerina's stance puts her at odds with her neighbors, she says. "Well, I know of other families that they say, 'Oh, you know, we went to Toys "R" Us, and they chose a toy.' And I say, 'Oh, was it their birthday?' 'Oh, no. We just did it.' So it's foreign to me. The entire concept is like 'Oh, okay,'" she shrugged her shoulders, wrinkling her brow in confusion and disgust.

Most affluent parents say they do not buy much for their children. "I never, ever, ever buy stuff that they want," said Helen, an Arrowhead parent and a lawyer. "We don't go hard-core with the toys," said Kate, a social worker with a child at Oceanview. "[Other] families spend $2,000 and $3,000 on the holiday gifts." Megan, who has two children at Arrowhead, noted: "It is real different around here. We don't have all that stuff."

Like Katerina, upper-income parents compared themselves to neighbors, friends, or relatives who were real consumers. "One family . . . ," recalled Shoshana, who held out as long as she could against buying a Game Boy, "I mean the kids' rooms are just decked to the ceiling with stuff, and . . . when we talk about what to get kids for birthdays and things, the mother admits, 'I don't know, there isn't anything they don't have already.'"

As with Katerina, however, when these parents talked about specifics—what they did for that birthday, what they packed in yesterday's school lunch, what they arranged for this vacation—a very different story emerged. While individual families might conserve in one or another arena, with a low-key Christmas or a ban on gaming electronics, on the whole, families described a pattern of substantial buying. Upper-income parents talked about spending $450 on a five year old's birthday party, thousands of dollars for a family vacation to Cambodia, and hundreds of dollars on Halloween costumes. And the expenses went beyond commodities, to the experiences they worked to ensure their children could have. Schools could command $15,000 for private tuition, summer camps might be $3000–$4000, and they might spend $1000 a month on extracurricular activities like carpentry, dance, soccer, horseback riding, or piano lessons.

In affluent communities, however, critiques of consumption are prevalent. Many parents feel strong cultural sanctions against excessive buying and will themselves argue that buying leads to materialistic or spoiled children, wastes the world's resources, or supports the aggressive tactics and shocking values of corporate marketing. In one poll, women said they felt guilty and uncertain even being asked about their children's consumption patterns. At the same time, affluent parents are supposed to give their children the best that they possibly can, to cultivate their children's individual talents and needs, and to provide for a safe and happy childhood. As Ellen Seiter observed, "while giving in, adults often harbor profound doubts about the effects of children's consumer culture today and worry that their own children are learning from the mass media an ethic of greed and a proclivity for hedonism." Trapped in the cultural vise of two contradictory cultural edicts, then, affluent parents claim they do not buy much.[1]

When people magnify the meaning of a certain practice, they load it with symbolic value that points away from the trend it conceals, cultural scholars tell us. In the same vein as John Gillis's notion of the "family we live by," then, are the market practices of good parenting that parents deploy. We might call these symbols "consumption we live by." Affluent parents appear to be relying on certain practices to signal to themselves and others that they are worthy members of their communities, not materialistic or "spendy," as one parent called it. I came to call these practices "symbolic deprivation," the means by which affluent parents take their children on a journey through consumer culture as if they were Dr. Doolittle's pushmi-pullyus, the storied two-headed llama going in opposite directions at once.[2]

It is important to attend to opposing feelings and actions, as they are flags for the cultural contradictions that lurk beneath people's lives. Feelings like dread, anxiety, and guilt—and the public finger-wagging that often precipitate them—act as markers of the cultural fissures beneath the ground of social action. Like working mothers, consuming parents feel bad because while one set of priorities demands they do what they do, another set dictates an opposing course of action. Their feelings point to powerful, durable cultural ideas that resist the reinterpretation and redesigning that might adapt culture to people's perspectives and experiences, cultural ideas that structure people's lives as well as the way they feel about them.[3]

Symbolic deprivation helped upper-income parents express their ambivalence about consumption. "I can't get into the mounds of presents. The competitiveness of it all," said Tracy, who then hesitated to tell me the price of her sons' Halloween costumes because she was "embarrassed." (At $700 for the handmade pair, they were indeed on the extreme end.) Letty, who is half-Jewish, described one year when she felt pressured by the comparison with her in-laws to provide for a big spectacle during the holidays, in order to somehow compete with Christmas. "I was just throwing toys at him! And it was ridiculous, because it was just . . . it was ridiculous. First of all, Christmas always wins. You just can't fight Father Christmas! And it's just too many toys at once. It's just too many toys."

Symbolic deprivation may also have allowed parents to resolve tensions arising from just what it was the children desired. Often children desired "the wrong thing," games the parents considered violent or addictive, dolls the parents thought were silly or "junk." Such goods were not expressing the "right" taste, for wooden playthings, for noncommercial, simpler toys and games that typified middle-class preferences. Parents not only despised consumption; they despised "cheap" consumption that failed to do the sort of distinction work that researchers have reported adult consumer practices seek. Symbolic deprivation allowed parents to assent, but at arm's length. But it raises the question, why did they feel they had to assent?[4]

DIGNITY: THE DRAWBRIDGE
TO THE FORTRESS FAMILY

In thousands of small decisions, which together form their particular approach to consumer culture, Katerina creates her own family's way of doing things. Through "the traditions that I have instituted in this family," such as the practice of throwing the baby tooth on the roof so that the *pondiki*, or "little mouse," will bring you a new one and a small treat in its place, Katerina establishes what is, and what is not, an occasion for gift giving. Some of these decisions are still in process. About TV viewing, for instance, Katerina says: "I don't know how I feel about [her son asking to watch while he got dressed]. That has crossed a little bit too much for me." About allowances, she says: "She wants to make money. That is a legitimate thing. [But] the fear I have with allowance is how sometimes the money is constantly in your mind. Like, okay, 'if you pay me I'll do it.' You know?" Other policies are settled—such as those about Barbies (Katerina does not like them, but while she won't buy them, others can buy them for her daughter as gifts)—and these rules create a kind of fortress against the commercial onslaught. Nonetheless, there remains a way into the fortress, a drawbridge across which consumer culture traipses, gaily, like a Billy Goat Gruff into Katerina's family life, and that is the call of her children's dignity. Katerina responds when her children say they need something to belong, to participate in their social worlds.

Take school lunches, a fertile area for examining the sometimes yawning gap between children's desires and parents' intentions, where what gets sent to school in a lunch box (and sometimes gets returned home uneaten) reflects an often subtle negotiating process that is ongoing in many homes with young children. Parents invent their own approach to the tension between children's desires—often for sweet, salty, or branded foods, and for food their peers talk about—and their own concerns, about health, cost, or establishing good habits, for instance. Katerina, for example, did not pack her children sandwiches. Instead, they got more unusual fare—often leftovers from the dinner meal of the night before, like cold salmon. "Apparently not everybody does that," she said. "What do I know?" But when her children urged her to buy other items because they heard about them at school, Katerina listened. "Once in awhile, they would come to me and tell me something very cool that I needed to buy. Like the gummies. That's how I discovered about the gummies. Or the fruit roll-up. I'm like, 'What is a fruit roll-up?' So I bought those for a while. I understand you need to fit in, honey. I'll buy you the fruit roll-up, I don't care."

Gradually, a picture emerges from her calm and reasoned parenting narrative: Katerina is passionately, determinedly focused on her children's social integration, and this above all makes her vulnerable to dignity concerns, children's anxieties about fitting in that can emanate from their peer cultures like a virus. She is gratified that Oceanview, as a public school, does not bring up religion, because "I don't want her to be singled out as different [as a half-Catholic, half-Jewish child]. Because at that age they don't see it as anything positive. So I want them to leave it alone." She second-guesses her restrictive rules on television because, she says, "sometimes I worry. I don't know if that's the thing to do, because in the school they talk, and other children have seen so many shows." Katerina pays close attention to what other children (and their parents) think and do in crafting her own child rearing.

The same logic prevailed in other affluent homes. Kevin, an Arrowhead parent, told of allowing his seven-year-old daughter Sarah, a martial arts fan, to watch one scene from the 2000 movie *Crouching Tiger, Hidden Dragon*, which is rated PG-13 for "martial arts violence and some sexuality." "I showed it to her once. Showed her a five-minute scene where they're dancing or they're fighting across the rooftops. It's kind of magical," Kevin explained. "She went back and told everybody in the class that she had seen *Crouching Tiger*, and they all told their parents, so all their parents said, 'Well, if Sarah can see it, then . . .' So six kids got their parents to let them see this movie. So then we got . . . we had a couple of phone calls." He laughed. "Yeah! I thought it was completely inappropriate and said, 'No, absolutely not! She's not going to see it until she's thirteen!' It was just awful. I was really embarrassed."[5]

Children were often the reporters who kept track of the standards being maintained by other families in the community, although relying on them for the word on what other families were doing could sometimes prove unreliable. In the case of the movie *Crouching Tiger*, parents were led astray because they used only their children to keep apprised of such community practices. Most affluent parents relied upon children, parent networking, school communication, and other means to gather a sense of common standards, to calibrate their own forays into consumer culture in response to the moving line defining what we might call the "good-enough childhood."[6]

Almaz, an Arrowhead parent who also worked at the school sometimes, told me in an interview how she had witnessed another mother's lightning-quick response to her child's dignity lament:

> A good example. Yesterday there were some Pokémon cards. I was working lunch duty. [One mom] came for lunch, and [the kids] were all exchanging cards and stuff. And the most expensive one there [was] in a plastic thing. That means it's something valuable, I guess. And she said, "Oh, that is a valuable one?"
>
> [Her son said], "Mommy, I don't have any of those cards." He was whining and stuff. She said, "Really?" So she grabbed one of the cards, and I saw her looking at them. And in the evening we had the author's night at the school. She came, and I saw her with that box full of them, and I thought "Wow!"

Almaz was shocked at this parent's immediate purchase of the coveted Pokémon cards, but most parents demonstrated a similar, though perhaps not as frantic, affinity for their children's dignity concerns.

THINKING ABOUT DIFFERENCE

For Katerina, as for many affluent parents, the successful management of difference was the main determinant of her children's social happiness. On the one hand, affluent parents cultivated their children's individuality through personal differences, searching for strengths or talents and diagnosing particular emotional or intellectual needs best met by this or that service or school—a process I investigate further in chapter 7. On the other hand, parents feared differences that threatened their children's social belonging.

All children faced the likelihood of differing from their peers at some time or place, be it camp, school, or the neighborhood. Their differences stemmed not only from personal or social categories we are perhaps used to considering consequential, such as their social class, race, gender, immigration, or family structure. As we have seen, they also experienced interactional differences, which were rooted in more mundane details, such as where they had gone on vacation, what they brought for lunch, or whether they had seen a particular movie. Despite the ubiquity of difference, however, it posed a challenge to many parents, who feared their child's abuse, ostracism, shame, or envy as a result of being singled out.

While Katerina's immigrant background might have produced more differences to manage than those experienced by affluent native-born families, all parents must resolve the dilemmas presented by difference. As the anthropologist Gregory Bateson famously asked, when—and how—does a difference make a difference? What kind of differences should be hidden or, perhaps with the purchase of a coveted toy or piece of clothing, erased? What kind of differences form part of one's core identity, worth declaring sacrosanct, even celebrated, such as the Three Kings extravaganza for Katerina? Furthermore, what are the stakes posed by difference? How important is it, for example, that children have the same toys or clothes, or the same experiences, like films or theme parks, as do their friends? What would happen if they did not?

How parents answer these questions, as well as how they interpret the stakes involved, determines how they handle their children's dignity claims, and their consumer yearnings.[7]

Parents and children often disagree about the value of difference. For Katerina, for example, her Greek identity was part of her core self, even as her daughter Marina was born and raised in Oakland's affluent hills, spoke accentless English, and chose "Kit," the plucky Depression-era survivor, as her favorite American Girl doll. There is some evidence that Marina viewed her family's "Greekness" as a difference worth sacrificing. "In preschool she had—a couple of times, she said something like, 'Don't speak Greek when you pick me up,'" Katerina said with chagrin, lamenting that Americans, perhaps including her daughter, did not admire bilingualism.

Marina Simon was by any measure an anxious girl, albeit one with a strong personality, as I witnessed during fieldwork in her classroom. The Oceanview second grader wore the same outfit to school every day, a pair of jeans and a purple T-shirt, and refused her mother's suggestions to do otherwise. Marina worked strenuously to control other children's access to her best friend, Shari. Vivian, a mother who occasionally volunteered in the classroom, told me that Marina constantly sought approval for her efforts. "Every single five-minute segment—'Is this okay? Do you think that's okay? Is this okay? I'm not sure. Is this okay?' Every minute. Every minute."

Listening to Katerina, it is not clear which came first: Marina's anxiety, as part of the temperament she was born with, or her mother's attention to (and purchases because of) the perception that "I understand you need to fit in, honey." On a field trip on which I accompanied her daughter's class to a local science museum, Katerina and about eight other parents gathered in the cafeteria while the children made chemical solvents and tested them for acidity in a large hall next door. The conversation quickly turned to child-rearing challenges, and the parents compared notes on how they handled electronics—polices about watching television, shock and chagrin at the mature content of video games, tales of children's fall and redemption through restriction of their screen time. Katerina told the group a story of calling a toy retailer to complain about a wooden toy that was missing a piece, and having him inquire how old her son was (he was six). She reported: "When I told him, he said I should go online and look at the other toys to see the more appropriate toys for him. I was outraged. It says '3 and up'! I am happy with wood. I don't want to buy him these electronics." The other parents looked briefly uncomfortable, and the conversation turned to homework troubles, but later on Katerina was thoughtful. "I had a very interesting conversation on that field trip," she mused. "Everybody has these games but me. I was like, 'This is interesting.' I didn't know I was so out of touch with life! But I guess I am!" Katerina cared about being "in touch," and the revelation was unwelcome.

WHOSE BELONGING? DIFFERENCE
AND THE DRIVE TO BUY

Ostensibly, Katerina discovered on the field trip that her children were among the few without electronic gaming systems. But by using words like "me" and "I" to declare "Everybody has these games but me," Katerina frames these discoveries as if they were about her, and her own exclusion from "everybody else." Katerina might be particularly sensitive to her children's desire to fit in because she herself has felt that she does not belong. As I concluded our first interview, packing up my tape recorder after several hours, Katerina paused and said she wanted to "throw an experience in your research. Because I think this is going to give you something to think about." She proceeded to spend another half hour describing her fury and outrage that her son Niko's preschool teacher had asked parents in the school to bring in kosher cupcakes on birthdays because of another child whose family observed kosher dietary laws. For Katerina, the incident crystallized her passion for religious privacy and managed differences, and her impatience with separatist doctrine. The depth of her feeling, however, and the visceral nature of her indignation, pointed to other than cognitive disagreement. But for her Jewish husband, her reaction might have been rather glibly read as anti-Semitism. Her soliloquy soon revealed another source. "Half of our family is Jewish, and many of those people will never accept Niko's mom [herself] into the family because I am not kosher and because I am not Jewish. And I said . . . and because I am not going to be," she said.

> So I told [the preschool] that if you insist on presenting this kosher and what it means, maybe I'm going to have to explain to Niko that the same boy excludes me from a certain environment because he has the mother. And I said, 'And if you know how to explain that to a five year old, go for it!' Because I am going to go for it. And then Niko is going to maybe develop something else for that boy that he shouldn't. Because I don't have anything against the boy. But I don't want to be asked to be kosher for him.

Katerina's experience of exclusion from her in-laws still rankled enough for her to issue vague threats about her son's predicted animosity toward his kosher classmate. Clearly, the wound was still sensitive, even to the unthinking touch of a preschool teacher's casual, well-meaning suggestion. To Katerina, difference is personal, important, and risky, while belonging, well, belonging is the font of much feeling and some pain.

It is very possible that Katerina's acute sensitivity to issues of difference and exclusion was bred in early family dynamics in Greece, but the task at hand is less to pinpoint its origins than to understand how it might create a certain sympathy for her children's efforts to belong. And while Katerina's specific history of her in-laws' rejection may be uncommon, her more extreme story highlights dynamics in other parents' lives.

Many affluent parents had experiences, characteristics, or family backgrounds that made them more attuned to their children's desire to fit in. Indeed, the constellation of such factors helped to shape what we might call parents' "social antennae," or the means by which parents would feel, ignore, or be oblivious to their children's yearnings. Parents' capacities to attend to their children's emotional connection to others are shaped by the parents' own histories and experiences, leading them to be more or less sensitive to their children's dignity claims. Parents' emotional biographies thus animated their own response to the prospect of their children's experience of being different.

Memories of being poor certainly contribute to some parents' emotional sensitivity to their child's needs, as others have reported. The writer Carolyn Kay Steedman recalled a searing moment when she watched her low-income mother cry as the health visitor strode away, having left behind her judgment: "This house isn't fit for a baby." "I will do everything and anything until the end of my days to stop anyone ever talking to me like that woman talked to my mother," Steedman vowed. Thus would affluent parents who grew up in more constrained circumstances shower their children with compensatory material privilege. "I don't want my kid to ever feel like I did when I was in sixth grade and had to wear those Joe Knuckle tennis shoes," avows one of several upwardly mobile informants in Karyn Lacy's thoughtful book *Blue-Chip Black*. The idea is the stuff of cliché—parent gives child all that he or she never had—and several of my sampled parents pointed to neighbors or acquaintances who were acting out this story.[8]

The cliché makes that kind of compensation more visible, because we have the cultural framework to see it. For many affluent parents, however, even those who would reject the notion that they had survived any particular difficulty, other kinds of memories exerted the same sort of influence. Tess, an Oceanview parent who grew up in a wealthy home, remembered how her parents restricted her TV watching. "And I thought because I never was able to watch TV, and all my friends would talk about all this stuff at school, I always felt out of it. Out of touch. And it made me feel alienated, really, from my peers," she said, pledging to be different for her sons. "So I kind of put all that together and thought—you know what, I would rather he played Nintendo here where I can see what he's doing and watch it and have conversations with him about it and be open about it."

A parent's sensitivity to a child's need to belong comes not just from a parent's past experience but also from a reckoning of the child's own prospects of being different in the here and now. When children experience social or personal differences due to their gender identity, their race, their class, their family structure, experiences of divorce or trauma, any developmental delays or physical disabilities—these characteristics can lead parents in turn to be particularly sensitive to their children's risk of interactional differences, and to their desires to fit in. Let us turn now to examine this process in the case of an affluent African-American family navigating the complex terrain of race and class in Oakland.

"YOU GOT A WOMAN?" RACE, CLASS, AND BELONGING

Most families I talked to, affluent and low-income, tried to mitigate their child's experience of being different. Deborah Lamont and other affluent African-Americans I spoke to appeared to seek it out, constructing what I termed "exposed childhoods" by sending their children to majority-white schools like Oceanview and majority-poor extracurricular activities like Little League in West Oakland. In chapter 7, I explore this practice as a unique form of "pathway consumption" that reflected the particular challenges of being affluent and black in the United States. For now, however, I focus on the challenge to belonging such a strategy poses for the Lamont children, and its implications for the way Deborah Lamont and other affluent African-American parents approach buying.

In Oakland, as in the United States generally, public schools with mostly white students produce higher test scores, employ teachers with more experience, have more active parents, and raise more money than public schools with predominantly students of color. Like their white peers, affluent African-American parents at Oceanview were sending their children to the best school they could afford to live near. At the same time, they relied on the extracurricular activities with poorer blacks and Latinos to give their children a certain fluency with street culture. The mélange meant the three Lamont children were rarely if ever in contexts where they did not stand out.[9]

Deborah had few illusions about the children's experience of being different at school. She did not expect that Oceanview was going to be devoid of the racism that came with the majority-white territory. The children had, after all, already experienced a few incidents of explicit racial hostility—just recently, her daughter had told her that an older child at Oceanview had announced around them, slowly and distinctly, "There are a lot of brown people here all of a sudden." But handling racism is one of the tasks for which the children would have to develop skills in order to be successful, she maintained. She had become a mathematician precisely because a high-school counselor had told her that girls do not do well in math; you have to grow from adversity, she argued. She was not going to sacrifice their education so they would be more comfortable. Other affluent African-Americans made the same choice, refusing to exclude themselves from the "best" schools because of the anticipated intolerance they would find there. In fact, difficult as it is, that environment imparts important skills to the children, they attested.

That is not to say the parents did nothing to prepare their children for their journey. Deborah Lamont was highly attuned to her children's peer culture, her hand always cupped behind her ear to catch the word on the latest must-have. While she did not expect them to run through the dignity gauntlet unscathed by exclusion or bigotry, Deborah used the family's affluence to equip her children for the trial.

For example, the Lamont children had all the gaming platforms at home—Sony's PlayStation 2, Nintendo's GameCube and Game Boy, Microsoft's Xbox—an unusual situation. ("Most parents you will find don't have all of the systems, although the Xbox is better for older kids, and the PlayStation and Nintendo are better for younger kids," another Oceanview parent told me. "But most families don't want to buy the games for all of them, so they pick one and then buy them.") Each year, the children had birthday parties where they invited everybody in their classes, which Deborah regarded as something of a challenge, but important for their social life. "Birthday parties are a lot of pressure," she said. "You have to come up with these ideas that are fun and the children want to go to. And that are novel, and . . . in addition to being expensive. It's really common to spend $500 on a birthday party." Yet she didn't question the necessity of the practice nor the influence it wielded in the children's economy of dignity. "Party bags are an important thing," she observed. "You have to have cool things for the guests." For Deborah, making sure her children had the right commodities was—like coaching socioeconomically integrated baseball, like walking them to public restrooms in low-income areas—part of introducing them to difference safely. We might say, then, that Deborah Lamont exposed her children to social difference but protected them from interactional difference.

At Little League, the impact of the Lamonts' material wealth was more complex, since it highlighted what made them different from the rest of the team in the first place. On a field trip with Vernon's class, Deborah told the other parents that in the Babe Ruth League, one of her sons had a jersey signed by the famous San Francisco Giants hitter Barry Bonds, "and when he got to his locker, it was gone." Sometimes, however, the extensive goods in the Lamont home did serve a purpose in giving the children something with which to make their claim for social acceptance. Deborah Lamont reported a conversation her husband overheard when he was driving nine-year-old Caleb home with two teammates whose parents hadn't come to pick them up after the game:

> And [one of the teammates] said, "Yo, man, you got a woman?"
> Caleb said, "A woman?" [She laughs.] He says, "I have a Game Boy." And he talked about that.
>   "My woman takes care of me." And it just confused [Caleb]. I think because he was embarrassed because he thought they meant . . . he was afraid to say anything. Because he wasn't sure what they meant. And he thought he'd get cool points by saying he had a Game Boy, you know? Because at this age that's what's cool to the children.
>   So he knew enough to ask questions after Rick dropped him off. "A woman? A girlfriend? Why would they want that?"

Thrown off guard by the question about "a woman," Caleb reached for the powerful symbol of his possessions to establish his status. Here was a totally unfamiliar economy of dignity, one in which "women" were potentially useful, although for what he wasn't sure. In response, he relied on the symbolic scrip he knew, that of object goods. The children appear to use their class privilege when they need to defend their status, particularly against unfamiliar cultural standards. Consumption was the lingua franca when other social facts were upended.

Like other affluent African-Americans, Deborah Lamont knew her children would be viewed by others as different at school and at play in Little League and other such venues. She regarded that prospect with a pragmatic mix of expectation, resignation, and some defiance. She kept alert, however, and through her practice of full provisioning, she worked to ensure her children could at least join in the conversations in their social world.

As with racialized distinctions, other differences from the white middle-class norms that prevailed at these affluent schools also served to make parents sensitive to their children's belonging needs. Gender or sexuality differences can be particularly threatening in peer groups of children, scholars report, and parents with unusual children sometimes spent money to shield them. Kevin, a middle-class white father, chose to send his daughter Sarah to Arrowhead, even though the tuition amounted to almost a fifth of the household income, because Sarah had an unusual gender identity.

> Sarah was a different kind of girl, you know? She's a girl who . . . I had it in my head that she'd be eaten alive at a public school. And maybe not every public school is the same. But I went to public schools from K through high school, and I was a pretty traditional . . . I was a typical boy—baseball, football, everything. And I still got teased. I went through . . . I thought a girl whose favorite thing is to practice martial arts day and night—she can almost cut through a block with her hands—I just couldn't see her fitting in.

At this point, upon entry into kindergarten, Sarah had not experienced much shaming by peers, even though she wore boys' underwear and a cap on backwards. But a parent's sensitivity can be shaped by the kind of difference a child poses, or rather by the cultural meaning of that difference, and how intensely the normative culture reigns. Kevin's own experience of gender-based teasing made him fear for his daughter, so much so he was willing to pay for private school.[10]

We can view race, gender, and sexuality as mostly involuntary social differences that accrued to the child—albeit ones whose meaning and signifying practices varied across contexts—and regarding whose reception parents had long had to adopt a particular posture: of expectation, of resignation, of preparation, of celebration. In other families, the differences at hand were of a more recent vintage, and parents' attunement to their children's belonging needs were so new they were raw. The next case study, that of Tess and her son Artie, explores the way such difference in children's lives can mingle with parental guilt and set parents' sensitivity afire, leading them to prioritize dignity above almost all else.

TESS LATIMER: EVERYTHING FOR MY CHILDREN

Artie Latimer was a happy, lighthearted boy with a lot of friends at Oceanview. His mother, Tess, an open, analytical woman who worked as a therapist, had recently bought a house in a largely white, affluent suburb about twenty minutes from Oakland but worlds away in its demographic profile. Having recently emerged from a harrowing divorce, Tess sought to make her children, above all, safe and happy, by making most decisions guided by the needs of their social life. In partial compensation for the upheaval of recent years, Tess considered it a priority to provide for her children's every desire, even to the extent that she knew, and imposed, practically no limits.

The pets in Artie's house, for example, attested to his mother's total devotion to her children's pleasures. This family had one dog, two cats, a lizard, two hissing cockroaches, a frog, two rats, two bunnies, a mealworm, and guppies. In the past they had also had snakes, hamsters, a bearded dragon, and other lizards. Tess did most of the pet care, she said. "It's not a big deal. It's almost therapeutic for me."

Similarly, she used to try to make "healthy" lunches for them to bring to school, but now simply tries to make them something they will eat. "I wish there was a better way!" she sighed.

> I used to always make them sandwiches and try to make it healthy . . . fruit and all of that. But those always came back. So now I've gotten vitamin-fortified candy-bar things. Not really candy bars. Granola-bar kinds of things. But they have chocolate in them. Or just plain granola bars without chocolate. And then they have a juice, but I try to get the vitamin-fortified juices. They eat those.
>
> And then I give them money to buy from what is in the cafeteria at school. But it's a horrible selection. I used to try the carrots, and it all just came back, and they wouldn't eat. So I just figured I'll give them something they'll eat. And then I'm hoping at the new school where they have a real cafeteria with lots of choices for food, then they'll eat. Because they'll see their friends picking food.

Tess hoped the economy of dignity at their new school would reinforce more positive eating habits in her sons. In the meantime, however, she was packing them bars, juice, and money.

This pattern of emphasizing children's happiness to an unusual degree was evident in other realms as well. Artie and Cliff had Game Boys, Nintendo, and computers, without much of a regimen governing their use. A recent birthday party involved scores of invited guests ("It's pretty much everyone"), two hired teenager helpers, and hundreds of prizes ("I spent so much money!"). Good parenting, Tess maintained, prioritized children's fun.

Focused as she was on her children's happiness, Tess was concerned about the effect of moving them. For that reason, she was proud that she let Artie and his brother Cliff finish out the year at Oceanview, even though she had to drive them there and back every day.

TESS: They have been able to keep their friends. Those friends—
most of them—have been out here. Cliff had his birthday party
here, twenty-three kids and twenty adults. People now know we
haven't moved to some other planet.

AJP: Right. And they can picture all the animals and—

TESS: Kids love . . . I walk into after-school care and they're like,
"When can we come to a playdate?" "When is it my turn?"
Monday, Victor was here. Tuesday, Bill was here.

For Tess, the honorable parent prioritized children's social lives.

She also worked hard to make sure her children already had friends
from the neighborhood, thanks to her open-door policy and her total
provisioning. "He knows most of the girls and boys who go to Park
Meade that will be in his class," she said.

> They just come over. They love it here. Last night there were six
> boys visiting. They come. They do their skateboarding. They do the
> jumping, and they play Ping-Pong. They love the trampoline. They
> play with the animals. They're on Nintendo. We've got computer
> games on the two computers. They'll have different guys on differ-
> ent computers, playing. Yesterday was so funny—I was just kind of
> wandering around. There were a group of people on the trampoline,
> there were two kids playing Ping-Pong. There were two kids on
> Nintendo. So there might have been more kids here. And then the
> computer in the office. So it was like every activity center was being
> used. And then a lot of times a bunch of them are staying for dinner.
> So I have gotten used to just making big meals. Costco is my friend.

Attending closely, almost fixedly, to her children's sense of social
belonging, Tess spends her resources to ease their experience. "I think
it's really nice for my kids to know that people like to be here. It's a little harder for me, but I do enjoy it,' she said. "But it's best for my kids to
feel loved and welcomed, and like everybody just loves it here. They like
that. They just love it."

Tess is certainly unusual in the degree to which she pursues her children's social integration. Most homes, even affluent ones, do not have

twelve pets, and most parents do not feed dinner to the neighborhood children with such regularity. But many parents kept a watchful eye on their children's friendship circle, and divorce was one of those factors that often led them to be particularly sensitive to their children's belonging. Zoe, a white professional, suggested that she became attuned to her children's dignity claims after her divorce, when her daughter became depressed, and it seemed like her son "didn't have friends." "[My son] went through a whole . . . he also has the Game Boy Silver or Game Boy Gold, you know, like he was really into that, and 'So-and-so had the GameShark, and that is what I want. I want the GameShark.'

AJP: And so how would you respond to that?

ZOE: And so I would go out and get him the GameShark. "Oh, okay, you can have it." "How much is it?" "Where do they have it?" And I would go out and get it for him. I mean, I did do that. I think maybe it was a birthday or maybe it was birthday money or whatever, but it was like I was on a mission. I had to go to Sears in downtown Oakland to find the GameShark.

AJP: And what was that about? Why was it all of a sudden a mission?

ZOE: Maybe because he had never asked for anything before, or maybe because I wanted him to have friends, and his life was in a period of time when he wasn't, you know, he didn't have friends. You know, maybe because I was feeling insecure.

Zoe recognizes how her own feelings made her particularly attentive to her son's desires, in this case for a Game Boy when she feared he did not have enough friends to get him through a time of family disruption.

One of the most important cultural changes in the past half-century has been the democratization of suffering, the social analyst Eva Illouz tells us. "Psychic misery—in the form of a narrative in which the self has been injured—has now become a feature of the identity shared by both laborers and well-to-do people," Illouz observes. "Neglected childhood, overprotective parents, secret lack of self-esteem, compulsion to work, sex, food, anger, phobias and anxiety are 'democratic' ills in that they no longer have clearly defined class membership." For Tess,

Zoe, and other upper-income parents, affluent suffering situates the experiences of being different for children and adults and helps shape how they spend.[11]

With their sensitivity heightened by perceived or potential suffering, these parents appear to share and even prioritize children's consumer desires generated by their economies of dignity. Sometimes, however, parents' goals differ from those of their children, as in the next case study, of Dorothy Winston and her daughter Olivia.

REARING AFFLUENCE: PARENTS AND
CHILDREN MANAGING POSITIVE DIFFERENCE

Olivia Winston had a giant tree house in her backyard, one with several rooms and a deck large enough for a hammock. In the affluent hills of Oakland, where multimillion-dollar homes were perched cheek by jowl on relatively small lots, that made the second grader special. A few months after they moved there, Olivia came home and told her mother, Dorothy, that a friend had said she was "bragging because I have a tree house." "Were you?" Dorothy asked her. Later, she told me: "I made light of it, but she got the message. You have to be careful not to even talk about it very much. Because it is extraordinary to have a tree house like that in this neighborhood. Most people don't." A creative and skillful mother, Dorothy went so far as to take out a few dolls and stage a role-play, with her daughter looking on.

"I was showing the difference between talking about the tree house, like, 'Oh, I hope you'll come over and play in it. It's really fun! Do you like to climb trees? I hope you come over and play in it sometime.' As opposed to 'We have a tree house, we have a tree house,'" Dorothy said. "There are different ways to talk about it. And *this* kid [meaning the Olivia doll in the second conversation], she's not going to have a lot of kids who want to come play with her, right? And *this* kid [the Olivia doll in the first conversation] is generous and has a lot of people that want to come hang out and play."

Born in Wisconsin, Dorothy considers herself a "funny combination of Midwestern frugality and higher income than I ever expected." She would buy trinkets for party bags months in advance if she came across a good bargain at a garage sale, but also described an affluent lifestyle of frequent entertaining, vacationing at Tahoe and other resorts several times a year, volunteering at the school, and living in a house "that looks like a rich person's house."

Such affluence was another kind of difference, distinct from the narratives of suffering and exclusion that animated other parents' fears. Dorothy considered it a central challenge to manage how her children experienced the kind of difference that might incur envy, as opposed to rejection. She handled this affluence by attempting to instill a sense of *noblesse oblige* in her children, starting with the tree house. "I try to be really generous, with the space and also with our home, which is kind of . . . it can be exhausting, but I think it's important. It's a responsibility that goes with having it, you know?" said Dorothy, who had donated the use of their backyard, and the tree house within it, that summer to eight local groups, such as the Girl Scouts and a local day care. "'That's all right. You have the space. That's a very lucky thing. So what are you going to do with it?' And trying to do that without going overboard and losing my mind."

Dorothy also viewed her biggest task to be not further accumulation, but a constant process of purging. "Our kids—and probably most kids around—have too much stuff already. And it's more a problem of trying to keep it controlled. Keep pushing stuff out," she said. With a big extended family sending boxes of clothes, toys, and art supplies to her kids, Dorothy said she gave most of it away. "There are two huge plastic black bags and a box on the way to the garage of stuff going to Goodwill and the cleaning lady's sister who is having a baby. Just a huge pile of stuff going out. And keeping on top of the stuff is much harder than finding enough stuff for [Olivia]."

Dorothy used the purging to teach her children about inequality and the responsibilities of the affluent. Every so often they would clean out their closets and send toys and clothing to the Central American town where Luisa, their housekeeper, was from. "I put a little guilt trip on them. 'You have so much stuff. Don't tell me you need four teddy bears or whatever. There is a little kid out there that doesn't have one. Think about where this is going. We're not throwing it away. We're giving it to kids that could use a cuddly thing. We're giving it to kids who will appreciate it more because they don't have one.' So they're well aware of where the stuff is going and that other kids are using it, and that sort of thing." She stopped short of putting the children in direct contact with poverty closer to home in urban Oakland, however. "I don't want my kids to have to see that much. I don't take them to most places where homeless people are. I honestly don't. I'd much rather write a check and deal with it on that level than expose them to anything."

Critiques of *noblesse oblige* have a long history, generally arguing that, however well-intentioned, it is nonetheless powerful class practice. In this view, parents seed in their children's childhood an embedded sense of righteous class distinctions that actually shores up the stratification of which these families are the beneficiaries. Like Dorothy, most of the affluent parents in this study seemed to prefer that inequality serve as an abstract lesson in charity and the responsibilities of the wealthy, rather than as a concrete experience in empathy and what we owe each other as fellow humans. While these critiques are surely important, the notorious antics of socialite heiresses in the tabloids can certainly make one yearn for a little more *noblesse oblige* on the part of the wealthy. Nonetheless, for our purposes here, I want to focus less on the politics of Dorothy's mothering than on the discrepancy between Dorothy's and her daughter Olivia's perspective on the kind of difference that matters.[12]

The difference Dorothy considered most important for her children's lives was their affluence, and her mothering tried to frame her children's experience of their privilege as something you earn, morally, through good works. For Olivia, however, as for other affluent children, the economy of dignity made more superficial differences—of lunch boxes or sneakers—more consequential in the moment; the interactional differences still stung, even as (adults might think) the social differences would seem to protect Olivia from invisibility. As we saw in chapter 2, the children's overall affluence did not give them free entrée into their economies of dignity; it still mattered socially whether or not Olivia had had an exciting birthday party or could talk knowledgeably about Hello Kitty pencils.

The persistence of these consumer criteria in their children's social world seemed to surprise some affluent parents. While she took time to cultivate and honor her daughter's friendships through playdates and treehouse parties, Dorothy did not think much about whether or not Olivia had the tokens of value to belong; she was not very aware of her daughter's efforts to navigate the economy of dignity. But there was some evidence that this was about to change.

A quiet, rather steady girl with two younger brothers, Olivia was not the center of attention in the classroom, although she enjoyed her share of friends. Still, she was beginning to care about being able to talk about the right stuff at school. She fought with her brothers for the Pokémon pajamas her cousins had sent her, she chose a Hello Kitty theme for her birthday party, and I watched her develop a singing act for the school talent show—a show that had almost all the second-grade girls gathering in little groups during recess writing lyrics and talking about how much they hated Britney Spears. One day, ironically enough, Marina Simon (whose mother Katerina sometimes packed cold salmon) teased Olivia about the kind of food she brought for lunch, a dumpling soup instead of a sandwich.

Even Dorothy was starting to notice. She recounted how Olivia complained about having to watch "baby videos" like the PBS series *Dragon Tales* just because she had younger brothers. When I asked how she handled that complaint, Dorothy hesitated. "I don't know. I agree, actually. Her friends know all the teenybopper songs, and she doesn't. I'm turning her into a little geek without intending to." Her social antennae starting to quiver, Dorothy was coming to understand the power of the economy of dignity to make small differences bite.

NOT JUST KEEPING UP:
DIFFERENT FROM THE JONESES

A few affluent parents were not ambivalent about consumption as a practice; they understood and even enjoyed the communicative power of goods. Dana Sands was a funny, charismatic Oceanview mother with an artistic flair and a frank manner when she talked about raising her two children in such an affluent context. While her husband Fred was more frugal, saying no when the kids asked him to buy something, Dana said she did not have mixed feelings about spending money on them. "I just tend to buy my kids what they want. My daughter doesn't ask for very much. And my son asks for a lot. I don't know. I just dole it out when it seems right. I really am into things that will teach them things. I don't see a negative in doing that. You know? As long as we really use it. It's a good thing." If the children ask for something in a store, she said, "for me it's like, 'Well, what do you see? What are you looking at?' I'm kind of interested, you know? I want to see Samuel do Lego. I think it's so cool. I want to see him discover how to put something together and make something. You know what I mean? It's neat."

Expressive, aesthetic affluent parents like Dana tended to cultivate a certain style for themselves, and if there was any distance between themselves and their children's consumer yearnings, it was because of what, exactly, the children wanted: their hunger for cheap, televised, and branded products. Generally, children's peer groups valued mainstream popular culture—in movies, in clothing, in music—and not the alternative or the uncommon, which for the parents signaled the knowing connoisseurship, the ironic detachment of those high in what scholars call "cultural capital."[13]

For our second interview, Dana chose the site: a new Thai café near her home that served bubble tea—large, sweet drinks with tapioca bubbles the size of small marbles floating in the bottom. She showed up sporting a large, red vinyl-looking bag with wood handles. At one point, our conversation touched on the paradox of being an unconventional high-end consumer. "I must say, even when you communicate you have style—it costs money to have style," she said. "You cannot do it cheaply. This bag, for example. It cost money! I spent $50 for it. I know that's not a lot for a bag. A leather bag costs more. But it's plastic! I love this bag because it's totally different and unusual. I love it."

"It says something," I offered. She agreed enthusiastically. "It says something! It's red. And 'I'm not what you expect,'" she said. "And so I love that. That's how I try to . . . that's what I do. I like that. I like that in my house, and I like that in my clothing. I like that in my kids. I like to try to push the envelope a little bit."

Dana had started out by homeschooling her daughter Trish but then decided to send her to Oceanview for second grade so that she could have more friend choices. In some ways, then, we can already see Dana's social sensitivity on behalf of her daughter twitching, bending, and attending to her need for peers. Yet Dana was mourning the loss of a more unconventional peer group for herself:

> At Oceanview, you know, I feel like a hippie. I don't usually . . . I mean, I think I show more like a hippie-ish kind of style. But with money. A little hippie with a little money is something probably what I'm looking like. There it's different. These are women wearing their big diamonds, and they're wearing their designer clothes. I don't have designer clothes, and I don't want designer clothes. I'm not interested in that. I don't even know how to puff my hair up! I don't even know how to do it. And I just felt like . . . I wanted to be . . . I want to play the violin and do art. And I don't think I'm going to find any friends here. That's how I felt. Trish is going to make some friends, and I'm not going to make one! I really didn't think so.

This pursuit of the alternative, the unusual, extended to food. "Trish is a weird eater. And I am a weird food person," Dana explained. "Trish's idea of a good lunch would be like a rice-cake sandwich with cream cheese—sesame tamari rice cakes with cream cheese. She's a weird kid. She would like almond butter in a container with crackers, that she could make little individual sandwiches. She'd be happy with pieces of feta cheese or Gorgonzola. These really intense cheeses. Not your typical kid, trust me. She's just really weird that way. She loves sushi." After Dana's interpretation of bags, clothes, and hair, we can see Trish may have been "not your typical kid" because Dana was not your typical mother.

Dana was right. Tall, ethereal Trish was not your typical seven year old. Despite her distracted air ("She's really whooo," her mother said. "You can say, 'Trish,' and she's not watching TV or something. Just, 'Trish? Trish? Trish!' She is just whooo"), she was unusually perceptive about interpersonal relations. As the new girl in the classroom, she once observed to Dana: "You know, mommy, there are all these groups. All these groups. And it's really easy to get into a group, but it's not easy to get out. I'm just going to stay outside a couple of groups." Still, from what I could tell during classroom observations, Trish seemed to pay little attention to the economy of dignity there. ("My daughter is so completely not aware of that stuff," Dana said. "There are some kids who wear jeans that have the little logos on them. I don't think Trish has any idea that it is something out there, that you can have designer jeans.")

In contrast, her brother Samuel, who had a minor speech defect, was keenly aware of the power and meaning of difference in his social world, Dana said. "He has these really cool surfboarding pants," she explained. "They are supercool. And he felt like they would laugh at him if he wore them to school because they're only supposed to be for surfboards." Samuel played T-ball, and one day he refused to go because he had left his hat at his grandmother's house. "Because that's the uniform. Samuel, my God—you have the shirt. I have seen other kids that didn't have the hat. Maybe they had lost the hat, or it had gotten dirty, or . . . but, 'I can't go without my hat.' And he's serious. He is," Dana observed. She tried to convince him to go, arguing that he would be letting his team down. But she was aware that his personal differences increased his sensitivity to interactional differences. "He just looked at me like 'I can't, without the hat,'" she recalled. "He really has a hard time feeling different in any situation already."

Dana is keenly attuned to Samuel's personal identity challenges, growing up with a small but noticeable problem in a world where being different can be really hard. So far, when confronted with Samuel's urgent desire for consumer goods that helped him navigate his peer cultures, Dana bought whatever he wanted, even when it went against her own highly developed personal style. "He has this friend from preschool. And he always wore necklaces, like a gold chain or something. And so Samuel wanted a silver bracelet," which Dana bought for him at Target. Then, at a jewelry store to have something repaired, "he said: 'Mommy, I really want a necklace. I want to have a chain necklace.' I just thought, 'You know what, he wants it; let me give it to him.' You know what I mean?" Her concern for his sense of belonging overrode any hesitation she might have felt for the gilding itself.

Other affluent, expressive parents followed the same tack. Tracy Patterson was a wealthy white mother of two Arrowhead children who spent upward of $24,000 to have two white cabinets custom-made by a Seattle designer. "The things that I have I think most people don't realize how much they cost," she said. "They cost more, but I know why they cost that. And other people aren't going to recognize it. That's fine. I'm not doing it for other people. [The designer] has a certain aesthetic that I completely get and love. I want it in my house. I love it. I get it. And I can afford it."

Nonetheless, Tracy did not require that her own children follow the same path, that of the cultural connoisseur. While drawing the line at "big, loud, crappy bullshit toys that break immediately," or, more significantly, "a mullet" (a haircut that signified white working-class masculinity), Tracy generally bought the children what they wanted, or enabled them to with their allowances. Her younger son Bobby was an avid collector of Pokémon and Magic cards who loved his Game Boy so much he once asked her to put her hand on his neck and steer him as they were going down the street so he could keep playing, a point at which "I said we have a serious problem here," Tracy recalled. Yet Tracy was open to her sons' desires, and when they said, "Mom, you have to get the Avatar

Wo [Pokémon card]," Tracy bought it. "You have to allow them to have the culture they're going to live in," she said. "We don't like it . . . but I can't be passing judgment on every single thing that is part of their school-yard culture and try to make them feel bad because they want it."

The expressive, aesthetic parent consumers seemed to appreciate the power of commodities already. Thus they did not clamp down on their children's consumer desires, despite the conflict between their own highly elaborated tastes and the mass culture for whose artifacts the children yearned.

WHITHER AMBIVALENCE?

While the aesthetic parents embraced consumer culture, they were unusual, as most affluent parents evinced the kind of ambivalence that led to symbolic deprivation. What were the sources of this ambivalence? Why did parents buy if they felt so ambivalent? Why did they feel ambivalent if they were buying?

On the one hand, children's desires were the source of deep ambivalence for upper-income parents. First, as we have seen, many understood their children's desires were linked to their social citizenship at school, their ability to participate and belong, and most thus sought to respond to their children's desires so that they could stand among their peers. In addition, part of the joy of upper-income parenting was in making "magic" or "childhood wonder" by meeting children's wildest dreams; parents found pleasure in being able to convey unremitting love with objects. "There's a certain age where I think it is really important for kids to feel magic," Melanie said. From the perspective of upper-income parents, knowing children's desires was also part of caring well, of listening, empathizing, and reflecting back to children their true natures, so that they grew to know and love themselves. Upper-income parents sought to understand their children as individuals, including their desires, as part of diagnosing their individual strengths and weaknesses—the central task of every upper-income caregiver before commencing on the path of "concerted cultivation." Plumbing the depths of children's desires was good parenting.[14]

At the same time, children's desires were also threatening to parents. Children's desires—particularly, intense desires—evoked a threat to the self peculiar to late modernity: they sketched the path toward the loss of self-control, where children would lose themselves in the very act of consuming. Children's desires could also be personally unsettling, ravenous reminders of parents' inability to satisfy. Children's desires forced parents, eventually, to say no—threatening a dreaded rupture in the parent-child relationship that parents feared for the damage it posed to the fragility of family emotions. Children's desires also reflected the inroads of other cultural forces into the middle-class home: the insidious creep of advertising, for example, and the spreading power of a peer culture that might not honor the same class-based distinctions in consumption, such as wooden toys. These forces felt like insistent alien invaders to parents, who paradoxically were often the ones who invited them in, through television and other practices. Lastly, parents charged with training upper-income children to succeed in their given trajectories must prepare them for the delayed gratification required by long years of education and training before most professional work; children's desires could distract them from that lesson. Caught in the middle, upper-income parents evinced all the ambivalence such a contest can muster.[15]

Electronics—including television, but, more important, gaming systems—drew the greatest parent ambivalence because they unleashed children's focused desire in ways that few other toys did. In a recent national poll, for example, almost a third of teenage boys confessed to having "ever been so into playing video games [they] felt addicted to them." Some upper-income parents talked about electronic games just as they might an addiction; their fear of children's intense, unfettered desire was evident. "It just sucks up their brainpower or something," says Melanie of her son's Nintendo. "They forget how to play and use their imagination because they get addicted to this screen thing." Tracy recalled the day she and her husband, Scott, gave their son Bobby a

Game Boy. "And I jokingly said when Scott handed it to him—you know, jokingly—'Good-bye, Bobby,'" she said. "But that was true."[16]

In addition to symbolic deprivation, parents solved these contradictions with two other strategies of distancing themselves from their capitulation to the consumer market: rules and allowances. Both allowed them to say yes to their children and no to popular culture at the same time, legitimating and codifying their ambivalence.

RULES AND ALLOWANCES: SAYING YES
AND NO TO POPULAR CULTURE
Rules

When they functioned well, rules accomplished an important sleight of hand: they evoked the Good Parent who knew how to set limits for parents who had already bought what their children wanted, at the same time freeing those parents from having to say no to spontaneous requests. Now, if the child wanted to play with his or her Game Boy, the rules gave or denied permission. Layla was open about relishing this freedom as she discussed setting rules about television for the summer:

> We have to talk about this summer, about what our rules are going to be. We have to meet as a family. Because I will not tolerate, "Can I watch a movie now?" every ten minutes. I'm not going to do that. It is just so messed up. So I want to make rules really clear so they don't have to ask me during the summer.

The ideal of restraint is being able to say no to children's desires, to teach children that satisfaction comes later, as a reward. By bringing the reward into the house, parents are already compromising that ideal. Imposing rules was a way for parents to pledge their commitment to self-control, even as they gave ground to the forces of gratification.

Rules that upper-income parents enforced also instilled a particular kind of class practice. Upper-income children experienced Game Boys and other electronics as unmitigated pleasure with limited supply; they learned to contain their fever in short, half-hour bursts; and they developed negotiation skills around gaining access. It is conceivable that these lessons had ramifications for their future trajectories; such lessons might even be supported or rewarded in the children's current interactions with institutions and authorities in childhood, as Lareau demonstrated for other child-rearing strategies. Even when children of different social backgrounds own the same goods, then, they may not experience the same childhoods.[17]

Some parents' rules appeared to be more symbolic than actual, even seeming quite slippery. "I personally feel like he should have no TV during the week. Say, Monday through Thursday night, no TV, period," said Martha, a teacher. By using the words "I feel," however, Martha softened the impact of her statement, turning it from pronouncement to preference, while in the next sentence the word "say" made it sound as if she were making it up on the spot. Perhaps then it should not have been a surprise that when she listed her son's favorite shows, she started off with "Maybe the Simpsons or something, during the week." Game Boy rules were just as malleable, it seemed. "And I don't want him to be doing Game Boy during the week," said Martha, and then added in the next breath, "As I said, sometimes things slip in."

Nonetheless, rules, or even the mere appearance of rules, enabled most upper-income parents to take steps to rein in their children's desires after answering to them in the marketplace. To the extent that they were successful, rules had practical value in demonstrating parents' values, enforcing a vision of time use, and protecting the parent-child relationship. At the same time, however, parents used rules to portray themselves to themselves (and perhaps to others) as honorable in their social context.

Allowances

Upper-income parents also invested heavy symbolism in children's allowances. Most families gave their children some sort of weekly cash gift, but the amounts and the terms of that gift differed for every family.

Like rules, allowances were a way to help children consume, while also maintaining the ideal of restraint, similarly accomplishing this trick so that parents were ideally left out of the moment of compromise.

By the time they were seven, most upper-income children in my sample received an allowance, even if it was just "in theory," as Layla put it. Amounts ranged from $.50 to $10 per week, with boys on average earning more than girls (meaning families with boys paid their children more than families with girls), and, within families, older children earning more than younger children. The terms of these gifts could be dizzyingly complex when tied to behavior or chores. In interviews, parents brought out Excel spreadsheets, charts with stars, and other artifacts of negotiation and planning. Allowances were clearly important symbols for the upper-income family.

Families doled out "the child's age, squared," "$2.50 a week, with a bonus of $.50 if she earns stars," "$10, with a forced savings of $2," and "$.25 per chore on the list, averaging out to be their grade level plus $1." Gavin, who went to Arrowhead, was given a list of chores he could complete, and then at the end of the week it was up to him to assess how many he did and what they were worth, up to $5. "He's like, 'I think I earned four bucks this week,'" his mother Donna said. Another mother scoured the Internet for three-holed piggy banks, finally finding something she could use in a give-away toy from a Burgerville in Oregon. She asked her children to put 10 percent of their $10 monthly allowance toward "donations, or tithing," and then apportion the rest between savings and spending.

The relatively stable financial situations of upper-income parents allowed them to consider allowances as a means of giving their children steady access to cash. Yet while this stability was necessary for allowances, it was certainly not sufficient. Why did so many upper-income parents award allowances to their children, and why did they do so under such elaborately constructed conditions?[18]

Allowances, like rules, enabled parents to solve the conundrum of meeting their children's consumer desires while wishing for spending restraint. They did so by hastening children's own consumer citizenship, granting them access to money before they entered the paid labor force. With children equipped with their own means of buying, parents then felt they could refuse to pay for goods or experiences they did not value, knowing that children could then "buy them with their own money." Without allowances, parents were in the hot seat, being forced to say yes or no to children's requests, evaluating the worth of children's desires, being themselves evaluated as gatekeepers to fun and dignity. Allowances permitted them to gain a little distance from that interaction, so that ideally the question became "Can I afford it?" and not "Would mommy give me the money?" Allowances also offered parents the same kind of solution as applying rules after a purchase: they allowed parents to act as if they were saying no when they were really saying yes. In addition, allowances let parents stand on the side as critical observers, maintaining their values in purity, without having to pit them against their reluctance to say no to their children. Allowances, then, were a kind of mediated parenting.

"Basically what they do with their allowance now is just buy these terrible cards, these Magic cards. Every opportunity they have they get another pack," said Janet, an Arrowhead parent. "Our house is kind of drowning in Magic cards." Donna recalled why they started giving her son Gavin his own money. "He started his Pokémon card collection. And we realized that he . . . we wanted him to have an allowance. That it was important to the family for him to be able to earn money that he could spend almost like he sees fit." The word "almost" is an important caveat; most parents did not give their children license to spend their money on anything they wanted. But cards, games, candy, even shoes—many of which are forms of scrip in the economy of dignity—these were goods for which parents were glad to have children use their allowances.

In addition to their practical use as a means for children to control their own consumption, allowances also had an important symbolic role in upper-income families. The elaborate conditions under which allowances were administered—the chore charts, the spreadsheets—

were testimony to the great ambivalence surrounding the practice of giving children money to buy what they wanted. By giving children allowances, parents carved out a special category for children's desires, but that move also had the effect of demarcating the rest of the money— the household income that was not earmarked for allowance—as not for children's desires. Furthermore, upper-income parents looked to often complex, almost contractual arrangements with their children to regulate their earning and spending, as if mere largesse was too much. Donna's system was among the most elaborate: once her son Gavin earned his $5, she transferred the money from her bank account to his; then at the end of the month he was allowed to spend 10 percent of his total balance.

> We decided that we didn't want him to just go willy-nilly and spend all of his money. And so we wanted to show him how he could save and how it was sometimes better to buy a bigger thing than to just buy little things all the time. You know, the five-and-dime things that break and get destroyed. I'd much rather have you spend $20 at the end of the month and really enjoy what you purchased. And what if it's something that's $60? You may have to sacrifice for three months in order to earn it. To be able to have that self- . . . fulfillment at the end of that three months and be like, "Hey!"—do the math—"So I can spend $33.80."

To be sure, like many upper-income parents, Donna used an allowance to train Gavin to save. Yet allowances also enabled upper-income parents to keep an arm's-length distance from the consumer desires their children evinced, such as Gavin's desire to augment his Pokémon collection. Parents tried to contain children's consumption even as they sponsored it.[19]

Children sometimes tried to negotiate the amount of allowance they would receive, or what they could spend it on. When Chloe, the elder daughter in an upper-income family, wanted to raise her allowance from $2 a week, she made a yearly budget that included items like "notebooks," "pens," and "gifts for family," which when averaged out over the year came to $6 a week. Her parents, a university professor and a stay-at-home mother, reviewed the list, noting sardonically that Chloe had made sure to list "gifts for family" in her budget. Chloe's efforts were unusual for their methodical nature, but they illustrated how some children match their parents' contractual approach to allowances.

Sometimes allowances seemed more symbolic than real, suggesting that they were less about training the children than about representing best practices for the parents. Parents who filled out a questionnaire affirming that they gave their children allowances would sometimes backtrack in our verbal exchanges afterward. "I will be honest. It is never consistent," Paulette said in a confessional tone. Adrienne, a writer, talked about how she had started, then stopped, then started again giving her daughters allowance. "I should be better about this. It's just that I feel like my life is in total chaos," she said, mentioning an upcoming deadline. "We never give it to them," said Layla. "But it is tied to some chores . . . hmm . . . which also never get done." But in making sure the response on my short survey read yes, they did give their children allowances, parents were relying on allowances' symbolic value in their presentation work. As with their claims about enforcing "rules," parents' claims about allowances— claims that did not match reality exactly—were a measure of the symbolic value of these practices for their sense of themselves as honorable.

Upper-income parents called on symbolic practices like rules and allowances to represent their own best parenting, in which they responded to their children's consumer desires but maintained the ideal of restraint. In these homes, allowances and rules both inscribed and surmounted parental ambivalence around children's consumer desires, allowing parents to accede to their children's wishes while holding dear the notion of childhood asceticism.

CONCLUSION

Parents' sensitivity to children's belonging depended on a set of emotional parameters that reflected their own past experiences of being "different" as well as their interpretation of the risk posed by their children's present-day differences. For many parents, memories of difference form part of the emotional backdrop to the conversation about what children need, a conversation that takes place in families nationwide. Social antennae help activate that memory for parents, and then they strive to reenact their own personal dignity by buying for their children. Consumption for children does not then only build bridges between parent and child; for parents it can also forge connections between the past and the present.

The claim of many affluent parents that they do not buy much for their children, however, suggests that, despite their privilege, they feel trapped by competing cultural edicts. On the one hand, parents want to give children what they want, to demonstrate care and connection, and to insulate them from potential exclusion. Are they not supposed to provide children the best that they possibly can? On the other hand, children often desire the "wrong" things, such as goods that are considered lower class, or they desire things too much, suggesting a lack of control that violates adult middle-class norms about self-control and gratification. For most affluent parents, consumer culture is the source of great ambivalence, as "we lament how affluence—the ownership, care and longing for goods—gets in the way of relationships and takes time and attention from 'real life.'" Still, for many parents, when their children's belonging is at stake, good care becomes provisioning.[20]

Born of this ambivalence were the symbolic buying practices of most of the affluent parents in this study. While seeking to meet many of their children's perceived desires in the marketplace, upper-income parents engaged in symbolic deprivation, instituted particular "rules" for playing with toys they had "broken down" and purchased, and distributed "allowances" that tried to set the terms of their children's debut as direct consumers. As common features of upper-income families, these practices constituted and reflected the commodification of childhood, and at the same time symbolized its opposite.

CHAPTER FIVE

The Alchemy of Desire into Need

Dilemmas of Low-Income Parenting

A few miles across town from Katerina Simon's leafy street in Ocean-view, Sandra Perkins sat at her kitchen table, bone-tired after a night shift working as a nurse's aide. Her house was one in a row of small bungalows, with weeds choking the yards, high chain-link fences keeping angry dogs in, and concrete broken into chunks in some of the driveways. Bleached by the sun and quiet on a weekday morning, the West Oakland neighborhood had a lazy menace, like a big cat before it stirs. Recently, a youth just nineteen years old had been shot and killed down the block, and the Perkins family was grieving. "I lost one of my best friends, just last month. I'm still mad about that," Sandra's thirteen-year-old son Darrin told me later. Sandra agreed. "He was like a part of our family," she said, recalling how the young man had helped her build a fence, how she was always telling him to pull his pants up, and how he would clean up after himself when he came over and ate cereal. The family sometimes felt like they were under siege by the violence and drug use around them. And the police? "They only come after people die," Sandra said with characteristic sardonicism.

An African-American single mother of four, three of whom were still living with her, Sandra was a calm, dedicated parent, whose gruff humor hid her devotion to her children, which was typified by her response when I asked her if she gave her children allowances. "When they're good. When I have extra money to give them. When they do what they're told. Most of the time that's never!" But Sandra's life was centered on her children—she didn't have many friends, was fairly suspicious of her neighbors, and kept to herself at work. Later she conceded, "My whole life just revolves around them." All three children, even Darrin, had an unusual openness to them, a sort of sweetness that alternated with the same kind of tough talk as their mother's.

Sandra supported her children on her salary of $26,000 in an area where a local research firm estimated $60,000 was not enough for a single-parent family to live comfortably. She did it by cobbling together their childhoods from a variety of resources, from kin (her mother stayed with them when Sandra had to work overnight) to community services (a "Section 8" federal rent subsidy, free public schooling where the children ate free lunch, subsidized after-school care, free basketball with the Police Activity League, and a Big Brother at Covenant House) to the formal and informal markets (she watched for sales, patronized discount stores, and paid a neighbor to teach Tae Kwon Do to Rasheed). Over the last twenty years, she had had two important relationships with men, both of whom sometimes came through with a little help; Darrin's father had health insurance to pay for his braces, and while I was at their house one night, Rasheed and Lexine's father pulled up outside their front door to give the children $2, which they excitedly ran out to get. Still, times were tight, especially during a temporary layoff over the past holiday season, during which no paycheck came, and unemployment benefits were slow to get started. "Thank God I had some money saved up," she said fervently.[1]

Given the struggle to support her family, Sandra had a jaundiced view of the commodities and experiences prized by children's consumer culture. "[Darrin] thinks he's supposed to have Jordans [basketball sneakers made by Nike]. But I tell him Michael Jordan is rich; I'm not trying to make him richer!" she said. "Better find some reasonable tennis shoes because all of them need shoes right now. Every last one of them. So you figure . . . let's see, maybe $35 for my baby, $55 for Rasheed, and $70 to $75 for Darrin. That's almost $200, you know?"

Other low-income parents shared her view. Clarisse, who worked in a nursing home to support her three children, recalled how she countered their desires: "If it cost too much, I would say, 'No no. I don't think that's going to happen.' You know? Like I might be, 'That's just too expensive.' Like some games, when they're like $60. I'm like, 'No, why don't you find a *couple* of games at that price?' Or something like that." Trinelle, another single mother of three, had a steady job working in data processing but still had had to move out of the city to find a place she could afford. Her children did not always understand "why they don't have some thing." "'Momma, you're rich.' I say, 'No, I'm not.' 'Yes, you are.' I said I'm just making it," Trinelle said. "But I . . . let them know. 'You know what? We don't have money like you think we do. So you need to stop asking for so much stuff.'"

These complaints were qualitatively different from the ambivalence typical of the affluent parents in the previous chapter. Unlike the affluent parents, low-income parents did not worry about the sheer quantity of stuff their children had. They were not too concerned about what a particular item might do to the child, such as the addiction to Game Boy and other electronics that affluent parents feared. They were sanguine about, even proud of, the values they were demonstrating when they bought their children what they wanted, because they viewed provisioning unequivocally as the sign of a good parent.

Many low-income parents did view children's consumer culture as a problem, however, not because it was a sign their children were out of control, but rather because it was dangerous. Children's consumer desires posed serious risks to the family's livelihood, to parents' ability to put gas in the car, to the odds of having food on the table. "Because we're not rich. It's not like we got piles and piles of money in the bank," said Erika, who was looking for work as a certified nurse's assistant, having finished her training recently. "You know? The bank account is zero, zero—you know? You're writing checks off of . . . you know, air and stuff. Sometimes." In this context, parents viewed children's consumer desires with caution but not dread, with regret, annoyance, even defiance, but not angst.

Yet these very same parents had felt the knife edge of longing and belonging. For most of them, no one needed to explain the psychological power of possessions, no one evinced a surprise that such things would matter to their children. Rather, most of these parents knew why their children wanted what they wanted, even as these parents fretted about the pressure to provide that they felt as a result. Darrin wanted Michael Jordan-branded sneakers because "he has to be in the limelight of everything," Sandra said. "He thinks that he's going to be some big record producer one day."

Similarly, Askia, who with her three kids had escaped an abusive relationship, lamented the stress she felt because of the things her children wanted. "The thing that I hate about society is that they put so much emphasis that things have to have a certain name brand," Askia said. "You know, it has to be . . . with our kids Sean John, Rocawear, Air Force 1, Jordans. You know, these are the styles that my kids like to wear and that they see other kids wearing." Askia pinpointed the source of her children's desires: "styles that they see other kids wearing." Yet while she complained that those styles were name brands, she did not begrudge her children their yearnings for what other people wore.

How did these low-income families reconcile their children's desires to have particular commodities and experiences—desires they largely honored as visible and understandable, if not always possible—with the fact of their relative poverty? How did they manage to construct "good-enough childhoods" for their children, when, as Askia put it, "there is no money. I mean, it's like . . . I mean, even though we are existing—we are not living"?[2]

Like affluent parents, low-income parents engaged in symbolic buying for their children and hoped their spending would accomplish particular presentation goals. But while affluent parents pursued a tactic of symbolic deprivation to convince themselves and others that they were not materialistic or shallow, that they valued self-discipline and restraint, low-income parents adopted another strategy. They engaged in what I term "symbolic indulgence," the practice of buying for their children specific goods and experiences that would yield the most social impact for their dollars. Through this practice, they aimed to mitigate their children's experience of "interactional difference," those moments in which they did not have what they were supposed to have in order to participate socially at school.

Sandra Perkins railed against buying Michael Jordan-branded sneakers for her son, who thought he was going to be "some big record producer." Yet other purchases were unavoidable, despite her disinclination:

> Well, I do Halloween. I buy Rasheed and Lexine costumes. I really don't like to because I really think it's a waste of money, really. To spend all that money on a costume and they're only going to wear it one time. But I do it because they have the parades and stuff at school.

Sandra knew that the "parades and stuff at school" meant that having a costume would be an essential component of dignity, marked by peers if absent, just as we saw in the vignette that opened this book, when Rasheed's classmates Simon and Marco reminded their peer interrogators that "the humans were the scariest part of *Dawn of the Dead*." For Sandra, the symbolic import of Halloween costumes meant that the children needed them, even if those "needs" were psychological.

The task for low-income parents, then, was to find out which possessions had symbolic power and which did not, so as to conserve resources for the most meaningful acquisition. Low-income parents struggled to make the purchases their child considered the minimum necessary to hold his or her head up at school. For the severely constrained budgets of the families at Sojourner Truth, a pair of $40 Melissa sneakers was a challenge, not to mention a $200 Sony PlayStation or an $80 bicycle. But in low-income families, most parents made sure to buy *particular* goods or experiences for their children, those items or events that would be sure to have the most significant symbolic value for the child's social world. Thus most low-income children had costly electronic systems, but fewer had bicycles; many had name-brand clothing, but fewer had Legos, Playmobil, or Bionicles; many had collectibles like Yu-Gi-Oh! or Magic cards, but fewer had board games, trampolines, swing sets, or LeapPads.[3]

We can consider symbolic indulgence, then, as the way low-income parents managed their children's foray into their social world. By prioritizing the dignity of their social participation, low-income parents avoided condemning their children to the predicament of poverty first identified by Adam Smith more than two hundred years ago, enabling them instead to "appear in public without shame."[4]

BUYING WHEN IT HURTS

Why didn't these parents just say no? All of the families at Sojourner Truth endured significant financial hardship. When their old cars broke down, for example, they couldn't just fix them; they had to get by without a car until they were able to scrape together what it took to repair it—which meant walking the laundry to the laundromat, taking the bus to work, and putting off food shopping until someone could lend them a car. One parent slept on the floor until someone gave her a bed (although she had bought her daughter a bedroom set). Some parents talked about scrimping on food during the lean times, before the next check came. Thus each pair of sneakers, each Game Boy, was an additional strain on the family budget, a strain parents absorbed by withholding their own desires, taking on extra work, delaying paying the rent or other bills, getting deeper into formal or informal debt, and even cutting back on food. Purchases for their children were not ones these parents could make casually. Why did they make them anyway?

Some critics argue that such spending patterns are a reflection of various forms of parental irresponsibility. They contend that low-income children lack discipline and wield too much influence over parents, who do not control them. Others dust off the claim that low-income people are less able to defer gratification, an idea largely abandoned by social science but still making the rounds among bloggers and politicians on the left and right. Still others point out how low-income parents fail to encourage their children to eschew status-seeking materialism, perhaps because of the adults' own yearnings. Even sympathetic critics express exasperation with low-income children's consumer desires, and observers often lay the problem at the feet of the parents.[5]

Of course, there are surely irresponsible parents among the low-income population just as there are among the more affluent. Some adults express their own consumerism through their children or fail to set limits and abide by them or neglect to model for their children the sort of moderation that might inhibit their buying habits. As the following case studies will reveal, however, these existing explanations have not captured the whole of the dynamics behind low-income parent spending.[6]

DISCIPLINE, DESIRE, AND EMERGING CONSTRAINT

Some critics contend low-income families bow too much before the will of their undisciplined children, with certain commentators linking the problem to family structure and the absence of fathers in particular. Yet while some low-income children are indeed undisciplined, and to be sure, some parents too compliant with their wishes, research largely contradicts the implications of these claims—that there is less discipline in general in low-income homes, or that low-income children wield greater influence than do affluent children. In fact, it appears low-income parents spend most of their time not giving wider and freer rein to their children but rather instilling "a sense of emerging constraint," as the sociologist Annette Lareau described it.[7]

Like other low-income parents, Sandra Perkins often mentioned her efforts to contain her children's consumer dreams.

> Christmas. Christmas is—I tell them they can have two things apiece. Because every time I buy them toys, before the week is out they can't find any of them, or they're destroyed. So I told them: 'You pick two

things that you really, really want the most, and then you'll get it.' And then that will be that. Because I stress to them: 'See all the homeless people on the street with nowhere to live and all these kids begging on the corner for change? That could be you, you know? Be grateful you got a place to sleep.' So that's how I do Christmas.

In the last chapter, we saw Dorothy Winston of Oceanview also call up an image of "kids who have less" to help her children appreciate their good fortune. But while Dorothy reminded her children of faraway needy children to instill the responsibility for charity that comes with wealth, Sandra pointed to people her children saw every day, and did so as a cautionary tale that conveyed their humanity, because "that could be you." And while Christmas offered a cultural moment—durable across many subgroups in the United States—in which children were invited to share their consumer desires, Sandra reported here the stance she adopted vis-à-vis those desires: don't ask for more, be grateful for your survival. Sandra narrated a negotiating process of defining children's needs—the result of a contest between children's attempted advances and her attempted retrenchment.

Other low-income parents described their efforts to stem the tide of their children's desires similarly. "My thing—and I tell my kids all the time—my job is to provide your needs, and some of your wants. Not all of them. All your needs, some of your wants," Askia said. Exhaling after Christmas, Trinelle started preparing her children early on for the next year. "I always tell them, 'Oh, next year we ain't celebrating no more.' I say that every year. 'We going to be Jehovah Witnesses next year! We're not going to celebrate.' And I say that every year! Because—whoa—I'm by myself."

Symbolic indulgence, then, did not just entail ascertaining what was truly important for children's dignity at school, but also involved managing the children themselves by corralling their expectations. Parents mounted this campaign in part to counter the message of boundless desire they viewed as coming out of pervasive cultural outlets, such as music videos and television advertisements.

Yet, for Sandra Perkins and other parents, the conversation with their children about consumer culture was never over. On the one hand, Sandra said she held the line against her children's expanding desires, especially those of her son Darrin:

> I refuse to spend that kind of money on tennis shoes. He gets mad at me. He was telling me just this morning: 'Momma, I heard that such and such got a new tennis shoe coming out, and it's only $100.' And I said, 'Oh, really?' And I said: 'You know, I'm tired of you telling me about how much these tennis shoes cost. You really think I'm going to spend $100 on some tennis shoe when I've got three of you running around here? No!' So he gets mad at me.

As Sandra describes how she stands firm, we can also hear the tactics her son employs. He draws her attention to new desires continually ("I'm tired of you telling me"), he deploys the pressure of negative emotion ("He gets mad at me"), and he ties his desires to his future ambitions ("He thinks that he's going to be some big record producer one day"). Sandra's words echo negotiations with Darrin over his consumer desires.[8]

Nonetheless, Sandra does consider her children's consumer desires when they can convince her that they are needs. Contrast the above excerpt taken from a one-on-one interview, with the one below, taken from a conversation when Darrin and five-year-old Lexine were present, while the family was in the kitchen making hamburgers.

SANDRA: I get what I want them to have. What I can afford and what I think they—

DARRIN: Especially on shoes for me.

AJP: Is that right?

DARRIN: I got to beg to get the shoes that I really, really want.

AJP: What shoes do you really, really want?

DARRIN: Jordans.

AJP: Really?

DARRIN: I had to beg to get the first pair I got.

LEXINE: I want to get the Air Force 1's.

SANDRA (to Darrin):   If you ever get another pair, you'll be begging
for those, too.

Despite her tough talk about getting "what I want them to have,"
Sandra actually paid some attention to her children's dignity needs,
when they could persuade her, sometimes by begging, of their necessity.
Through repeated argument and reinterpretation, Sandra aimed to
limit her children's horizons of desire, but these efforts were in constant
tension with her hopes for them to have the sense of basic humanity that
social participation brings.

While these examples emphasize the conversations about desire that
are ongoing in these homes, more often low-income children did not even
ask. It is not that low-income children nag their parents more than affluent children; in fact, research has found that the opposite is true. In my
sample, children varied in how much they made their wishes known.
Some children, like Darrin, kept up a steady drumbeat. Margaret, a talka-
tive mother of three, shook her head as she reflected on the stubborn will
of her eldest son Anthony. "He rather us to not pay rent so he can get what
he wants," she said. "Games. Computer disks. Anything that involves his
computer. Printout paper, whatever it is. I don't care if it's $100 or $1000,
he wants it. And he'll bug you until I break down and give it to him." Yet
other parents noted that their children rarely voiced their desires directly,
perhaps silenced by their visible poverty. Angela Lincoln, who worked as
a janitor on rotating shifts, said her children knew to stifle their urges.
"They already know. They work with me. They know what we working
with," she said. "So they're not tripping. They're not tripping. They know
Momma is doing what Momma got to do, or what Momma can do." In
several instances during fieldwork I observed children actively restrain
themselves from asking for money or items they wanted when opportunities presented themselves, during shopping trips or at pick-up time, when
other parents were buying their children treats from Ms. Graham.[9]

I was not the only one watching this prevailing restraint. Low-
income parents also saw their children hold back, and it made some of

them feel bad. Parents described trying to compensate for their children's inhibition by buying what the children wanted when they could. Trinelle recalled that after she moved the family into their new home, out of an apartment where a bullet had come from the street through the living room, she bought a Christmas tree for the first time. "And everything they asked for, they got it," even her son's Game Boy, she said. "Because you—like I say, he really don't ask for much." Parents compensated for poverty, for fear, for constraints, for the many no's that had to come before they could say yes. "I never like having to tell my children no," said Askia, the mother who said her poverty meant her family was "existing" but "not living."

Whether their children were demanding or restrained, most low-income parents knew what their children wanted, or, perhaps more important, *that* they wanted. The parents often adopted a defensive posture toward their children's consumer desires even as they respected their children's social needs, simply to manage the tension between their limited resources and their children's seemingly unlimited, even if unvoiced, yearnings. Like the children of affluent white divorced parents, then, buying by low-income parents had an acutely compensatory quality. Following the alchemy of their children's desire into need, low-income parents practiced symbolic indulgence as the best compromise they could make between their keen sensitivity to children's belonging needs and their own intermittent ability to provide.

WINDFALL CHILDREARING, PLANNING, AND INSTANT GRATIFICATION

Critics who argue that low-income parents lack the ability to plan or delay gratification betray a lack of familiarity with the experience of money in low-income settings, where it is not only scarce, but also unpredictable. Due to the cyclical nature of much low-wage work, the lottery-like rarity of public largesse such as Section 8 rental subsidies, and the way in which social obligations tend to ferret out any surplus or savings in the kin network, money falls like desert rain for low-income families—unexpected, irregular, and given to flash floods (if we can call them floods). The implications of this unpredictability for parenting are profound, resulting in what I term "windfall childrearing."[10]

Many low-income parents cannot predict when they will be able to afford many expenses that might go beyond rent or food, which impedes any of the sort of regular, planned payments considered routine in more affluent homes—from weekly allowances (in contrast, recall in the previous chapter the elaborate symbolic edifice affluent parents built around allowances) to after-school lessons or activities. The scarcity and unpredictability of money also meant that most purchases of "extras," like an outfit for Easter or new soccer shoes, required extensive planning. Research has demonstrated that low-income parents may buy many of the same items as more affluent parents for their children, but that their buying practices differ dramatically. When affluent families might stop in at the ShoeMart on the way home from dinner, low-income parents look for sales or coupons, buy far in advance, or put money away for long periods before buying, for example. These practices embed class patterning into the experience of growing up.[11]

Erika Henderson was an African-American mother of three, although she lived only with her two youngest girls, as her oldest, a son, was living with his father. She had the most troubled background of the Sojourner Truth parents in my sample, beginning with her mother deciding she couldn't raise Erika as a young girl and "giving" her to a friend, and then years later swooping in to take her back, before quickly dying of cancer, all without explanation to the bewildered child. A former addict, Erika had been homeless, and she said she was "full of rage," a claim that seemed to bear itself out when I saw her react angrily and loudly to a store clerk who didn't hear her requests for help in pricing pumpkins. Most significant, Erika had had her children taken from her for almost three years due to what she called "corporal punishment." Her turnaround began when she met Otis, an African-American man with a drinking problem and maybe worse, to whom nonetheless she felt a profound sense of obligation, because he gave her a home when she had none, and stayed by her while she was struggling to get her kids back. Times were tough: Erika had worked for Sears but had been laid off, and had since retrained as a certified nurse's assistant but had not landed a job, while Otis worked in roofing sporadically. Together, they made $1120 a month.

For Erika, parenting was about training her daughters in good habits, but it was not going well. They were generally viewed as an undisciplined, reckless pair, particularly the oldest sister, nine-year-old Loretta, whose unpredictable lawlessness earned her a grudging wariness from kids and watchful disapproval or stern reprimands from adults. Both children were required to see therapists and social workers regularly at school, while at Sojourner Truth, staff opinion of the girls' behavior was low. Erika seemed to share this prevalent view, as when she described grocery shopping with them:

ERIKA: Okay. Go the grocery store. We're parking in the parking lot. Before you get out of the car you tell them: "Don't touch nothing, don't ask for nothing, don't do nothing. Just stay beside me and walk wherever I walk with the basket. Don't swing on the basket, don't get in the basket. Just hold the basket."

AJP: And that doesn't work?

ERIKA: You know, like Albertson's is really, really clean. They'll slide on their knees. They'll run real fast and slide. I'm like, "You better get up off that floor." "Mommy, can I have some cookies? Mommy, can I have some chips? Mommy, can I have—?" And it's just on and on and on. And you forgot half of the stuff you're supposed to buy. You come out of the store, and you get home you're like, I spent all this money, and I don't even have the things that I need. Oh, it's very embarrassing.

She viewed her children as unreasonable, almost alien to her—"Maybe because they was away from me for a while"—and certainly not responsive to her efforts to control them.

While for Erika, parenting was a constant struggle—she admitted to not knowing what to do about her children's misbehavior, now that striking them would bring in the authorities—her skills as a low-income provider, given her severely constrained circumstances, were undeniably strong. Like many low-income parents, she had considerable experience in and talent for extending the reach of her money. She described the way she handled the bills.

> We juggle a lot. I really never usually get a second notice. Because before I get a second notice I'll put something on it. Even if it's not at least half, a quarter—something. That keeps them off of my back. And before they can call again I'm going to put something else on it. Or before they can send me another note I'm going to put something else on it. So that's how I do it. I don't pay the whole bill. Because I can't. If it's $70, I might put $30 or $40. If it's $80, I might put $20. Like the phone—you can give them $10. They don't care. Just as long as you give them something. So it's different companies they have different ways, cycle billings and stuff. The way they do stuff. So it has been working out. I can say that.

Erika endeavored to learn different companies' billing practices and then ensured that she gave them some amount in order to keep them from sending her account to collection, shutting off her utilities, or taking other direct action. It is important to note that had she been talking about credit cards or more informal debt mechanisms, her skill and attentiveness at "keeping them off her back" would also have extended the duration and amount of her indebtedness, effectively increasing the total amount she paid, due to interest and fees, against most financial analysts' advice. The poor certainly do use debt to be able to pay for expenses they deem necessary, research has shown. In this specific case, however, Erika was talking about paying monthly utility charges, and for Erika, the strategy of paying them a little at a time "has been working out."[12]

She learned how to manage various vendors and their representatives through years of practice, she said.

Because you kind of get a feel. [For example,] I have had so many apartments. But this is the first time I have ever paid water. So that first whole year you have to make a really good impression. Let them know you're going to pay the bill. So if you ever do get in a situation—they know. "Oh, don't worry about it. Pay us when you can." That's the kind of relationship I build with PG&E, phone, cable, and water. You have to. Because there are going to be times when you are not going to be able to pay it.

Erika planned for the eventuality of need, and the unpredictability of money, by working to establish a relationship with particular vendors.[13]

Erika described the way the unpredictability of money affected how she managed to pay for her children's dignity needs. Most of the time, she tried to get her children what they wanted, she said. "When I get my unemployment check I make sure they get one thing that they want. Like if I'm at the beauty supply, I'll let them buy a thing of lip gloss. Just one thing that they want. They don't necessarily need it. I make sure I do that. If I don't buy them that, then I'll give them their own dollar, and at Sojourner Truth they can buy gum." She did this to make up for all the no's she had had to say up to that point, but the consequence was to pass down to her children the same experience of money as windfall—random, unpredictable, and not linked with particular behaviors or attitudes. Erika partially recognized this process and lamented it, even as she knew it was happening:

And that's the worst thing that you can do—is buy a child something or do something for a child that has not earned it. I don't care if it's as simple as taking them to McDonald's. You know? Because I've done it. I mean, it's just like somebody just eating you up on the inside. Because you know they don't deserve it, and you sacrificing, too! Oh my God, that's the worst feeling in the world. You know?

The unpredictability of money shaped Erika's spending (and her parenting) into a form of windfall childrearing; she felt compelled to respond to her children's boom-and-bust experience of enforced deprivation with a compensatory period of released desire. For Erika, the result was her maternal anguish, "the worst feeling in the world."

For bigger-ticket items, however, Erika handled the situation differently. She just did not have the wherewithal to buy what she wanted for her children when she wanted to, even after "the check came." She explained:

> I can't wait until Easter comes, or the night before Easter to say, 'Okay, I'm going to buy [shoes].' No, when I have the money and I see them I just get them. Know Easter is coming. It might be four months away. You know, Christmas—you don't wait until December 20th and think you're going to get gifts. You start working on that in October. You know—get the most expensive thing first and then work your way down. That's how . . . that's the only way I know how to do it. So that's how we deal with Christmas and the big holidays and birthdays. Start shopping ahead of time.

Only through extensive planning could Erika provide for the gifts and celebrating that made annual American family rituals meaningful.

Like Erika, many low-income parents talked about the foresight and methodical preparation necessary to make a life out of what felt like barely a living. Askia could see the day nearing for her oldest daughter's sixteenth birthday, but she thought she might get some help for a party from an old friend whose mother had recently died. "And if I have to put a little money away here and a little money away there—it'll get taken care of. It always does," she remarked. "And I think that a lot of people are amazed how people on fixed incomes or whatever can do the things they need to. I should probably get a degree to be a mathematician or an accountant or something. The way that I juggle the numbers to make stuff work."

This kind of planning ahead required a longer-term horizon than most affluent families maintained for spending, and seemed to stand in sharp contrast to the mythology of low-income instant gratification. The irony behind the unpredictability of money for the poor was that low-income parents were forced to lie in wait for months for a few punctuated moments, those moments in which they could engage in the brief symbolic indulgence allowed by "windfall childrearing."[14]

From the children's perspective, windfall childrearing meant that sometimes their parents had money and sometimes they didn't, and little that the children did had any effect on the matter. Although some low-income parents said they gave their children an allowance, almost none of the children in these families actually received a regular, weekly sum of money that they could count on, because it was not always clear whether the money would be there for such a predictable doling out (I discuss one family's exception in the next chapter). Instead, children got a few dollars here and there, or knickknacks at the store "when the check came." Thus every icey, every candy, every yes from their caregiving adult felt like a windfall, as unforeseen and unrelated to their actions as a dollar you find on the street. "Well, I don't give Theresa allowance," Margaret said. "But if she wants—like if I have the money and she wants something at the store, I give it to her."[15]

In addition, even though their parents were the ones saying yes and no, it was repeatedly clear to children that the windfalls originated from somewhere behind their parents, as they didn't seem to be in charge of when there was money or not either.

ERIKA: They know when I have money. They don't know like we know. But they know when mommy has money. Because I'm going to the store myself! "Ooh, I got some money. Ooh, we got to go here, we got to go there. We got to get some gas, we got to go—" They know when I have money. It's obvious.

AJP: It changes everything.

ERIKA: Yeah. Everybody is happy. Oh, yeah! You know? Until it's all gone! Then we're like, Oh, we got to wait another week. You know, every family goes through that.

These experiences taught children that their parents shared the sense of money as windfall, that the real control over how much was available lay outside of the family, a lesson that perhaps contributed to the parents' diminution.

The windfall effect also removed some of the backdrop of moral deservedness behind possessions, because if you had money or belongings in this context, it wasn't that you were good, it was that you were lucky. For all sorts of American families, the Tooth Fairy and Santa Claus are conduits of money and things to children, conduits that use myth and ritual to obscure the true parental origins of this largesse. In a very low-income urban environment such as Sojourner Truth, however, it all felt like the Tooth Fairy.

MATERIALISM, DESIRE, AND FANTASY: EXPRESSIVENESS UNDER CONSTRAINT

Other critics argue that materialism is the scourge leading to widespread buying, and some research has found greater prevalence of materialism among the poor. Yet even if low-income parents were more "materialistic" than the more affluent (a finding that depends on the word's definition), there is disagreement about the degree to which parents can effectively transmit their values to their children. Furthermore, even useful definitions of materialism—like, for instance, Douglas Holt's elegant concept of it as the sense that "value inheres in consumption objects rather than in experiences or in other people"—often skirt the question of how things come to have more value in the first place. In a sense, and as the experiences of the children at Sojourner Truth bear out, "materialism" describes the symptoms but not the etiology behind a certain way of being in the world.[16]

A few of the low-income parents I interviewed did seem to take the same sort of pleasure in consuming, or thinking about consuming, that animated mothers like Dana Sands or Tracy Patterson, two of the affluent, expressive, aesthetic consumers we met in the previous chapter. These parents took a different stance than that of Sandra Perkins and those like her—less suspicious, more joyful about commodities, even as their constraints kept many commodities out of reach. Their virtual embrace of consumer culture echoed that of some of their affluent counterparts, with the critical difference that most of the time the low-income parents could only peer in through the windows, wishing. These low-income parents also seemed to entwine materialism with their identities as mothers and fathers, invoking possessions as part of good parenting.

Margaret Roa, a Filipina woman living with Rick, an African-American, was an intensive mother who, like some affluent parents, derived much pleasure from buying when she could buy, and musing about products when she could not. Margaret had three children, a seventeen-year-old boy Anthony, an eight-year-old girl Theresa, and an infant son. The geography of her house spoke volumes about her priorities: the five of them lived in a tiny two-bedroom apartment, the two older kids each with their own rooms, while she, Rick, and the baby slept in a cramped living room the size of a small car.

With Rick laid off from work three months before, resources were extremely tight. Margaret reported $888 in monthly "official" income, including food stamps, while their rent alone was $985. Dribs and drabs from her first son's grandfather, her ex-husband's drug dealing, and some gambling winnings had been making up the difference until Rick could find steadier work than part-time construction, her welfare check increased, their housing subsidy came in, or some other hoped-for eventuality developed. But Margaret was definitely sacrificing some comforts due to their financial hardship; at the time of our first interview, she wasn't able to leave the tiny apartment often. "I don't have a stroller, so I'm having a hard time. You know, we can't afford one," she said frankly. Her son's grandfather was going to buy her one, and then decided against it. "So I told Rick, and he said, 'Well, buy one this week when we get paid.' Well, the rent is behind. I mean, bills—" and she broke off. Poverty meant adult needs—like Margaret's desire to go outside with her new baby—got put on hold. Poverty also contributed to her periodic bouts with depression, which sometimes got in the way of the intensive mothering of which she was so proud; last year, Theresa, a smart girl whom I had watched win several awards at school for achievement, missed nineteen days of school because her mother couldn't get out of bed to take her.

Margaret talked at great length about her older two children as individuals, including long soliloquies about her son's penchant for getting out of housework and her daughter's social problems with the girls next door. When I accompanied her on a shopping trip, my fieldnotes reflected how Margaret's children's individual likes and dislikes fueled her food-buying decisions:

> As she is shopping she is always assessing who likes something, and who doesn't and who she is buying for. Cereals: "Theresa likes this, while Anthony likes that, so I buy this, which they both will eat, because I am not buying a new one and have it go uneaten, and then I just have to give it away, to someone else who has less than we do." "Theresa will eat sausage links, while Anthony likes bacon, only Rick eats baloney"; "Tony likes chili beans that are hot, Theresa likes them not hot," etc. This is the most detailed, focused narrative I have heard while shopping—and she says, "I think I'm a good mother."

Good mothers were also involved in the schools, Margaret maintained. "I'm an outspoken mom," she said. "And I go to every meeting they give. I mean every meeting. I go. I volunteer. I donate. I cook if they need lunches. I do all that. I'm into it."

Margaret also reported that she decorated the house, cooked special food, or gave gifts for Christmas, Easter, Valentine's Day, Halloween—even St. Patrick's Day, she said. "I dye green food—for rice sometimes! I do food coloring for the cupcakes. We do a lot of stuff. I'll pin a dollar bill on Theresa or something." Attending to the rituals of childhood was an important part of good motherhood, she said. "I do it for the kids. My kids. It's fun. And I'm a good mom. I like to do all the stuff. I'm a fun person. I just want to. The kids want it, you know? And so I'll do it. I think all parents should take the time and do things, you know?"

Margaret admitted to what she perceived as moral compromises in many other arenas—how she was embarrassed to have three children by three different men ("It's so bad. I have three baby daddies"), how she relied on Theresa's father's drug dealing to pay for Theresa's clothes ("I hate to ask him. But if I'm short, I will ask him"), how she does not feel upright enough to go to church ("I don't know if I should go yet . . . right now I smoke cigarettes. I cuss a lot. I'm not actually married yet to Rick. So that, to me—that's a sin").[17]

But her core moral identity was as an intensive mother, attuned to her children's individual characteristics and needs, and devoted to fulfilling them. Included in this panoply of tasks was paying close attention to the consumer landscape for children. So attuned to the call of dignity and its role in her children's social lives, Margaret monitored, encouraged, and even initiated efforts to get information about valued commodities.

Sitting in their living room putting on nail polish together, I asked Theresa how she found out what was cool for kids. Her mother proved an active participant in the conversation:

THERESA: When everybody comes to school wearing it.

AJP: Everyone comes, and they're all wearing the same thing?

MARGARET: Well, no. What about Melissa's shoes?

THERESA: Oh, Melissa's.

AJP: Who is Melissa?

THERESA: It's the shoes.

MARGARET: Shoes for teenager girls. It's the new thing now.

THERESA: Or Bee Fly shoes are just like them, but they're fake. And they have a "W" on them. Melissas— the tongue right here says, "Melissa," and then it has an "M" right there.

AJP: And where can you get those?

THERESA: Hilltop Mall, or—(to her mother) what's that other one?

MARGARET (proudly): And how did you find this information? Who found it out for you?

THERESA: My mom! She asked some girl at the Wash
            Out that was wearing them.
MARGARET: She wants them so badly.
AJP: You want the Melissa ones or Bee Fly or the—
THERESA: I want the Melissas because the Melissas are
            the real thing.

Unlike Sandra Perkins, Margaret did not try to hold off consumer culture with one arm extended, waiting for her children's constant lobbying before she decided the item must have enough social cachet to be worth buying. Instead, Margaret's awareness of "the new thing for teenager girls" and her initiative in bringing up the subject in the first place suggested a different relationship to the symbolic tokens of her children's economy of dignity—one at once more playful and more serious, in which she herself kept track of what counted as scrip. She even rendered an opinion on children's objects:

AJP: Who has them? How did you hear about them?
THERESA: Everybody got them.
AJP: How much are they?
THERESA: There's three kinds—low-top, high-top, and slip-ons.
MARGARET: And they run from $40 on up.
THERESA: You should see the high-tops. My mom thinks they're—
MARGARET: On the top they're like high-tops up here, but they're all
            open like this over here. And they come out like little
            collars.
THERESA: I think they're ugly.
MARGARET: They're gorgeous.
AJP: Which ones do you like?
THERESA: The low-tops or slip-ons.

Margaret played an active role in monitoring and creating her daughter's experience of the economy of dignity through goods, and her playfulness made consumer culture sound like something fun, as opposed to something threatening. Like Dana Sands, the affluent mother who greeted her children's in-store requests not with annoyance but with "Well, what do you see? What are you looking at?" Margaret was more curious than resigned, interested than suspicious.

Margaret's extreme poverty makes some of her claims unlikely—all that decorating and cooking and gift giving would be expensive even for a budget above survival levels. In all likelihood, Margaret gets pleasure from *talking about* special activities just as she enjoys talking about goods like the Melissas; while it is not the same as owning a pair, Margaret knows where to get them and how much they cost, and she has an opinion about which ones are "gorgeous." But this level of consumer engagement serves a purpose as well, as we have seen. Through talk, Margaret indulges her own delight in consumer fantasy, gathers cultural knowledge valuable in Theresa's social milieu, and equips Theresa for the facework she might have to do at school.[18]

A few other low-income parents shared this kind of enthusiasm for consumption. Malcolm Clarke took particular pride in his ability to provide for his son, Malcolm Jr. The married father of two, Malcolm was a union carpenter whose wife was training as a health technician while holding down a retail position. A confident, handsome man with a pleasant, straightforward demeanor, Malcolm was one of the only African-American fathers in the Sojourner Truth sample who was both living with his children and employed in the formal economy. It was unusual for a Sojourner Truth child to have two parents still living together, both working and contributing, and it offered Malcolm Jr., their son, a radically improved financial situation. The Clarke family actually owned a house, albeit in the depressed housing market of West Oakland, from which they derived rental income to pay the mortgage. Still, they made little enough to qualify for Sojourner Truth, and Malcolm Sr. reported $2400 a month in income.

Malcolm Sr.'s response to children's consumer desires was as enthusiastic as Margaret's, as eager as the aesthetic, expressive parents at Oceanview and Arrowhead. Pleased by his ability to provide for his son, he indulged his own desires as well as his son's for consumer goods. For example, Malcolm Jr. had five Game Boys, more than any other house-hold in this research project, bought by his father "so his friends could play with them on sleepovers." The boy celebrated his birthday this year at the indoor recreation area called the Jungle, inviting relatives and, unusually, all his Sojourner Truth friends. On his eighth birthday, he received a small motorcycle, which he rode up and down the street until the police pulled him over and told him he had to restrict riding to a parking lot. "I gave it to his older cousin," Malcolm Sr. said. "But when we move I'm going to get him a four-wheeler." Malcolm shared the gleeful sense of play that these kinds of parents seem to have for their children's consumer desires, in his case enhanced by his delight in being able to buy. Nonetheless, while Margaret and Malcolm may represent a form of "materialism" among the Sojourner Truth cohort, most low-income parents were less like them than they were like Sandra, evincing not pleasure in their children's consumer desires but suspicion, even defiance, softened by a knowing pragmatism.

THE PRACTICAL VERSUS THE SYMBOLIC: CONSUMPTION AS PUBLIC SAFETY

The foregoing case studies explored common criticisms of low-income families. Instead of wanton consumption, however, I found "emerging constraint"; instead of uninhibited gratification I found a regimen of waiting and planning imposed by the unpredictability and scarcity of money; and instead of widespread materialism I found just a few parents experiencing the joy of consumption, a joy certainly shared by a few of the affluent. The most common criticism of low-income consumption, however, centers not on *why* these parents buy, but *what*. Some observers contend that under the constraints of poverty, low-income parents should prioritize their families' basic survival, such as food and rent, and eschew nonessentials like Easy-Bake ovens and Game Boys. No matter why they bought these luxury items, in this view, it was an irresponsible choice.[19]

Even if these critics recognize—which not all of them do—that some affluent families demonstrate as much or even greater extravagance, some of these observers put such habits in a different, more benign category, as if they were comparing a tipsy great aunt to a homeless alcoholic. In this view, affluent overspending is a bad idea, but low-income overspending is indecent. It may be slightly over the top for an upper-middle-class child to have her own horse or a $2000 collector's edition doll, so the argument runs, but it is shameful for a low-income child to have expensive electronics when there is not enough money for food at the end of the month. At least the more affluent parents can afford their mistakes, these critics say. When low-income parents make such a mistake, it precludes them from spending that money more wisely, on books, tutoring, museum trips, or even a better neighborhood, with better schools. Such choices on the part of low-income parents, these critics contend, serve to mortgage their children's future.[20]

Yet I found that low-income parents had practical as well as symbolic reasons for their purchases. In contrast to the affluent families at Arrowhead and Oceanview, for example, these families lived in neighborhoods where danger was palpable. One Latina woman recalled when a strange man stalked her last winter, repeatedly following and threatening her. Another mother saw me at a local Halloween festival and proceeded to pour out her desperate concern for her daughter, because a pimp who lived nearby had recently made suggestive comments. Trinelle's family moved to the outskirts and took on an hour-long daily commute because of a bullet that whizzed through their living room one day. A friend of the Perkins family had just been shot down the street. Margaret and Erika lived next door to a crack house. Though only a few miles away from the panoramic views and the towering, fragrant forests of bay laurel trees in the Oakland hills and their million-dollar homes, the houses of Sojourner Truth families were in another world, and they viewed it as a dangerous one.

Toys had a role to play here. Low-income parents wanted goods that would keep their children enthralled, because they often refused to let the children outside when they got home from school in the afternoon. Those children who may have had bicycles or scooters were severely limited in when they could use them. Erika talked about giving her daughters roller skates, a "big-ticket item," as she said. But "a lot of times they don't even get to use it because . . . unless it's the weekend, and he's out there barbequing or something like that—we'll close the gate. It's just so dangerous around here. You know, with all the drug traffic and everything." In this light, toys that kept children inside and happy, especially particularly effective ones like Game Boys or Nintendo, were a boon, and their extensive use was fundamental as a public safety issue.

The extreme practical value of objects that keep low-income children from going outside and getting hurt is of course undeniable. This finding certainly suggests that the challenges of parenting in a low-income environment serve to shape consumption and other behaviors in ways not immediately discernible to those who live free of these concerns. Yet, at bottom, my argument is not that these purchases had a hidden practicality whose urgency absolved their buyers of all criticism. Rather, I contend that these parents, like their affluent counterparts, considered the symbolic value of things just as significant as their practical import.

SYMBOLIC INDULGENCE: AN OASIS OF BELONGING

For low-income parents, the symbolic value of certain possessions and experiences is manifold. First of all, dignity needs can seem particularly acute in contexts where dignity is scarce or disputed, or when it plays a critical symbolic role in attenuating perceived deprivation. Low-income parents do not just reject their children's desires out of hand, for example, in part because of these multiple meanings of dignity. Recall that even as she complained about Darrin, Sandra did not disagree with his claim that feeling accepted in his social world was crucial. As we have seen, her response, like those of the other low-income single mothers of color at Sojourner Truth, was almost matter-of-fact in its assumptions.

Children's dignity needs also recalled for parents their own memories of deprivation. Scholars attest that low-income mothers seldom forget the sense of longing and shame from their own childhoods. "I'm trying to give [my son] things *I* always wanted," said a low-income single mother in one recent study. "Like if my friend had new sneakers, and I'd be like, 'I really wish I could wear them.'"[21]

Meeting children's dignity needs worked its symbolic magic for parents as well as their children. Doing so reflected on parents as good providers, showing that they were able to plan, save, and otherwise accumulate enough to meet a stated need. For low-income parents, part of parenting well was engaging in the acquisition work Erika demonstrated. Through buying they showed they could maintain the long-term horizon to keep important upcoming ritual moments—and their necessary accoutrements—in focus well before the day arrived.[22]

Moreover, buying for children did important symbolic work in representing the low-income family as not "in trouble." At the low end of the moral hierarchy of families in the United States, these low-income, single mothers of color operated against the prevailing assumption that they were unable to control or provide for their children, described by one scholar as the notion that that they were not just "flawed consumers," but "flawed mothers."[23]

Toward that end, some goods seemed to matter more than others in representing that families were not "in trouble." Ironically, television and electronic gaming systems, the very same objects that represented everything problematic—addiction, excessive violence and sex, passive experience—about consumer culture for affluent parents, carried a particularly heavy symbolic load for low-income parents as well. The television was often mentioned as a sign that someone had not fallen over the precipice, could still keep it together, owned at least that much. When Yvette's father, just returned from jail, offered to have Yvette stay over with him, for example, Yvette complained about his empty house. But her mother assured her: "He's going to . . . he'll progress. You have to take it one step at a time. But as long as he has somewhere to sleep and you have a TV." Similarly, Askia defended her dire economic straits to her children. "I'm not really concerned with the fact that we don't have cable right now," she said. "As long as I can provide a roof over the head, and you can flick or turn the TV on when you want to. Even if you don't have 250 channels. You have about ten of them."

Electronic gaming systems had even more emotional value. Angela Lincoln, the janitor, reported struggling to make the food last for herself and her three children before the end of her monthly paycheck. Yet when she talked about getting her son a PlayStation, she was matter-of-fact. "You have to manage your money," she said, dolefully. "You can't neglect the kids, though."

Thus children's consumption desires, transformed into needs by the economy of dignity, were a top priority for low-income parents, sometimes even pegged ahead of other basics like clothes, food, or even rent, and worth extraordinary efforts to procure. "What I do is I just sacrifice something. I'll work extra hours somewhere just so this can be the Christmas," said Shirley, an African-American single mother of three, describing how she manages to buy her son the electronic games he wants. Despite the steep challenges such buying posed for a low-income budget, parents went out of their way to do it.

CONCLUSION

Most Sojourner Truth parents were responsive, even enthusiastic, consumers for their children. Yet it is important to remember that for people on the lowest end of the income ladder, as they are, the choices they make are painful ones. These are families who have known hunger, who wait for the check to come at the end of the month, who have had to learn the skill of how to juggle creditors, paying one, calling another, putting off a third. Thus even to be as responsive as they are is often difficult; their decision to respond to the economy of dignity is more than a casual one, and it is one that comes at some cost to them. But their particular sensitivity to dignity is in part, perhaps, due to their own social location as low-income people of color, subject to their own dignity injuries, both now and as children. If, as scholars suggest, cultural knowledge turns on the emotional energy of experiences, these encounters have a searing impact. As Richard Sennett and Jonathan Cobb suggested in their classic work *The Hidden Injuries of Class,* "no more urgent business in a life can exist than establishing a sense of personal dignity. If forces beyond one's control call the dignity into question from the time one is a schoolchild, it becomes a prior question to power and possession, and indeed a reason why power and possession are sought after at all." Who among people who have felt the shame of lacking could consign their children to the fate of indignity?[24]

Very few families, lower- or upper-income, were able to eschew their children's dignity for other priorities. In the next chapter, I explore the unusual circumstances that enabled certain parents at certain times to mute the desires their children brought home from school. But for most of the Sojourner Truth parents, the call of dignity was particularly loud, at times drowning out other needs. The sacrifices, the extra jobs, and the extensive planning that heeding that call required were evidence of just how high a priority children's consumer desires were. The urgency of dignity shaped the emotional topography on which parents and children made childhood together.

CHAPTER SIX

Saying No

Resisting Children's Consumer Desires

Kevin Yardley laughed in sheepish horror when he described the rules about television he established for his children. A genial, lanky father, who had sent his daughter to Arrowhead in part because of her unusual gender identity (see chapter 3), Kevin instituted for Sarah and her sister Maggie "the exact system that I grew up with"—a half hour of watching per week, each. "I can't believe I'm doing this! I hated it growing up!" he cried, with good-humored dismay. Why did he hate it? "It wasn't enough television," he said, simply. "All my friends were talking about *The Munsters* and *The Green Hornet*, and—'*The Green Hornet*—that sounds so cool, I'd love to see that.' Or 'Batman—he did what?'"

Kevin recalled the economy of dignity of his childhood, one that made his own family's television restrictions particularly odious. He remembered talk of television programs as a form of scrip, part of what gave him, as a child, that momentary sense of belonging or not belonging. And yet he decided to limit his own children's time with the television anyway. He did so, he said, because he did not like the way television affected his daughter Sarah, who became so absorbed by the characters she saw that she would act them out obsessively, almost disappearing within them. "For a week after she saw Aladdin . . . she was the Genie character, you know, the one Robin Williams played? At dinner. Everything. She was the Genie," Kevin chuckled at the memory. "It got to the point where we were saying, 'We want Sarah back. Will you give us Sarah?' It's that way."

Helen Barber, a lawyer who sent her son Jimmy to Arrowhead, was another affluent parent who viewed consumer culture askance. Efficient, capable, and opinionated, she considered herself fortunate, she said. She had two sons who were eight and five years old, and yet somehow she had escaped the fate of her peers: she had never—until recently—given them a birthday party. "Jimmy has never wanted a birthday party," she said, explaining that she had always hated birthday parties as a child. "Most kids want a party," she said. "I personally can't relate to it." Then last year her younger son Andy saw a ubiquitous party-favor catalog in the recycling bin and after looking at it, decided he wanted a party after all, and one with a Batman theme. Helen invited his preschool class to the family's swim club, made a cake, and had party bags, but the entire time she was looking back with a rueful nostalgia. She said: "I realized how lucky I was—and I always have realized how lucky I have been, that I have not had to give a party. I have two kids, eight and five, and I had my first party last year."

Jimmy did not own a Game Boy, and though he had asked for one, she was not buying it for him, standing firm because she thought electronic games substituted virtual experience, skills, and benefits for real ones. "I do disapprove of it!" she exclaimed. "At a certain point, especially when they're eight—for crying out loud!" Most children today lived too sedentary a lifestyle, she argued, and the Game Boy was partly to blame. "There are no kids Andy's age—zero—that can ride a bike. There are a lot of kids *Jimmy's* age that can't ride a bike. We have a lot of fun, going on little bike trips and stuff like that. And we've had a great time. I don't know—I just think [the Game Boy] is a pathetic thing, really. I mean, it would be like just putting them in front of the TV all day. I'm very strongly opposed to it."

To Helen, if you're an eight-year-old boy, you should be outside. "I think if your choice is doing a video game, skateboarding, or snowboarding you should be learning the real skill," she said. "And so I say that to him, you know: 'You should be outside. You should be riding your bike. You should be playing tennis. You should be running around.'"

Standing in her front yard, looking out past the neat white picket fence, I was charmed by the picturesque view of the quiet, safe street that wound its way past her house and through the hills. Not for the first time in doing the research for this book, I was struck by the pervading sense of peace, such Rockwellian calm, so close to the drug trafficking and "perverts" that marred Sandra Perkins's and Margaret Roa's neighborhood. The leaf-strewn pavement and stately trees outside Helen's house served as potent, silent reminders that the uneven distribution of public safety played a role in shaping parents' stances toward children's consumer culture. Like most affluent parents, in all likelihood Helen never had a reason to make that journey to Sandra's and Margaret's neighborhoods; thus, certainly from the vantage of Helen's front yard, her edict about outdoor activity seemed eminently sensible. "'You should be doing adventures of your own instead of sitting on your butt with a computer,'" she continued. "'Because there's all kinds of skills—physical skills—you're not learning. And social skills, too—no small thing.'" Game Boys ruined other eight-year-old boys, Helen thought, but they were not going to ruin hers if she could help it.

And yet, despite this vociferousness, Helen could see the day when she would reconsider her opposition. She would do so, she said, if the device became a necessary part of her son's social world, a point they were debating, much as Sandra Perkins and her son Darrin argued about sneakers. "Jimmy's starting to get to the age where these boys now have Game Boys. And they don't all. It's a very small percentage of them at Arrowhead. If he weren't at Arrowhead, it'd be a ton of people. I mean, other places it's like—but he knows I don't want to get him a Game Boy." Her own research—talking to other parents and listening to Jimmy talk about his friends—convinced her that there was not yet a critical mass of Arrowhead children who owned Game Boys. "So there may be a point, at a certain point, where he will need to acquire those skills and do that just to fit in. But luckily that's not it yet."

Sometimes parents decline to take part in children's consumer culture. If there were a spectrum of parent responsiveness to children's consumer desires, with parents who more frequently say no at one end, and those who more often say yes at the other, Kevin and Helen would be at the "no" end of the spectrum, as parents who were trying to hold off the call of dignity, to redefine what dignity meant, to redirect their children's interests, and to limit access to popular media and goods.

Most often, as we have seen, parents refuse to satisfy their children's desires due to resource constraints or as part of practices of symbolic deprivation. Parents do not normally sacrifice their children's social lives for this principle, however, and the occasions on which my informants heard about their children's social suffering and still held out were few indeed. Kevin recalled his own chagrin at his mother's television regimen and evinced dismayed surprise that he was replicating it for his own children. Yet his distaste for the policy stemmed from his own memories, not from any pressure from his children. For their part, Sarah and her sister Maggie were not actually arguing that they were missing out at school, perhaps because in their economy of dignity at Arrowhead, knowledge about television programs had less of a presence in the conversation among children there. Many of their friends lived under similar rules, Kevin said. "Part of [what has made it possible to limit television] is community. Arrowhead definitely has at least— maybe not in practice, but in philosophy—a no television [culture]."

As for Helen, she rejoiced in her years without birthday parties but considered herself lucky that her children did not want them, not that she had successfully overruled their desire for parties. Even when she held out on the Game Boy, a device that had perhaps a larger presence at Arrowhead than her own research into the matter revealed, she acknowledged that her decision was a contingent one. It depended on her understanding that the device was not yet a crucial component of dignity for an eight-year-old boy. Thus Kevin and Helen were among those parents who were more likely to deny their children, but like most parents, they were able to say no to their children's consumer desires because (they thought) these purchases did not (yet) really matter to their children.

CIRCUMSTANCES ENABLING RESISTANCE TO SPENDING

Still, there were a few isolated situations in which, despite children's arguments that they needed some commodity or experience to belong at school, the parents still held fast. Certain parents were also more inclined to resist than others. These parents would batten down the hatches against the marketing messages swirling around outside the home, ignore their children's entreaties, and try not to participate in the prevalent branding of childhood. What were the circumstances that enabled this resistance? When did parents say no?

The same factors that we saw shaping parent buying for children also shaped those moments when parents declined to buy. First and foremost, parents' own social location and history shaped their resistance, as those who could resist were those who had been relatively insulated from dignity injuries. As we saw in chapter 5, growing up low-income seemed to make issues of belonging resonate for many with a heart-stopping thrum. Even if parents could recall a few memories of feeling excluded—as almost everyone had been—their overall experiences of social class either threw a sort of protective bubble around them or did not, depending on their relative affluence. Parents who resisted consumer culture for their children now were those who did not live through the mundane horror of invisibility in the past, or, if they had such memories, like Kevin, they wore them lightly. Parents' social location thus helped to make them more or less sensitive to matters of belonging.[1]

Second, parents who resisted were aided by the particular context in which their families found themselves. Some "no's" were easier than others. Helen was able to say "Go outside and ride your bike" because her street was safe and quiet. Kevin's television restrictions were not too difficult to impose because the Arrowhead economy of dignity did not seem to center on knowledge about network programming.[2]

For parents who confronted acute child desire, two cultural distinctions also enabled their resistance. First, it helped if parents viewed interactional difference as a positive, often stemming from valued social differences. Parents who resisted more often seemed at times to have a sense of themselves and their families as outsiders, with superior customs and practices, so that the family's difference was not only different, it was better. Helen was suspicious about how few children Jimmy and Andy's ages knew how to bicycle, and amused when children who came over for playdates were not prepared for being outdoors. "The other kid [sometimes says:] 'It's raining, why do we have to go swimming? *Why?*'" Grinning, Helen acted out a little dialogue with a fictitious child, cold and outraged. "[Calmly] 'Well, we like to swim in the rain.'" [Her voice rose in a rendition of the child's scandalized horror]. "'What is wrong with you people?'" Eva, an Oceanview parent who later transferred her daughters to alternative school, said she had taken them out of Oceanview in part to slow down their exposure to a sassy, sexualized popular culture that she thought came too soon there. "So I feel that [their new school] is a good way . . . is more . . . is a way to control that more," Eva said. "Whereas when they would be in a traditional school you have less control of that." For Eva, difference meant a slower, more innocent childhood for her girls than the standard girlhood on offer at other homes and at Oceanview.

In addition, parents who resist must have a competing cultural idea, or frame, that enables them to withstand their child's potential social ostracism or other repercussions by suggesting something else is more important. One such idea was the importance of the family unit. Eva talked about deciding to allow her daughter Mona to go to Seattle with a close friend who had invited her, and then, upon reflection, backtracking and deciding against it, because "it's just too much, too soon." Then she had to tell Mona, she recalled. "It was okay. Because we [parents] have to do unpleasant things [like saying no], too," Eva said, "[even though] you don't want to keep doing that, because it's hard on the kids." Still, Eva, a fifth-generation Californian, maintained that family was more important than friends. "The kids still need to understand that whatever friends they run into, whatever bonds they form—that the family is always there for support, and we'll always be there. I want them to understand that."[3]

For some families, these factors, both cultural (such as values effectively competing with consumption) and material (such as the protective bubble of social class origins) existed in at least a limited way, enabling the parents to resist their children's desires. Even to talk about resisting children's desires as if it were some sort of challenge, of course, assumes a cultural backdrop like that discussed in the introduction, wherein children, their concerns, and their longings loom large in the family home. For a few families, notably immigrants from other cultures, such "resistance" was easier because they started with a different premise in the first place, a view of the child as less central, of individuals as less important, out of which grew a distinct vision of just what constituted adequate care, with implications for buying.

WHEN CHILDREN ARE NOT THE CENTER, AND CARE IS NOT CONSUMPTION

Anne-Marie Bujold and her husband, Vincent, moved to the Oceanview neighborhood fifteen years ago, before the housing market took off, and before their three children were born. Immigrants from Quebec, neither had gone to college, but Vincent now worked as a general contractor, and they had since bought and renovated several houses in the pricey district. Anne-Marie was very aware of how lucky they were, and how unusual their trajectory, given their origins. "We came from a very different—probably—background to a lot of people that live in this area. We're not your normal, typical Oceanview parents, I would say." Anne-Marie described years as illegal immigrants, of doing menial jobs, "whatever we had to do, workwise," and of living in "some rough enough areas and rough places." She laughed when she recalled Brian's teacher asking Vincent to come speak about being a contractor on "career day"; "I said, 'So all of these kids are going to go home—in this neighborhood—and tell their parents they want to be builders!' I said, 'Are you sure you want a contractor in there?'" She contrasted their own lives with those of their neighbors. "We have basically worked really, really hard. I mean, over the years we've had no big rich parents for handouts," she said. "We look at our lives and the lives of our kids here, and we just think, 'My God, these kids have so much.'"

While that recognition—"My God, these kids have so much"—fueled Anne-Marie's approach to consumer culture, so too did the sense that they were alone in that realization. "I think sometimes in certain areas— like here—kids get a lot of stuff," Anne-Marie said. "It's just like there is a lot of—'Oh, you want this?' And then they buy it for them. They just get stuff. Which I'm trying not to do. Which is not always easy." When I asked how she handled it when her children asked for things, she said: "I just say no. I just say no. I'm very conscious of that. This society right here, you know, there's a lot of give, give. And we just don't."

Indeed, for Anne-Marie, good parents enforced limits on their children's gratification, even if doing so threatened to impede their children's ability to participate in their social world. Buoyed by their social difference, they were not afraid of interactional differences. "I notice here a lot of parents just can't disappoint their kids," Anne-Marie said. "It's okay to be the mean one every so often. Just little things. 'No, you can't go to your friend's house today. It's not a good day.' 'Well, why can't I do that? They're all doing it.' 'No, some people can't.' Like Brian—we won't get him a Game Boy or PlayStation. 'Sorry, we're not buying one.'"

Anne-Marie exemplifies at least two of the factors identified as enabling resistance to consumer culture. First, we can see the value Anne-Marie places on her family's difference. Social mobility or immigration can provide a narrative of outsider superiority that bolsters parent refusals, although Katerina's example in chapter 4 is vivid testimony that this is not always the case. Furthermore, Anne-Marie's talk portrays her rather casual approach to Brian's participation in his economy of dignity—"No, *some people* [meaning you] can't," she tells her son, succinctly. But her words also suggest a more fundamental dissimilarity between her and her Oceanview neighbors: a different approach to childhood, and thus to parenting.[4]

The core of the problem, Anne-Marie felt, was that too many affluent parents did not like to deny their children, while she felt that children had to experience some limits to their desire as part of their character education. "You just have to—they don't always get what they want," she said, simply. "You have to be able to say, 'No, you can't have a sleepover with your friend.' Or 'No, I don't want your friend over here tonight.' Just little things. I notice some of our friends, they just—they don't want to disappoint little Joey or whatever. Because little Joey might be upset. It's okay to have them upset!"

Anne-Marie's sense of the importance of limits extended to allowances, which, as we have seen, other parents in her milieu used both to enable their children to buy what they wanted and to distance themselves from that very act. One day, Anne-Marie recounted, Brian said he wanted to buy a soda.

> And I said: "We don't buy sodas. Do I ever buy you soda? Why are you asking for soda?" "But I have my own money with me." And I say: "So? So what? So when you're fifteen and you have your own money to buy drugs I can say, 'Okay, as long as it's your own money, Brian. Sure!'" So this is the conversation we're having at the moment. And he says, "Soda is not like drugs." "Brian, I'm not saying it's like drugs. But still, I never buy it." We have this fight. We're standing at the corner, and he's like, [she starts half-shouting] "I want a soda!" "You're not getting one! You're not getting a soda!"

This is not to say other affluent parents would allow their children to buy drugs with their allowances; nonetheless, Anne-Marie was unusual for the extent to which she monitored what Brian could buy, even with his own money.

While parents ranged across the spectrum of responsiveness to children's desires, Anne-Marie was atypical: she ignored, for "just little things," the social impact of particular goods or events. In contrast to many parents I talked to, both affluent and low-income, she had a different formulation of good parenting (which she viewed as about setting limits, versus the more common notion of making children happy and fulfilled), children's desires (which she perceived as seemingly without end, and certainly not in their best interest, as opposed to some sort of natural outgrowth of their individuality), and peer culture (which she considered not as important as children's long-term character, rather than a social world to respect if not to understand). To Anne-Marie, consumer culture was the peculiarly American weakness of her neighbors, versus a sometimes regrettable sphere of pleasure and utility, as other affluent parents seemed to view it. Scholars report that first-generation immigrants like Anne-Marie and Vincent are more likely to look back to their cultures of origin for their "reference groups," the points of comparison they use as guides for norms and values. Their self-concept of positive difference surely spawned their ability to withdraw from local consuming practices.[5]

But further, and perhaps more important, Anne-Marie had a different notion of the child—as on the margins somehow, as a part of the whole to be sure, but with priorities and needs subordinated to that whole. Such a sense gave her license, indeed, a mandate, to set limits, even seemingly arbitrary ones, even when they were not warranted by resource constraints. Limits, just because they were limits, taught children their rightful place. Under this view, care was not only refusing to buy what children wanted; it was refusing even to hear much about it.[6]

IGNORING DIGNITY IN
A LOW-INCOME CONTEXT

Dignity was scarce among the low-income families of Sojourner Truth; those "no's" that low-income children heard stemmed from resource constraints first and foremost, and, as we have seen, parents aimed their assent at the goods and experiences that wielded the most social power for children. Most low-income parents at Sojourner Truth heard the call of children's dignity keenly, their ears already bent to the ground listening for it because of their own history of dignity injuries. Yet Mary and Emmanuel Deng, Simon's parents, were an important exception.

Simon and his family had moved to Oakland from a refugee camp in Kenya with $200 three years ago; since that time the parents had learned to speak English and to drive a car, they had each earned an associate's degree (equivalent to two years of university coursework), and they had bought a car, a computer, and—in a crowning achievement—a new house three hours away, where they planned to move in the summer. At the same time, however, Simon was a constant practitioner of the bridging work described in chapter 3; the owners of just three toys and two bicycles, he and his sister Bettina had the fewest possessions of any children in this study.

As we saw in chapter 5, the Sojourner Truth families generally listened to their children's songs of dignity and responded by sacrificing, planning, and prioritizing children's consumer desires. In contrast, Simon's family vaguely understood that their children liked some things, even yearned for them. The difference was what they did with this information.

Mary and Emmanuel had fled Sudan for a refugee camp in Kenya when Simon was four months old. They alone among the sampled Sojourner Truth families eschewed children's consumer desires with a stance best described as dismissive. They saw themselves as outsiders with superior cultural notions of parenting, and they were unconcerned about their children's social participation. Moreover, like Anne-Marie and Vincent's family, the Deng family was not "child centered," and caring was not spending. At day's end, the implications of this asceticism for their future trajectory through the country's social and economic fabric seemed promising, although the impact on Simon's daily life, his construction of self, and his interactions with peers was less clear.

"I Lived as a Princess, I Lived as a Refugee, I Lived as a Slave, and Now I'm Here"

Although they earned little, lived in the same dangerous neighborhood, and sent their children to the same strained schools as the other Sojourner Truth families, Mary and Emmanuel were very different from their son's classmates' parents in one important respect: their class origins. They were both from privileged backgrounds in Sudan, with Mary the youngest daughter of the first of her rich father's four wives, and Emmanuel a college instructor. When they fled the war they went first to Kenya, where they stayed in a refugee camp for six years while international bodies fretted about where they belonged. When they arrived in America they spoke only Dinka and Arabic, had only $200 in their pockets, and three children in tow. The International Rescue Committee paid their rent for four months, and then they were supposed to support themselves.[7]

They found training and jobs as certified nursing assistants— "exploited labor," Emmanuel said—and arranged their schedules so that during nonschool hours, while one was working, the other was taking care of the children. After a year, they had saved enough to buy a car. After a year and a half, Mary and then Emmanuel got an associate's degree, hers in accounting and his in business. After three years, they had saved enough to put a 5-percent down payment on a $352,000 house near Monterey, where Emmanuel had applied, been accepted, and arranged to go to school for a master's degree in international relations. They would move down there this summer, they said, spreading the blueprints of their new house on the living room table.

On the one hand, their trajectory from having just $200 and not speaking English to owning their own home and studying for a master's degree reads like an advertisement for social mobility in America. On the other hand, it certainly attests to the structuring power of social origins and the horizons they shape. As Mary summarized it, "I lived as a princess, I lived as a refugee, I lived as a slave, and now I'm here." Mary's years as "a princess", and Emmanuel's elite background, clearly gave them the tools they needed to succeed in unpredictable situations, tools that, when coupled with high expectations and the benefits of their close-knit partnership, enabled them to take advantage of opportunities in the United States.

The Dengs also benefited from Emmanuel's flexibility: a black man without a degree from an American college, he was quickly employable in part because he was willing to do what is traditionally women's work in the United States, where 86 percent of certified nursing assistants are women. Part of the reason Emmanuel was able to do this, of course, was because his dignity lay elsewhere, in a different cultural construct that framed his work in a different light—that of the "making do" of immigrants, as opposed to the feminization of service work in the United States. Contrast Emmanuel's ability to take on this work with that of Rick, Margaret's husband, who was reluctant to try for an open cashier's job for Toys"R"Us, taking a physically arduous, and temporary, construction job instead. "I don't know what is wrong with him," Margaret said.

> He doesn't want Toys"R"Us because he's used to being constantly in—
> he doesn't want to take a low position at the cash register. He can't . . .
> he don't know how to do the register—he's never worked a register. And
> I told him right now anything would be nice. Rick has a lot of pride.

Though Margaret does not mention gender, cashier work is a feminized job in the large toy warehouse chains. This fact, coupled with Margaret's hesitation, her characterization of it as "a low position," and her statement that Rick has never worked a register suggest Rick's pride kept him from taking a job that has been defined as "women's work"; scholars have documented the lengths to which other (U.S.-born) male workers shied away from the task.[8]

"Normally the Way We Are Is Different from Other Americans"

Another principal resource the Dengs called upon was their identity as outsiders. Mary and Emmanuel did not look to local culture for their sources of dignity. Here for three years, they had not incorporated themselves socially into American life, although they did periodically attend a church. "In Oakland here—I don't think we have a friend yet in Oakland," Emmanuel said. Their talk was filled with constant criticisms of American culture, offered politely, in an unruffled tone—Americans eat too much sweet food, Americans are too public about their love relationships, Americans swing too easily in and out of marriage, Americans do not take care of their own elderly, Americans do not greet each other or take care of each other's children. Their impressions were undoubtedly colored by the basis for their comparisons—they were comparing their privileged life in Sudan with their experiences among the American urban poor. Mary and Emmanuel looked to each other and the memories of their common practices in Africa for evaluation and esteem, not to their Oakland neighbors.

By keeping alive their emotional ties to the Sudan and eschewing more local attachments, the Dengs reflect the constrained choice of immigrant blacks within the American race-based system of inequalities, in which immigrants face a context that some scholars have called "segmented assimilation." Looking for a positive social and economic trajectory, according to this theory, immigrants of color have three options: they can either vie for a white middle-class model of success, a path that scholars suggest is largely unattainable due to racial discrimination; they can adopt the practices, culture, and stunted social mobility of the black underclass; or they can cling to their cultures of origin as a font of practical and cultural power.[9]

It is important to remember, of course, that the Dengs do not represent the trajectory for all black immigrants, as their originating culture was far less Westernized than other sending countries. Immigrants from the Caribbean, such as Jamaicans or Trinidadians, for example, are highly Westernized and much like Americans in their consumer habits, including celebration of such holidays as Christmas. The point is not to measure the breadth of the trend of which the Dengs are a part, of course, but rather to observe that they demonstrate just what would be necessary for a low-income family to be able to see past their child's belonging needs.[10]

The Dengs' daily practices emphasized their differences from the low-income families of color who surrounded them. They spoke Dinka to each other, although Simon refused to do so at school. They searched for African grocery stores that would sell them cassava, a staple of Mary's cooking. Their experience of shopping as a family was unique, especially compared to the laments of affluent and poor native-born American parents. First, the Deng children made the shopping list, as Simon's older sister Veronica reviewed what was in the refrigerator and what was needed for their regular meals. Second, the whole family, as was their custom, went shopping together, as opposed to the other mothers' practice of going alone. In contrast to Erika's narration in the last chapter, in which she described her daughters sliding down the shiny aisles of Albertson's on their knees and running away from her as she tried to collar them one at a time, Mary and Emmanuel did not have to reprimand their children to stay in control. Instead, the children themselves did the shopping, and at a breakneck pace. Here the whole family was intent upon the same task—they gathered before the breakfast bars for a few minutes and discussed the merits of one bar over the other—and individual desires for frivolities were visibly suppressed. I watched Simon and Bettina nudge each other and look up intently at a row of Easter baskets perched on top of the cereal aisle that were overflowing with pastel bunnies and candy, and then look away again, without commenting, as their mother stood nearby; later, Simon pulled out a Yu-Gi-Oh! card magazine from the rack, leafed through it, and put it back silently.

Mary also noted their differences from other families out loud and within earshot of the children (and the other families). As she was looking over her receipt at the checkout, she looked back at the next person in the cashier's line, an African-American woman with nothing but two cases of soda in her cart. "We don't buy soda," Mary said to me. (The other woman said "Excuse me" rather pointedly after she had paid for her soda and got by the Dengs as they were putting their wares in plastic bags.)

The Dengs intersected with native-born Americans most closely in two places—at work and at the children's school—and that is where they felt their differences most acutely. The kids sometimes came home with bruises or worse, and Mary and Emmanuel were not pleased with their environment. "Especially at school—where my children go to school— they—my children are with rough children," Mary said. "So in that way I think that also their parents are rough, too. So it's like we are living in a rough environment. Yes." The institutions corroborated their sense of exceptionalism: Mary told a story of having arrived to pick up Simon from school, and the white teacher stopped her:

> When you go to school to pick them up the teacher will say, "Oh, are you Simon's mother?" [I] say, "Yeah." "Keep doing the good job you are doing." He didn't tell me all the stories, but from what he tells me I feel like Simon—he saw that there is a difference between Simon and how other children are. And that difference comes from his family. "Keep doing the good that which you are doing for Simon." And then from there I see that . . . we are . . . maybe we are unique.

The Dengs' interactions with the school affirmed their sense that they were different from their neighbors, but also, according to the institution, better. The implications of this cultural understanding for their children's lives were powerful.

SAYING NO TO BELONGING

One day, I asked if the children had a Game Boy, and Mary answered with a gesture of her head to the back of the apartment.

MARY: It's one of the little things. No. We don't have that.

AJP: Do they have a Nintendo?

SIMON: No.

AJP: Do you have an Xbox?

SIMON: No.

AJP: Do you have a PlayStation?

SIMON: No.

AJP (to Mary): What is the thing that you think that they have?

EMMANUEL: Show her what you play.

AJP: It sounds like he's playing something.

(Simon returns with a free toy from a McDonald's Happy Meal, a small electronic item that beeps).

As electronic games go, a free one distributed by McDonald's in a child's meal offers next to no entrée to the economy of dignity at school. Simon took over the responses to my questions in this interchange because, as opposed to his mother, he knew the items about which I asked, and knew well that they did not have them. Mary and Emmanuel, however, evinced little knowledge of what would matter in his social world. When I asked them what Simon asks for, Mary answered, "A remote control car."

MARY: But we didn't buy that for him. We feel like because we are next to the street—

EMMANUEL: And also having this! (brandishes Connect Four)

AJP: I know what that is. That's Connect Four.

EMMANUEL: Yes.

Emmanuel brought out Connect Four, a plastic game somewhat similar to tic-tac-toe, as if that would bear any equivalence to "a remote control car" for Simon, as if it were even in the same category.

The McDonald's toy was tangible evidence of the few instances in which Mary and Emmanuel did respond to the children's desires. On rare occasions, school and work holidays when the whole family had been home all day, the children would convince their parents to go to a restaurant, and the restaurant they chose was McDonald's. Still, the parents would cook for themselves at home first. "We don't like it," Mary said. "Normally the way we are is different from other Americans."

Despite Simon's halfhearted attempts at reeducation, the Dengs didn't celebrate Halloween, Christmas, or Valentine's Day; the Tooth Fairy never came to visit their home. In fact, Mary compared her home country's folk practices related to lost teeth with American rituals, emphasizing the reductive materialism of the local version:

> MARY: Back home when you are growing and then you lose your tooth they will tell you to take it and throw it on top of the roof. You have to go outside and throw it there. And you call [to a white bird] and then tell it that come to take this old tooth and bring me the new one. Because the bird is very white. And then it will bring you the new, white tooth. So that is Africa, where I am coming from. So here we have to put it under the pillow, and then the Tooth Fairy will come and take it and will leave you money under the pillow.
>
> AJP: Does it happen in this house?
>
> SIMON: No.
>
> AJP: What happens in this house?
>
> EMMANUEL: He wishes it would happen!
>
> MARY: So here, what we will do is we still keep their teeth.
>
> AJP: You keep them.
>
> EMMANUEL: Hmm-hmm. In a box.
>
> MARY: That's it.

Simon's reply to my query about whether the Tooth Fairy came to the house was a simple "no," yet the word was nonetheless laden with pent-up emotion that his father picked up on and invoked with his rapid-fire exclamation. By remarking "He wishes it would happen!" Emmanuel demonstrates that he is aware of Simon's yearning, but that Simon's desire for the American ritual has no standing among the Dengs, and that indeed, his father can gently mock him for his feelings. Yet as we saw in the previous chapter, Tooth Fairy practices were not just part of home rituals but part of the economy of dignity—kids and adults talked about them at school. Recall the scene related in chapter 2 when Ms. Graham marveled at the generosity of Jasmine's Tooth Fairy. "Whoooee," she said. "I want *your* Tooth Fairy." Perhaps, we can surmise from Emmanuel's comment, Simon might, too.

The Dengs did not celebrate any particularly American holidays, and yet the pervasive power of Christmas made that a difficult holiday even for Mary and Emmanuel to skip. Yet skip it they did, as Mary recounted:

> Actually, we didn't buy nothing for them. We bought only just clothes for them. . . . But ourselves—we saved our big present, is to buy a home. And then we talked to them because they couldn't understand why we have to buy nothing for them. We didn't want to spend money for this Christmas for something which you will play and after two days you will just throw it away. It is special to keep this money and buy a big present for everybody.

While they opted out of the powerful symbol of intertwined care and consumption that is Christmas, they had to explain it to the children, and did so by reference to an even larger present. That big present was their new home near Monterey, off the coast of California, south of Oakland. Simon's parents were deaf to the call of local children's dignity because they thought they knew better as adults, and were better able to have what they considered the right priorities.

I argue that Simon's parents chose not to buy things for the children because they viewed the local children's economy of dignity as worthless, an unimportant value system that had no bearing on their child rearing or their consumption. But can we explain their child-rearing consumption, or the lack thereof, in another way? Did they, for example, not value dignity at all, thinking it more a distraction to their main goal of getting ahead? Or did they just not value dignity for children? Did they care less or differently about their children?

Perhaps the Dengs did not care about cultural notions of honor and participation at all and were just trying to make it economically, not getting distracted by concerns for particular standards of behavior or possessions. My first indication that this was *not* the case came when Mary regaled me, unbidden, with stories of how Sudanese ritualize getting married, including visits to the engaged couple to warn them of the difficulties of being married and a social test of whether the wife can adequately care for and provision a house. There are high standards of behavior there, she was telling me, and also much preparation for the responsibilities ahead. At the time of our interviews, it had been eight years since Mary had set foot in Sudan, and yet she still spoke warmly of her home country, to reaffirm the values of their cultural practices, to contrast them with American speed, materialism, and superficiality. Mary could have set aside such cultural concerns for now, concentrating solely on economic matters; yet her exposition on marriage rituals, and her institution of other rituals such as group shopping, family meals, and the like, suggested she cherished such meaning-making experiences as what enriched life, especially given her view of the culturally impoverished setting of urban America.[11]

Yet perhaps the Dengs did not buy things for children, not because they criticized local definitions of dignity, but because they did not think dignity was a project for children per se. Their words and practices, however, established their own version of dignity for children—one less about enabling them to hold their heads up with peers than instilling in them certain habits they deemed worthy. Emmanuel talked about how they handled it when the children misbehaved: "Because it is my experience— I do remember when I was their age, say, between . . . four to maybe eleven, twelve—it was my experience that when my father was punishing me I was becoming more and more aggressive," Emmanuel said. "More naughty—I can say that. But if he was treating me with dignity I was becoming a [better person]." The Dengs took pains to describe the chores each child performed. Their vision of children's dignity rested on children's full participation in the household, rather than children's status as practically useless but emotionally priceless objects of adult affection.[12]

Or perhaps the Dengs declined to participate in the local children's economy of dignity because they cared for children in a different way, not as intensely, or valued them less. Their pride and focus on the three children was evident in my repeated visits, however. They offered thoughtful individual analyses of the children—Simon is all quickness, curious and clever—"he lives on American time"—while Bettina is more methodical, slow, and thorough—"she lives on African time"— and quiet Veronica has an inner strength that helped her fight off aggressors in middle school. They showed me pictures of the children when they first arrived from Kenya. They were pleased with how the children were different from their peers, and paid close attention to their character education. Theirs was not the easy banter of the more informal parent-child relationships among other Sojourner Truth families, but the Dengs laughed, ate together, and took care of each other. It was not a cold home, nor one where only adults mattered, but rather one where the unit seemed more important than the individual parts.[13]

Allowances provided a good example of the approach they took to children's dignity. As we have seen, while most Sojourner Truth families gave their children money when they could, they could not do so often, resulting in windfall allowances of $1, $5, $10, or $25 when the parents were flush. Instead, Mary said, the Dengs gave each child a quarter every day, but they were not allowed to spend it. Then, every once in a while, the family—all five of them—would troop off to the bank to deposit their accumulated money in each of five individual accounts. All five, even young Bettina, received their own bank statements in the mail, and the children's balances were now around $200 each.

AJP: And do they ever get any of their own money?

MARY: Like one dollar to go and just buy whatever they want?

AJP: Yes.

MARY: I can't say yes. Because they don't have the time to just go to the store and buy something. No. We go together.

Children had access to money, and it was their own money, complete with institutional recognition and mail, and in this way was part of their own dignity. But it was not money they could spend, nor could they really use it in their peer economy of dignity at school. It was training money, not showing money.

POWER, CARE, AND THE
"COMPANIONATE CHILDHOOD"

As for Anne-Marie and Vincent, a central factor contributing to the Dengs' ability to ignore the local children's economy of dignity had to do with the distribution of power in the home. In the homes of other families, those affiliated with Sojourner Truth as well as Arrowhead and Oceanview, children were more central to decision-making, in their roles as advisors, consumers, and companions. But the Dengs relied on a cultural schema for appropriate child rearing that was closer to the adage "Children should be seen and not heard"—children were helpers who were nonetheless subject to parental vision, priorities, and will.

Other Sojourner Truth adults also said they knew better than their children, that they had better priorities. What made them less able to assert these judgments? Perhaps part of the answer lies in the broader social trends discussed in chapter 1. Scholars argue that in many American homes, demographic and other changes have led to the expanding influence of the child in the family. The rise in numbers of children spending time in single-parent homes and of mothers employed outside the home, as well as the increasing commodification of family life such as dinners and entertainment, has increased children's responsibilities as consumers for the home. Without another adult in the house, children's lives begin to resemble what we might call a "companionate childhood," as they become more like friends and less like subordinates to the adult who remains. As adults spend less and less time in the home, children play a more central role in shaping what goes on inside it—due to adult guilt and conflict avoidance, as well as a time crunch that calls on all participants to help. We can point to the cumulative effect of these changes to understand the shifting norms of parent-child relationships in the United States.[14]

The net effect of this elevation of children within the home (even while the home was perhaps shrinking in practical importance for adults) has been also to elevate children's dignity concerns. In contrast, however, the Dengs and to some extent the Bujolds called on a cultural schema for child rearing that assumed the adults' benevolent wisdom and diminished the child's contribution to family decisions. Under the logic of this collective representation, children's economy of dignity was a product of children's foolishness, and to the extent that adults paid it any mind, it was evidence that children did not have the right priorities. Why does today matter when tomorrow—as represented by savings, investments, and other long-term purchases—is at stake? According to this schema, only adults had the broader perspective to make the right decisions, because children did not know enough, had not experienced enough, to be able to dismiss what was not important. The distribution of family power influenced the ability of parents to hear beyond the call of the economy of dignity.[15]

CHILDREN, CONSENT, AND CULTURAL INNOVATION

The Dengs were also able to almost completely eschew children's local economy of dignity because their children cooperated. Enmeshed in the cultural world his parents had created for their family, Simon did not ask, did not beg, did not show them the pain that was his for not having his own pack of Yu-Gi-Oh! cards. He also did not push to redefine his family's meaning systems, through discursive and practical strategies that might have contested their paradigm of dignity and hope. Instead, Simon acquiesced to his parents' framing at home, and instead brought his cultural innovation to bear on the economy of dignity at Sojourner Truth.[16]

Children's lives can straddle vastly different groups, as Simon demonstrated. When two groups have dramatically different beliefs and practices, children must struggle to reconcile them in order to establish a coherent, honorable self. Yet they are faced with the question of where to try to move the culture. The answer for Simon was to concentrate his efforts at school—perhaps because his parents had proved implacable, or because the contested atmosphere at school lent itself well to negotiated meanings. Thus we heard how Simon never spoke Dinka at school, while at home he did not barter his emotional cooperation in exchange for a GameCube, say, or a coveted football. Simon did not engage in cultural reinterpretations at home but rather engaged in bridging, claiming, and other meaning work at Sojourner Truth to find his way into common measures of basic humanity among his peers.

Other immigrant children tried instead to move the culture at home to secure access to symbolic tokens of dignity, perhaps because their family proved more malleable for them. David, the Chinese-American boy who sometimes lent his Pokémon cards to Simon, took it upon himself to spell out for his parents the mystery of American rituals. When the dentist pulled out one of his teeth, he put it under his pillow and asked his mother to be the Tooth Fairy, recalled Sue, his mother, who had immigrated to the United States when she was in high school.

AJP: How much did you give him?
SUE: I put $10.
AJP: Did he tell you how much?
SUE: Yeah.
AJP: He said $10?
SUE: Hmm-hmm.

David's initiative was striking—and expensive. In his family, David was able to actively support his pursuit of dignity, in part because his parents were listening for his clues as to how Americans do it. In contrast, the cultural schema informing the child-rearing decisions of the Dengs made them dismissive of American ritual practices and deaf to local definitions of dignity.[17]

CONCLUSION

The acutely ambivalent feelings many affluent parents have about consumer culture mean they often believe they are resistant—or wish they were more resistant—to their children's consumer desires. Yet the parents who would deny their children "the essentials" for social participation were truly scarce. Those rare instances in which parents stood firm against the prospect of their children's social invisibility required the convergence of particular circumstances both "material" and "cultural," both "systems of social relations" as well as "systems of meaning." To do so, parents have to be inured to their children's wish to belong, by virtue of having been protected themselves from dignity injuries in the past by their social location, and also by their stance toward the value of difference in their own present-day social context.

Simon and his family occupy a paradoxical but central position in this analysis. As one of the most visible practitioners of bridging work and other means of extracting dignity from thin air, Simon is an essential example of the power of children's social worlds to shape what matters to children by making meaning and inequality through their everyday interactions. At the same time, Simon's parents are important exceptions to the way most Sojourner Truth, Arrowhead, and Oceanview families responded—with open ears, hearts, and wallets—to the siren song of their children's quests for dignity. Perhaps it is not coincidental: Simon had to make do with the least possessions of any child at Sojourner Truth, and thus resorted most visibly to bridging work, precisely because of his parents' inattention to his consumer desires, even as they focused intensely on securing for him better opportunities.

Other Sojourner Truth families, in contrast, who belonged to this social world, seemed to feel the pain of their children's need to belong more acutely. Without an alternative to the cultural schemas that ultimately asked what children wanted, most other Sojourner Truth parents were unable to distance themselves from the children's economy of dignity, and its definition of what matters. Yet Mary and Emmanuel had another option, another realm in which to locate their mandate, and thus their cultural schemas for family retained more interpersonal power for the adults, making the pursuit of what children considered worthwhile less important. These beliefs were not just dusty old ideas from the old country trotted out to justify their actions, but alive, vibrant, and enacted daily in family practices such as the family group visits to the bank, the food shopping lists made by Simon's older sister, and the three-day process of pounding the cassava into edibility. The concrete, realized nature of their meaning system proved an effective counterpart to the peer culture of Game Boys and Tooth Fairies, prompting Simon to reinterpret dignity at school rather than pushing the family to adapt.

Combined, these practices enabled the Dengs to win the lottery that is the American Dream, to become prime, and unusual, examples of the meritocratic ideology underpinning the U.S. myth of opportunity and success. Yet Simon continually faced a gap between what he had and what he was supposed to have, a gap he time and time again bridged with unusual initiative and innovation. His remarkable creativity and courage in doing so meant that he had friends, dignity, and pride at school, but it took a lot of interpersonal work to get there. In addition, his one-word but weighty answers at home, his quick perusal of the Yu-Gi-Oh! magazine at the store before putting it back unbidden, his silent glance up at the Easter baskets—all belied a deep reservoir of unexpressed feeling. Simon's longings were almost palpable, but he did not voice his desires, and perhaps never would, conceivably until it came time for him to consider spending on his own child. Thus we can admire the Dengs for most of the qualities that enable them to resist—their self-control, teamwork, and total dedication, their indefatigable energy. Yet we can also see in the parents a certain steeliness, a hard-heartedness about relegating Simon to an interpersonal purgatory, which seems perhaps a bit pitiless. The clear benefits of the Dengs' practices went to the family, but the costs—in a sense of belonging, in the relentless need to answer for his own consumer shortcomings, in profound yet unexpressed feeling—were Simon's to bear alone.

CHAPTER SEVEN

Consuming Contexts,
Buying Hope

Shaping the Pathways of Children

When Danielle Montgomery, a white stay-at-home mother of three, realized that a tighter family budget meant her twin boys would have to go to kindergarten at the local public school instead of at Country Day, the elite private school their sister Caitlin attended, she had an idea. Why not pay a tutor to supplement their schooling? If even ten families from their public school class of twenty put in just $5,000 each, she calculated, they could hire someone, maybe a retired teacher or perhaps a graduate student in education, to provide private tutoring in the afternoon, after dismissal at Oakland's half-day kindergarten.

"These Country Day teachers told me [if I did this] the kids would progress much further than the kids in the Country Day kindergarten," Danielle said, her deep voice rising in excitement. "I mean, I've heard estimates that only three and a half hours are spent learning [in the Country Day kindergarten], and the rest is social. But what kind of social? I mean, Caitlin is getting picked up for an eight year old's birthday party in a stretch limousine." She rolled her eyes. "That's not the social I want her to get."

Across town, Angela Lincoln, an African-American single mother of three, made it clear, if unsaid, how disappointed she was when her daughter—"a smart girl"—got expelled from her old middle school for fighting over a jacket. But she seemed to take heart as she described paying into a college scholarship search service for her daughter, keeping faith that the service would be all they needed to ensure she would go to college.

ANGELA: I have to pay them like a thousand dollars to fill out—the institutions, they do all that, you know, what you call that . . . financial aid! That's what it is, financial aid thing, they'll find her a college, you know, scholarships, they'll find her a college that's best for her, that has the best scholarships or whatever they do, they do all the paperwork, they do all the looking, they do everything, they do everything, so when she gets into twelfth grade, she'll be set. And all we got to do is worry about—

AJP: You had to pay a thousand dollars—

ANGELA: Yeah, but that's not bad, it's going to pay out. Because she's going to be somebody, she's going to be somewhere. So it's all good. And she wanted it. She looking forward to it. She already know what to do, going to school, she's getting extra credit and all that stuff go toward her points, volunteer work, everything, it goes towards her—the little college thing, whatever they got going on. So they say like, they do different schools and whoever got the best scholarship that's where they going to try to get her to go.

A janitor on rotating shifts, Angela didn't go to college herself, and she once gruffly told me she had to manage her monthly paycheck carefully to make sure the children had enough to eat at the end of the pay period. Broken down into small monthly increments, $1000 was still an extraordinary amount of money for her. But to Angela, a service—even an inauspicious one soliciting through direct mail—that promised to help her navigate the unfamiliar college admissions system, and "the little college thing, whatever they got going on," was worth it.[1]

"When she get in eleventh [grade] she ain't got to worry about nothing. I don't have to worry about paying nothing. I don't have to worry about her talking about 'Momma, I want to go to college and I need . . .'

It'll already be taken care of." Angela's hope and relief were evident. "So she going to be straight. She going to be straight."

The inequity between these two families—living, as they do, not four miles away from each other in Oakland—is striking, painful, and because of the segregation that continues in the United States, mostly invisible. Angela and Danielle could not be farther apart in their access to knowledge and opportunities, their understanding of how the education system works, their capacity to take advantage even of what is offered them. Their stark differences are apparent, not least in what is at stake. If Angela's daughter doesn't make it, the odds are she'll become another single mother with a high-school degree and a low-paying, unstable job, potentially sinking into lawless trouble, as the anxiety behind Angela's pronouncement "she going to be straight" reveals. If Danielle's twins don't make it, the odds are they'll go to a less prestigious college and have a slightly less impressive pedigree for their white-collar futures. Still, across this divide, both mothers are using their own private consumption to solve problems that are, broadly speaking, similar: the mistrust of what the public education system will do for their children, the dreadful uncertainty about their children's future, and the imperative of college for occupational success in America.[2]

Consumption—the private school, the tutoring, the scholarship service—is everywhere in these and other stories of parenting I heard while conducting research in the three disparate Oakland communities of this study. Parents—even very low-income parents—find market solutions to all sorts of problems of child rearing—from how to get children dinner to how to keep them safe to how to get them properly trained or educated. What counts as a child-rearing problem and what counts as its solution, of course, reflects greater forces that are at work—the particular configuration of public provisioning, the structure of opportunities and resources, corporate marketing and cultural expectations. For Danielle and Angela, one critical problem was their inability to ensure their child's future. They turned to consumption to provide social contexts—neighborhoods, schools, and other settings where child care takes place—that would serve as talismans to ward off their children's potential failure.

So far in this book, we have considered more conventional kinds of child-rearing consumption—parent spending on such commodities and experiences as expensive sneakers, fast food, and popular movies. As Danielle and Angela demonstrate, however, child-rearing consumption also includes the purchase of the social contexts through which children travel—neighborhoods, schools, day care, camps. It might include driving south to bring a child to live with grandparents for the summer, having a child attend a new public school in the neighborhood to which the family has moved after planning and saving, or sending a child to the local YMCA for swimming lessons. All of these contexts have greater or less potential to shape a child's future trajectory, through social contacts made or strengthened; skills acquired; job, school, or other opportunities encountered; or psychocultural lessons of empathy or individualism experienced that affect how children act toward others. We might call this activity "pathway consumption," and families undertake it seriously, particularly, but not solely, those on the upper end of the income ladder. "Pathway consumption" involves spending on the opportunities that shape children's trajectories, and as such, in contrast to dignity, which refers to their efforts to belong in their everyday lives, it involves a combination of aspiration and uncertainty we might identify as hope.[3]

Some "pathway consumption"—such as spending on schools or a house in a particular neighborhood—is considered an "investment" rather than a form of consumption, a distinction that conventionally refers to whether one buys something for one's future benefit or for one's current use. Many consumption scholars have largely acknowledged this distinction, mostly by ignoring varieties of pathway consumption. While useful for some purposes, these traditional categories carry an implicit normative judgment (investment in the future being viewed as surely better than consumption merely for use now). In addition, the distinction is not always made easily (How to view the purchase of a tennis racquet for a child? A tennis racquet for a tennis pro? A tennis racquet for a child who turns into a tennis pro? At what point does spending become an investment?). The distinction also serves to obscure some important linkages between the two, which I discuss below. The sociologist Eva Illouz argues that "the cultural critic ought to use the moral criteria at work within a community" as a starting point from which to launch an analysis, dubbing this practice "an impure critique" (as opposed to a falsely pure ideological one). Following Illouz, then, I define consumption broadly to signify family spending for the present and the future; I do this from the point of view of the impure critique, because I start from the perspective of the families in this study, who have to pay for either or both out of the same pot.[4]

Not all caregivers value the same sorts of pathway consumption to the same degree, however. While all caregivers might want a good neighborhood or a good school for their children, some would measure those in different ways, valuing test scores or a particular pedagogical style, for example. Just like commodities, certain pathway purchases are more precious for some parents than others, and more precious for some parents than for their children. Yet the kind of schools low-income children go to—as characterized by their resources, their teachers, and their peers—matters in terms of shaping their opportunities for the future. Other research points to children's neighborhoods as affecting outcomes such as rates of school completion and teenage parenthood. An extremely uneven distribution of urban resources is often part of the picture of parents' pathway consumption with regard to schooling, making their choices more portentous. Research has consistently found that vast inequality in the contexts of children's lives contributes to inequality in the outcomes they experience.[5]

A principal factor intensifying these differences between families is the disinvestment by the state, making some options much worse for children, as private monies intervene in some locations but not in others. In some locales, there are public schools and private schools, and in between there are not-so-public schools, in which enormous private, school-based contributions make a difference. In-school fund-raising campaigns such as those involving Sally Foster products raise an estimated $1.3 billion annually, for example, but the schools with the most affluent populations raise the most money. These private efforts to augment particular public schools serve to create a sort of gated community of public education.[6]

As we saw in chapter 1, the landscape of school context in Oakland was dramatically uneven, with most of the schools characterized as "apartheid schools," as the Harvard Civil Rights Project termed them, and a handful of majority-white schools availing themselves of hundreds of thousands of dollars in parent-raised funds. In addition, the schools of Oakland were vastly unequal compared to other school districts in the surrounding area, so that the schools of neighboring Orinda, Albany, and Piedmont offered superior educational opportunities to the children living in those bordering communities. These differences were apparent in funding (including public and privately raised monies), teacher experience and certification, parent involvement as evidenced by PTA activity, and other areas.[7]

The impact of the twisted strands of race and class on this landscape is as powerful as it can be in America, affecting the whole continuum from the unequal distribution of resources to culturally informed tastes. Research has demonstrated that even if a school is fully funded, its racial composition can scare off white families, and poverty rates can frighten away affluent families of any racial identity. Pathways are a type of consumption good that reflect and shape racialized class inequity. Such inequity contributes to the way families perceive their choices; further, the contexts themselves actually mold inequity through the opportunities, skills, and contacts they promise for the child involved.[8]

Unequal contexts for children thus act like geological forces, making the landscape of opportunity crimp and buckle. Yet contexts do more than mold the future; they also shape the present, in the guise of their own particular economies of dignity. As we saw in chapter 3, the particular flavor of an economy of dignity can have significant impact on the specific forms of scrip and facework children must master to achieve the social personhood of those who belong. Contexts shape children's relationship to consumption, to need and desire, and to difference, as well as their capacity for empathy and tolerance. Contexts shape not just where children are going, but how it feels to be where they are. Like Danielle, who considered limousines "not the social I want [her daughter Caitlin] to get," parents—intentionally or not—arrange for their children's economies of dignity when they establish where their children's childhoods take place.

COMFORT, DIFFERENCE, AND CONTEXTS

The examples of Danielle and Angela illustrate a crucial point: low-income and affluent families are in some ways remarkably similar in their goals and yet worlds apart in their practices of pathway consumption. Underlying those goals and practices were parents' evaluation of their children's contexts through the prism of difference. Parents on both ends of the income ladder focused on their children's "comfort" at school, a priority that often rested on a particular and widely held interpretation of difference as risky, threatening, and sometimes coded for racial/class meanings. As we have seen in the preceding chapters, the fear of interactional and sometimes social difference contributed to what we might consider a "commodities arms race" for elementary-school children. As I will elaborate below, the same fears led most parents to engage in pathway consumption practices that seemed to rely on and augment a racial/class segregation already in place in the school contexts confronting them. Only affluent African-American families took a different approach, deemphasizing "comfort" for other goals.[9]

MOVING OUT: A PATHWAY
CONSUMPTION MYSTERY

During the period of this study, some of the families at each site moved away from Oakland—some to Oregon, Massachusetts, or Florida; others to nearby Bay Area suburbs. These moves were classic examples of pathway consumption and seemed to portend significant effects on children's lives. Affluent families who moved did so in whole or in part so that their children could attend the local schools in their new towns, pulling out of Oakland neighborhoods for the express purpose of pulling their children out of Oakland schools. But the story was more complicated for low-income families. Some low-income parents told me they wished they could move, offering comments like "I'm through with Oakland," but noting that they were stuck there because of budget constraints. At Sojourner Truth, however, there were several low-income families who lived outside of the intake zone yet commuted to drop off and pick up their children from this school. In essence, these families had moved from their homes in the urban core but kept their children in schools there.[10]

This latter behavioral pattern presents a bit of a mystery, particularly because the widespread media reports of the abysmal Oakland schools actually referred less to the experience of upper-income children than to the overwhelmed and underfunded schools that their low-income counterparts attended. If anyone was going to take their children out of their schools, one might predict it would be these underserved low-income families. Of course, most critics of "school choice" proposals such as vouchers contend that low-income parents lack the resources, networks, and know-how that affluent families have to make real "choices." And to be sure, the uneven distribution of knowledge affected the decisions of several Sojourner Truth families, as Angela Lincoln's reliance on the scholarship search service would seem to poignantly attest. At the same time, those parents who moved out of the city but kept their children enrolled there were not just choosing the default route, but rather taking specific action, requiring more intention than just sending their children to the (new) neighborhood school. We should at least consider that these families were acting not out of apathy, inertia, or ignorance but out of their own predilection. What could be causing the difference in pathway consumption between these two groups?[11]

Trinelle Harris had a steady job that gave her the wherewithal to get her three children out of Oakland. Trinelle, whom we met in chapter 5, had bought her first Christmas tree when her family moved to Vallejo, to celebrate not only the holiday but also their freedom from the physical danger of their old apartment, where a bullet had passed through their living room. But Trinelle kept her children in Oakland schools, despite the widespread reports of budgetary woes and bottoming scores that plagued lower performing schools in the district, and even though her oldest daughter had already been kicked out of one middle school for fighting.

The schools in Oakland were fine, she argued, if a child wanted to learn. "It's not the schools, I feel. It's what the kids make of it, basically," Trinelle said.

> If the kid is going to school, and all they're going to do is sit and talk—that's just going to happen. They go in, and they put their mind to working, then they can do something. They can improve. They can move on into the next grade and be something. But if they go to play—hey, that's what comes out. Because they can go to a good school and then go in there and do the same thing they was doing there.

Malcolm, the carpenter we met in chapter 5, agreed. As a married homeowner, he contemplated moving out of Oakland just because he could, but if he did so, it would not be because the schools were hindering his children's social mobility. "It ain't got nothing to do with the school," he said. "Because . . . can't nobody teach your kids but you. And instill the good values in them. Any school they go to, they should be able to learn. It's up to the family to instill the good values. They've got to want to learn. You have got to want to learn."

It is not that Trinelle, Malcolm, and other like-minded parents are unthinking about their children's future. Rather, they believe a child's future depends on a child's motivation rather than a child's context. In seeming echo of some pundits' words about "personal responsibility," these low-income parents contend that what matters most is whether a child will take personal responsibility for learning. What kind of context encourages children to want to learn? A comfortable, friendly environment, these parents suggest, where the child knows people and feels situated—in other words, where a child is not too different.

Some of their comments had a racialized undertone, in which "comfortable" seemed to mean schools where children were not among a tiny minority, as African-American children were at Oceanview, for example. Why would he move his son Malcolm Jr. from Bryant Elementary (and from its after-school program at Sojourner Truth) where he is comfortable? Malcolm asked. Moving might just stir up bad feelings, he said.

> Then they start rebelling for some odd reason. Because they're not fitting in with the new surroundings. It might be a better environment or whatnot, but [the old school was] where they was comfortable at. . . . It's up to them. If he don't want to go, he ain't going. You know? Because he's the one that's got to learn. He's the one that's got to go to school. I done went to school already. She has got to go to school. So I want them to be as comfortable as possible. It's not on me.

Malcolm suggests that comfort is the root of student achievement, and part of that comfort stems from "fitting in." For Malcolm, difference at school threatened not only the children's sense of belonging, then, but also their motivation to learn.

To prioritize something else is to risk their rebellion, Malcolm argues, and worse, it is doing them no favors. "If you take . . . you're taking them out of their comfort zone and putting them in there because you want to be there. That's being selfish." Malcolm even argues that to move the child is a self-centered act, one parents are willing to consider because they are not the ones attending school anymore. The caring act is to keep the child in comfort, in surroundings he is used to, with his friends.

There was some evidence that for these families "discomfort" referred to the potential costs of encountering racism. Trinelle had moved to Vallejo, a city about forty-five minutes from Oakland, with approximately 24 percent black residents. Its plurality of racial/ethnic groups does not really mix, and a *New York Times* article about Vallejo bore the headline "A Diverse City Exists Equal But Separate." Trinelle heard about racism in the schools from a local woman who braided her hair, and that was part of what gave Trinelle pause about moving her children to the schools there, she said. "I heard little stories about Vallejo schools—the teachers are very prejudiced. They do a lot of jumping on the kids." Malcolm, who considered moving to join his cousin in Benicia (a town that is 5 percent black), said racism was common once you left the inner city. "They [whites] feel like this is where we [blacks] should be. The flatlands. And they feel like, 'How did they [blacks] get to live out here?'"[12]

Similarly, Angela, the janitor who had bought the financial aid service for her daughter, moved to the outer reaches of East Oakland without switching her son Derrick and his siblings' schools. What she said about the move echoed the words of Malcolm and Trinelle. "They don't really want to go to none of these schools out here because they don't ... they're not familiar with them, or the people. I didn't want to change the atmosphere for them."

Racial safety is an important part of child rearing for parents of color, who must protect their child from the "mundane extreme" environment of racialized denigration and prejudice, as the sociologist Lynet Uttal reported in her research on child-care choices. The prospect of their children being among the few black people in their school made some Sojourner Truth parents fearful their children would be labeled as troublemakers or worse. In other, whiter schools, would race become a form of scrip in the economy of dignity, and would their blackness deny them their belonging, their ability to participate?[13]

Furthermore, while the children's discomfort elsewhere may have stemmed from racial differences, some of their current comfort stemmed from their success in the local economy of dignity. Malcolm Sr. did not want to move Malcolm Jr. because he was doing well in Oakland. He described his son as "grounded" because he "shares all his things."

He lets the little kids ride his motorcycle and everything. That's why I don't really want to move right now and take him out of the element. Then he probably will think—you know? Start thinking that he's better. So that's why I try to stay grounded. The working mentality. I work every day. I want him to—you got to work to get over. You got to work to be a product of your community. You've got to work because that's what makes us . . . that's what sets us aside from other people. To where he sees somebody else's daddy out there on the corner selling drugs. But he sees me getting up and going to work. And we've got more than what they've got.

Malcolm's contradictory feelings about the links between dignity and context are captured in this soliloquy. On the one hand, he wants his son, a popular, poised third grader, to stay "grounded," and not think he is better than other (low-income African-American) people simply because he could move to the suburbs. On the other hand, he clearly wants his son to understand that they *are* better because "someone else's daddy [is] out there on the corner selling drugs," but Malcolm Sr. is going to his legitimate job every day. And the clincher he offers is that "we've got more than they've got," so that in addition to the stigma of illegal money, the drug dealers' families cannot even compete in the commodity arms race. Malcolm clearly values their (moral and financial) differences from other neighborhood African-American families, particularly those involved in the drug trade, even as he fears the impact other kinds of difference, perhaps racialized ones, might have on his children's motivation, were he to change their schools.

Based on observations of their children in the Sojourner Truth afterschool setting, the folk theory of "comfort equals motivation equals success" applied to some of the children, but not all. Malcolm Jr. was doing well, both academically and in terms of the economy of dignity; when he was a second grader, he was obviously but silently proud of being able to do two-digit multiplication, and the other children vied for the chance to catch his footballs. He had not been identified for the gifted-and-talented program, a designation that often disproportionately omits African-American boys, but he was "comfortable," and he was learning.[14]

Angela Lincoln's son Derrick, on the other hand, was not yet reading when he was seven; one day he "read" to me an entire book, but his smooth missteps revealed that he was narrating the book almost completely from memory, a classic sign of a reading disability that he had compensated for with intelligence. Derrick's teacher, a sympathetic man, reported that the school district would not be able to test him for a learning disability until the following year, somehow because of a district policy that he confusedly described as requiring that a student be performing two grades behind before he qualified for special services. The family could test him privately, but that was unlikely, Ms. Graham said, as Derrick was a child most often "picked up by his grandmother." Three months later, a letter came home announcing that Derrick—a tall, hulking, well-meaning child who was nonetheless not above using his bulk to get his way—would repeat first grade. The prospect of Derrick towering over his peers but becoming increasingly frustrated in school seemed likely, as did the sorrowful possibility that he might then lose his affability and become a bully. While Malcolm Jr. may have benefited from the "comfort" of his surroundings, Derrick looked as if he was falling through the cracks between the school's delay in handling what appeared to some to be special needs and his fragmented family's inability to attend to matters beyond "comfort."

RACE, INEQUALITY, AND PATHWAY CONSUMPTION

In addition to their concerns about racial safety and difference, low-income parents considered another important factor in their decision to keep their children at Sojourner Truth: their availability for mandatory pick-ups due to school discipline. In her rich, thoughtful ethnography *Bad Boys*, Ann Ferguson tracks the disciplinary practices of an urban public school, noting that African-Americans, mostly boys, but girls, too, are disproportionately subject to teacher reprimand and being cast as troublemakers. Calling relatives is a common event when children have been formally disciplined. "The moment when mother, sister, grandmother, and in rare cases, father come in to pick up a child or to have a conference about a child's behavior is a traumatic one," Ferguson writes, describing the wrath of relatives risking their jobs.[15]

Similarly, Trinelle, Angela, and others reported that their pathway consumption depended on their ability to make a plan for when they are called to pick up their children from school, which they considered part of being a responsible black working mother. In this way, then, everyday experiences of racialized class shaped the situations confronting these mothers, and the decisions they felt compelled to make.

Both Trinelle and Angela relied on other relatives to form part of their network of care, and for both, those relatives were part of the children's safety net, just in case someone other than the parent needed to come pick them up. "My momma live over there [where Sojourner Truth is located]," Angela explained. "So I take him to school. Like on my days off, I'll pick him up. But when I'm at work, like if I've got to work swing, she pick him up. So it's convenient for her, because she don't drive at night. So we got to make everything convenient and safe. And close together for all of them." When Trinelle's son's father was arguing for him to go to a particular middle school, one with the highest test scores in Oakland, Trinelle was unsure. "I mean, I don't even know where James Madison is. All I know is it's up in the hills somewhere. I don't even know where it's at. I need to know where the school is at just in case they call me and I need to go get my son."

To plan so carefully and extensively for the possibility that the school will call the mother to come get her children, to consider unfamiliarity a deal breaker even when the school is a distinct improvement by "objective" measures, might seem to a middle-class audience unusual, certainly pessimistic. But these women were confronting very real eventualities. Having to come to the school was not a hypothetical event for these mothers, and good mothers (and good employees) planned for it. Trinelle's cousin even lived in the same complex in Vallejo and had offered to stand in for her just in case, if she wanted to send her children to Vallejo schools. But Trinelle declined.

> There is nothing like me being here. I will never make it. It's too much traffic. And something about my child—I don't know what I would do. So it's better for me to leave them where they are. Everybody [else] is there [in Oakland]. My mother is there; their dad is there. Their grandmother, their aunties. Everybody is there.

One relative, even a willing cousin, was not enough to make up for the fact that Vallejo was too far away for Trinelle to get there quickly herself from her job in Oakland.

Trinelle was not being overly cautious. When Trinelle's oldest child was in middle school, Trinelle began to feel that her job was at risk for all the time she was spending traveling to and from her daughter's school, leading Trinelle finally to lay down an ultimatum for her daughter to shape up.

> I went through a whole lot. And I was at the point—the last time I went up to the school, and I cried. I said, "I'm not going through this no more. If this is what you want to do, if this is how you want to live your life, go ahead. I'm washing my hands with you. If that's how you want to do it, go ahead. Because I can't keep leaving my job. I'm a single mother. I try to do y'all—everything y'all want. And you have $100 tennis shoes, always have money—why am I getting treated like this? Why do I have to keep coming to the school behind you?"

Part of Trinelle's sense of outrage stemmed from an implicit bargain her daughter Cecilia had violated; Trinelle had provided for her daughter's dignity needs—the sneakers, the money—and yet her daughter kept getting in trouble, forcing Trinelle to come to the school in the middle of the day and take responsibility for her.

In keeping their children in inner-city schools, avoiding situations of white racism, and ensuring their own ready availability, these parents

opt for pathway consumption that serves to amplify the school segregation they already face. This result would be regrettable for the dream of
social integration and its implications for democracy and the social contract if schools that were separate were nonetheless equal. But the stratification of opportunity in Oakland and other urban districts made these
patterns potentially tragic for the children involved.

"WE HAVE A CHOICE": THE MANDATE
OF AFFLUENT PATHWAYS

It would not be overstating the case to say affluent parents in Oakland
organized their lives to some degree around the matter of where their
children would go to school. Parents talked of spending thousands of
dollars on enrichment and camps and tens of thousands on private
school, or, if their children went to public school, most parents reported
a dogged purpose in buying in a particular neighborhood. As Harvard
professor Elizabeth Warren has noted, middle-class families often pour
enormous energy and nearly all of their economic resources into getting their children into decent schools; she argues that increased bankruptcy among families stems not from "overconsumption" but from
parents' prioritization of children's needs. Many families choose a
neighborhood based on the local public school, struggling mightily to
afford real estate in the area of a good public school or opting to buy a
cheaper house or stay in a rental so they can afford private school. Parents change jobs or work overtime to pay for their choices. In my sample, three families out of twenty moved out of Oakland in just the six
months I observed in the Oceanview classroom, and cited "the schools"
as their primary reason. Pathway consumption, and in particular school
choice, determine much for the upper-income family, including where
they live and what they do.[16]

Perhaps not surprisingly, then, most affluent families who relied on
salary income talked a lot about making ends meet, even on six figures.
Layla reported that despite her husband's $250,000 annual salary, the

family was putting away nothing in savings. "It's kind of shocking to me," she said. "We always have enough to get through the month. But we go down to zero." When Kevin and his wife, both full-time professionals, examined their finances recently in preparation for buying a new car, they realized they didn't have the $158 left over at the end of the month to afford it. "We both kind of panicked," he said.

For upper-income parents, pathway consumption often started by choosing either private schools or what are essentially "private neighborhoods." Time and time again, I heard parents say what Dorothy told me, in anticipation of her plans for Olivia's middle school, that although they valued diversity enough to try the public schools to "see if they are good enough," at the same time "we're not going to sacrifice our kids' education for a principle like that." "I spent a day in the public school classroom and thought, 'I . . . I don't have to send my kid here.' It was just so boring," said Adrienne, an investment counselor. "And then you go to a place like Arrowhead. I mean, I know this is so arrogant and so unfortunate. But you have the option. So . . ."

The Mackenzies, who mostly live off income from their investments, agonized over where to send their boys to middle school, once they graduated from Arrowhead. But after researching all of the public school options, they chose an elite private school with a reputation for stellar academics and a wealthy student body. "We kept finding ourselves saying, 'They'll do just fine [at the public school], they'll do just fine,' and it was kind of a survival thing," said Anne. "But when it came down to it for us, and we walked into the classroom, and there weren't enough chairs for the kids, and some kids were sitting on the floor, and you read about them not having enough textbooks," that was when they just couldn't go through with it. It was not that they felt that they *had* to spend money to buy a good education. "It's not about what it costs," said Richard, her husband. "If you can find it without—I mean great." But a safe and challenging learning environment for middle schoolers was not available for free in Oakland, they thought, and at the moment of that realization, they opted out.

"For us ultimately the decision came down to what can we give our kids," Richard said. Anne chimed in: "It's sort of an embarrassment of riches, you know, but at a certain point you just say, 'If we can give this to our kids, what else is there, but to give them a great education?'" And the extent to which others could not make the same jump was certainly regrettable, but not something to sway their decision. "You know, some people don't have a choice, and they make the best of what they can do for their children," Anne said simply. "We have a choice." By implication, Anne seemed to be saying that if one has the choice of acting on behalf of one's own children, one is compelled to make it. For affluent parents with sympathy for lower-income families, the problem was that the system forced them to choose between their politics—their intellectual commitment to diversity or community or equity—and their child's pathway to the future.

BEING UNIQUE, BEING THE SAME: THE POLITICS OF DIFFERENCE FOR THE AFFLUENT

Affluent children were nothing if not different. Parents offered long diagnoses of children's individual traits—"Dennis just constitutionally is a very empathic guy. A soft, low-toned guy, and there's something just . . . sweet about him. Deeply sweet and just. He was born with a certain nervous system, a certain anxiousness. And the obsessional qualities— he's a risk-averse guy." Their soliloquies emphasized their children's uniqueness, and how it would be best served in particular settings and not others. Donna, an Arrowhead parent, described her son Gavin as needing "constant challenges." "I just didn't sense that in the public school system he'd get that," she said. When I asked her what happened when he did not "get that," she responded by acting out a dialogue in which I was a teacher and her son was my student.

DONNA (said all in one breath):   "Allison, can I tell you about the jaguars that I want to go see when I travel to Africa? I know you want to

talk to me about this stupid reading
program that the Oakland public
school district forces down the kid's
throat, but I want to tell you about
what I'm going to do when I go to
Africa." "Gavin, I really need to get
through this about this reading program." "Allison!"

AJP: So he kind of . . . unless he is chal-
lenged his brain is somewhere else?

DONNA: Oh, yeah.

Affluent parents who chose private school often did so after deciding
their children required a more individualized educational match for
their particular needs and strengths—in other words, their differences.

As we saw in chapter 4, affluent parents were leery of the power of
interactional differences—such as what children owned or experiences
they could talk about—leery enough to respond to children's desires,
often despite their own ambivalence about spending. Yet at the same
time many affluent parents, particularly mothers, felt responsible for
searching for and recognizing their children's psychological and intellectual differences, what we might call "personal differences." In upper-
income families, this celebration of "uniqueness" was tied to spending
through pathway consumption, just as the fear of interactional difference was linked to spending through commodity consumption.

This cultivated uniqueness is generally not part of a low-income
childhood. When asked to describe her eight- and seven-year-old
daughters individually, the girls for whom she had worked so hard to
retrieve from foster care, Erika responded: "They both like mostly the
same thing. They like the same. Because they just . . . they're so close.
They both Capricorns. They both stubborn." This broader view—in
contrast to the close-in scrutiny of the affluent—might be due to a
different parenting style, as Annette Lareau's family ethnography
suggested. But it might also be due to the resource constraints of

low-income families, who struggle to meet even the most pressing problems—such as Derrick's delayed reading—let alone those needs that might require parent examination and analysis to identify. Because of the contrast between this constrained response and the upper-income parents' expanded ability—and propensity—to deal with their children's unique needs and talents, I came to view the affluent approach as the "luxury of difference."[17]

THE LUXURY OF DIFFERENCE

The luxury of difference gave upper-income parents a mission, to serve their children's unique needs as identified. The luxury of difference also gave parents a justification for skipping the public schools, a decision that needed to be explained in the politically progressive environment of the Bay Area. Private school parents, or public school parents who were planning to pull their children out later (at middle school or high school), had plenty of reasons why schools organized for mass education were not right for their children. The luxury of difference also lent an added urgency to the process by reframing the question. The question was no longer "Which school/program/teacher do I like?" It had become "Which school will best provide what my child must have?" As we have seen throughout this book, when children's desire turns to need because of the call of dignity, the word "need" can order social action precipitously. The luxury of difference, then, performed a certain magic for upper-income parents by producing urgent needs, the same magic that the economy of dignity performed on commodities, particularly (but not solely) for low-income parents.

Upper-income parents strategized about plumbing the depths of their children's characters, and then matching them with schools that promised to bring them from where they were in the present to where the parent wanted them in the future. But while choosing schools was thus partially driven by the task of meeting the child's unique needs, the process was also often informed by a fear of the difference of others. And like low-income parents, when affluent parents talked about the fear of difference, they often used coded references to what sounded like racialized class.[18]

Difference could be polluting, as when Oceanview parents contemplated the school district plan for children from other less pristine neighborhoods to attend Oceanview, which had been newly revamped to expand its capacity. Said Dorothy: "As long as it doesn't cause . . . as long as it doesn't pull down the—it'll be an adjustment for everybody." Difference could be dangerous to children's physical or mental well-being, as when parents traded scare stories about (white) children navigating the halls of the high school Oakland Academy getting accosted for their money, or when parents discovered their child had been bullied at previous schools. "They were in fights almost every day," said Janet, who quickly transferred her sons to Arrowhead. "I mean, physical fights." Difference could threaten the innocence of children shielded from the experiences of poverty. In this way, my informants echo the feelings of a San Francisco woman quoted in the local newspaper: "People say, 'Don't you want her to see the real world?' I say, 'Not yet!'"[19]

Thus we can say most of the affluent parents in this study sought out their own children's differences—often in personal characteristics, such as how they learned or whether they were shy—but avoided the differences of others—often in social characteristics, such as racialized class. This observation held true even in the diverse Bay Area, where many parents would announce their own preference for diversity. At Arrowhead, which had an explicit commitment in admissions, curriculum, and school culture to respecting and articulating difference, parents frequently said they elected to send their child to the school because of this approach, welcoming diversity along racial/ethnic origin, sexual orientation, family structure, or other lines. Few of the affluent families I interviewed, however, pronounced dedication to racialized *class* diversity, instead stating their appreciation for immigrants, say, or a school with students of color, but not articulating a preference for low-income others.

Studies have shown that U.S. households became more geographically segregated by income between 1970 and 1990. Coupled with the stratification of circumstance across race and class in Oakland's land-scape of opportunity, the perceived risks of social difference and the perceived mandate of personal uniqueness encouraged upper-income parents, particularly white and Asian ones, to choose segregation. In an environment of great disparity among schools, these choices replicate the social inequality that make them reasonable decisions in the first place, as racialized class identities self-segregate among radically dis-parate pools of educational and career opportunity. Only one group—affluent African-Americans—handled difference differently.[20]

AFFLUENT AFRICAN-AMERICANS AND EXPOSED CHILDHOODS

Caleb Lamont is the African-American third grader we met in chapter 4 who plays Little League in one of the toughest neighborhoods in Oak-land. Even though someone checks the field before every practice, they still sometimes miss a syringe or two left behind from the nighttime drug activity that takes place among the bedraggled weeds. When some of the parents, many of them single mothers, African-American and Latina, line up on the bench to watch the practice, Caleb's mother, Deb-orah, sits among them. But Caleb and his family are different from the others, and according to his mother, this was never more obvious than one day when Caleb put down his baseball bag.

DEBORAH: He really embarrassed me. We were at another field, and he yells across all the other little mommies, "Hey, Mom, is this one of those places where I can leave my stuff and it won't get stolen, or should I take it with me?" Well, you can imagine the eyes that I got, first of all! And then I had him come over to me, and we walked away from the other mothers.

   He didn't do it intentionally. I had been on him about getting his things stolen. [But I told him] if you have something like that to ask me, you come and you do it quietly. So we all learned a lesson.

AJP: So you're down there with them as they're having
practices.

DEBORAH: Oh, I don't . . . I'm not to the point that I leave them. No.
I mean, I walk them to the restrooms.

Caleb and his family live in Oceanview in a beautiful three-story house. Caleb attends Oceanview public elementary school with his brother and sister. His father, Sam, earns a comfortable six-figure salary in a research lab and coaches the baseball team. His mother left her job as a mathematics professor to devote herself full-time to her three children, advocating for them in school, planning their schedules, carefully tailoring their environments to their perceived needs. The Lamonts spend more on the children's tutoring than the average West Oakland resident makes in a year. Caleb's life, when he is not in Little League, is so different from those of his teammates that in many ways he is as alien as his question about "leaving his stuff" belies.[21]

Why, then, does Caleb's mother actively seek out for Caleb this team—and another similar one for Caleb's brother Vernon, coached by their uncle? As we have seen, most families handle these kinds of disparity by finding relatively homogeneous environments for their children, where they won't be confronted with others of different racialized class locations. Oceanview fields its own team, of course, on which most of the boys from Caleb's school play. The Lamonts certainly have plenty of other choices for this particular kind of context, choices that their white neighbors are making instead.

It is not that Deborah puts her children on this team for herself, say, because she can relax with the other mothers there, away from the social pressures of her affluent, white neighborhood. In the vignette above, we can see her essential discomfort when Caleb "blew her cover" as just another mom of color, revealing her to be an affluent woman skulking in low-income surroundings. In East Oakland, Deborah Lamont feels that she has to watch herself closely. "I stay away from topics that could get me into trouble," like where they live or what school Caleb attends, she says. "So I try to be cordial. I try to strike up conversations. I try to talk to people. But at the same time I'm careful about how much I volunteer."

Nor is it likely that Deborah is hoping that her children will absorb character lessons from these low-income African-Americans that differ from those they derive from their affluent white friends, values that researchers have found prevalent in African-American communities, such as the importance of kinship, of giving back to the community, or of redefining success more collectively. These themes are not part of her lexicon; she does not articulate or demonstrate such a social critique in other venues. In fact, on several occasions, she revealed her critical perspective on the East Oakland families, as when she began a story about what the low-income children were like with the explanation "The values are just totally different, so Sam had to take two little boys home whose parents just left [them] there, and [they] didn't have a ride." The dream of many of the other bleacher moms, as she saw it—that their son would be the next baseball star and would take care of them—"it's just sad to me," she said. Caleb and Vernon are not there in the fields of East Oakland to gain heart.[22]

Rather, the baseball team offers a different kind of prize for Caleb and Vernon, a set of skills Deborah Lamont anticipates will be as beneficial to their future as how to write a science report: that of adaptability. By surviving in a variety of settings where they are continually the Different Ones, the boys become social chameleons, familiar with a variety of cultural styles and practices, and intimidated by none of them.

> Vernon told me when he started—this is his second year—children were mean to him. Well, I immediately noticed, first of all, that he didn't observe—[you and I] are at the polite talking level. They talk LIKE THIS, and Vernon wasn't used to that, and there were a lot of mannerisms and the talking loudly. And then I realized it was his experience level—well, [Vernon and Caleb] have learned to adapt.

The payoff will be considerable, she believes, when they are older and she can no longer control their environment, when they are confronted with difference more regularly as their social world widens.

In some ways they're going to come in contact with these children who are in your face and speak differently. And I want them to know how to act and react. Like Vernon being afraid and intimidated. Better at six than at sixteen, when he runs into them in downtown Oakland or at a party at Highland Point.

For the Lamonts, East Oakland baseball is a type of pathway consumption they choose as carefully as they choose tutors for their children.

In fact, the Lamonts are not unusual among the affluent African-Americans in my sample, who purposefully enroll their children in mostly white schools and mostly black enrichment activities. Some middle-class African-Americans choose particular after-school settings for their children in order to help them craft African-American identities from lives spent mostly amid white people. In her excellent work *Blue-Chip Black*, Karyn Lacy called these practices "strategic assimilation," through which middle-class blacks pursue a "deliberate limited incorporation into white mainstream, American life." Lacy contends that "scholars have . . . failed to acknowledge just how much work middle-class black parents put into nurturing and sustaining their children's racial identities." Further, she argues: "This work is compounded by the fact that in addition to teaching their children to negotiate the black-white boundary, these parents must also prepare their children to manage class-based boundaries between different groups of blacks." Deborah Lamont provides an example of this extensive labor, most often taken on by affluent black mothers.[23]

But the Lamonts are not just finding people of color wherever they exist, and putting Caleb and Vernon in among them, hoping they'll learn what it means to be African-American in the process. They are much more precise than that; for them, for example, that the teammates are more "street" than "decent," to use Elijah Anderson's terms, is an important factor. Theirs is a particular approach to constructing childhoods, one that contrasts sharply with that of the low-income African-Americans and Latinos, and that of the affluent whites and Asian-Americans discussed previously—one that strives for what I term "*exposed childhoods.*"

In my sample, most of the affluent African-Americans—seven of the ten such families I followed, including all those in Oceanview—to some degree constructed "exposed childhoods" for their children. The Lamonts, and others, are thrusting their children in environments of difference all around, hoping they'll learn to carry themselves with aplomb everywhere.[24]

CONSUMPTION, PATHWAYS, AND EXPOSED CHILDHOODS IN ACTION

The broad pattern of choosing segregation makes the Lamonts, and other like-minded families, particularly interesting, because their children, unlike others, experience difference. They are put in situations where they carry the weight of being the odd one out, either on the basis of race, as some of the only African-Americans in majority-white schools, or on the basis of class, as some of the only affluent children in their majority low-income enrichment activities.

An "exposed childhood" rests upon consumption, that of pathways and commodities. Parents choose contexts for children that present challenges of adaptation to them, because of their contrasting racial or class composition. Like all pathway consumption, geographies of inequality framed these choices, especially the availability of mostly two kinds of public schools: the "apartheid schools" failing the children of color who made up their student bodies, and the high-scoring majority-white environments of the handful of hills schools. Against this backdrop, then, parents pursued three goals in three particular contexts: (1) in a setting where race and class to a large degree overlapped, affluent African-American parents enrolled their children in the majority-white schools to prioritize academic learning over social comfort; (2) they sought out social engagements with affluent blacks like themselves to combat simple cultural equivalence of race and class and show "all kinds of black people"; and (3) they arranged for extracurricular contact with lower-income children of color to encourage their children's wide-ranging social skills, as well as to school their children in the everyday meanings of their own elite status. Through this welter of complex social dynamics, families trained their children to be anthropologists in a world in which everybody was an Other.[25]

"SO YOU LEARNED THAT YOUR DAD WAS A SCIENTIST"

Deborah Lamont and other parents I observed were extraordinarily purposeful in their production of exposed childhoods. In the example of the baseball team, we see her choosing the team, managing the conversation with other mothers, preparing Caleb in advance for a different environment, teaching him about discretion by pulling him away from the other mothers, "getting on him" about keeping track of his property, and walking her sons to the restroom at the Little League fields. This is intensive, watchful mothering. At the same time, while those parents actively constructed their children's environments, what happened inside those contexts—the economy of dignity that prevailed, for example—was in large part beyond their control.[26]

This was particularly evident in Vernon Lamont's classroom. Vernon was one of only two African-American boys in his second-grade class at Oceanview, where I observed children in the classroom, at lunch, and at recess, went on field trips, and interviewed parents and staff. A small, handsome boy, he was nonetheless not popular in a milieu where popularity was unusually salient. In contrast to the noisy cauldron of teasing, crying, and laughter that was the ambience at Sojourner Truth, his was a quiet but fairly mean classroom. Friendship groups changed members frequently, and some girls and boys seemed to be continually working to be accepted—it sometimes felt a socially dangerous place.

Vernon was an unusual child, not because he was boisterous and bright, but because he was also detached somehow, insensitive to social cues—prone to making jokes to himself or repeatedly approaching another child after being rebuffed. It was as if other children were years older in their social sophistication, as was demonstrated when the teacher told the class to get in groups or work alone on a special classroom project:

> Vernon says to Garrett he wants to be in his group, Garrett must have answered about being in a group with Brian, and Vernon says, "You are always in a group with him"— his arm is draped around Garrett's neck while he is saying this. . . .
>
> Brian and Garrett refuse to work in a group with Vernon, and the way they do it is they say, "No, we can't work together" (as a threesome) and say, "No, we each want to work alone," but later when Ms. Sullivan is in the bathroom I see Brian and Garrett working together at the same desk and kind of grinning, finally collaborating after all.

Vernon was not very well socially integrated in the classroom. In addition, Vernon's white teacher, Ms. Sullivan, who intimated that she thought he should have to repeat second grade over his parents' objections, sometimes made comments that the children seemed to interpret as tacit approval for classroom censure of Vernon. A science presentation Vernon gave provides one of several examples:

> Vernon's project was on pH and involved a lot of paper plates with litmus strips of different colors. The class kept asking, "I don't get it—what's pH?" and Ms. Sullivan doesn't do a lot to curtail it—making fun of Vernon is not unacceptable, it seems. He doesn't seem to notice. Ms. Sullivan doesn't hide her unimpressed face. "So what did you learn from this project?" Vernon says, "That my dad was a scientist and—" "So you learned that your dad was a scientist," she says, with barely hidden scorn.

In all likelihood, Vernon's marginality was brought on by a combination of his own personality issues and an invidious institutional racism at Oceanview, in a school district where class and race generally overlapped in scores and preparation. But Ms. Sullivan, a competent veteran teacher made cynical by years of teaching, seemed to allow a social system whereby Vernon's "weirdness" made him somewhat of an outcast.[27]

On one level, this was clearly not the classroom experience Deborah Lamont hoped for, and despite her active participation in the school, she was not completely aware of it. But on another level, she didn't care if Vernon had lots of friends in class; she cared that his education was rigorous and challenging, which she considered it to be. She had no illusions that Oceanview was going to be devoid of the racism that comes with the majority-white territory. But handling racism is one of the tasks for which her children will have to develop skills in order to be successful, she maintained. "They have already had situations happen. And they're going to," she said. "And they're going to have to deal with it."

Similarly, Felicia, another African-American parent at Oceanview, argued that surviving in a difficult environment, one in which you are the Different One, offered a powerful lesson:

> It's instilling a sense of self-esteem in your children. That you can go anywhere and do whatever you want. You can fit in. You can't worry about the race issue. And then also what—well, my husband and I, the career paths that we've chosen. We're just used to generally being the only ones, the only African-Americans for miles. . . . If I can do it, you can do it. You know, just . . . you can't worry about that. You just have to worry about being the best that you can be—and take the challenges as they come your way. And that's all you can do.

School is not like home, then, but neither will other environments be for these children, now or in the future, these parents said. From their perspective, as a given context Oceanview was perfect for Vernon and his peers, even if—and maybe because—it was not that comfortable.

"OH, BLACK FOLKS HAVE BIG HOUSES, TOO"

Many affluent African-American families have their children in majority-white schools but seek to expose their children to other elite black families, on the principle that this will teach them "there are all kinds of black people." This principle animated exposure in only this upward direction on the class ladder, however, as parents worked to counter stereotypical equations of black with poor, uneducated gangsta culture.

In this vein, several informants belonged to Jack and Jill, the national social club for affluent black families, who attend events together, hold birthday parties, and arrange for monthly social activities. Jack and Jill can be "a little snooty, frankly," said Letty Owens, another affluent African-American parent at Oceanview, in an interview in her comfortable home overlooking San Francisco Bay.

> But what you wind up is getting your children in a social circle with other black children with parents that are educated and the kind of children you are willing . . . you want them to see. "Oh, black folks have big houses, too." And I mean Big Houses! And that's sort of the value of doing that.

African-American parents could not ignore the surrounding cultural messages equating race and class, even as their own homes provided resplendent counterpoints to reigning stereotypes.

For Deborah Lamont, the benefit of exposing children to other affluent African-Americans was the "values" the families shared:

> And it's because they're not around a lot of African-American children. And the children in this particular organization tend to be well-off. They tend to do more social things, more academic things. They tend to go to college. They tend to—so we went to [the Museum of Modern Art] with the group. They do things like that, and it's a group of black children who go to private schools, who go to public schools, but who within their families can have the same type of values.

"Values" can be a code word for other social categories delineating difference; in this case, Deborah makes clear reference to middle-class practices like going to museums and college, as well as noting simply that they are "well-off." Similarly, Letty talked about getting together with a group of other black professional families, a group that "grew out of a need to have the children around other children that looked like them," and who shared their middle-class values.

"HE WALKS DIFFERENTLY WHEN HE'S IN EAST OAKLAND"

Caleb and Vernon's after-school life on the baseball team provided a sharp contrast to their everyday classroom environment and the rarefied outings of Jack and Jill. On the team they learned the components of an entirely different demeanor, that of low-income African-Americans. Deborah Lamont valued this exposure for the skills it engendered in her sons, whom she hoped would become, to use Karyn Lacy's term, "authentically black." Better now than later, Deborah maintained.[28]

Other affluent African-Americans agreed. Andrea, who owns several homes in the Oceanview area, said she had to "supplement" her children's Oceanview experience with activities that are not all-white. She related her own history as a cautionary tale guiding her own efforts to construct exposed childhoods for her children:

ANDREA: Like, it was very awkward for me when I went to college. I
            did join a black sorority. I had to make that choice. I had to,
            or else—I didn't want to not be—I wanted to be able to be
            in all of the worlds, not just here and not just here. It went
            well. My roommate was white. And I felt comfortable in
            that world. Because that's how I grew up. And I joined this
            sorority, and I felt comfortable in that world. But I had to
            make . . . I had to do it.

AJP: You had to do the leap. Right.

ANDREA: And I did. And it was fine. And it's great. I can talk to my
            sorority sisters about it. We talked about it—how I came
            from this one world and—we talk about it, even to this day. I
            get teased all of the time. They kid me all of the time. So it
            worked out. It was fine. So in terms of the children—I want
            them to have that now. And not have to think about it later.

Despite her assurances that "it was fine" and "it's great," Andrea's experience charting her own racial and class identity so late in life sounds like it was a discomfiting journey that she does not want her own children to have to repeat. The activities she thus plans for her children are not just populated by nonwhites, however, but rather by lower-income people of color, as when she signed her children up for the city's subsidized art camp or events at the local YMCA. She wants them to learn "how to be able to be in all of the worlds, not just here and not just here."

Children emerge from these circumstances with newfound skills of talking, walking, and other bodily practices, and parents collected the evidence of their exposed childhoods with a mixture of pride and humor. Deborah said she laughed sometimes when she watched Caleb walk. "Because Caleb has a different walk. He walks differently when he's in East Oakland. Once he got to Oceanview and he's like, 'Oh, I forgot,'" she recalled. "So they know that you do, you have two different manners." Or as Andrea put it: "In their life it's working out, you know? I mean, I giggle with my girlfriends about 'Oh, God, they get ghettofied over there.' That's what I say. I kid. I can say it. But there is a part of me that actually appreciates it."

Just as important as learning a new code, however, is learning when and where those codes apply. Deborah Lamont is amused by, even proud of, Caleb's new walk, but she is clear it doesn't belong in their neighborhood. She patrols the borders of these codes vigilantly:

> And then we have this joke, because they were talking. Something like, "Mommy, where we be going?" And I said, "What? Oh." And I shouldn't make fun. I'll say, "Caleb, do you know what we be doing today?" "Mom, we don't talk like that." And it's probably not a nice thing to do. But I also think it's very important for them to be aware.

The children get immersed in environments with low-income African-Americans so they learn the skills of handling themselves in that environment, but parental humor keeps these skills where they belong—dormant, except in those contexts where they are useful.

Humor can patrol these boundaries, but it can also act as a flag for our discomfort, a divining rod for transgressive behavior that violates expected social codes, even as it paradoxically "expresses pleasure at subversion." Letty Owen recounted one story when she realized she had gone past the point of her own comfort in search of authentic blackness for her son Nicholas:

> And I remember I was sitting there watching—this is funny—and I told [my husband] Lawrence, I saw this woman . . . two black women were there with three or four children and there was a . . . I'd say she was between nine and ten—a little chubby black girl. And she was dancing. And her mother turned over to her and said, "Ain't nobody out here doing no booty dancing." Which is like a joke now, we say that. And it's the kind of thing where I want Nicholas to be comfortable in a situation that is very diverse, but I don't want him to use that kind of language.

The line between just enough and too much exposure to street culture was a fine one, but you had to get it right, these parents said. "Because otherwise you have—they're overprotected, and they're not comfortable around black people," Letty said. "And there are all kinds of black people. And I'm sort of interested in having exposure to the range. But you know, [the 'booty-dance' episode] was the kind of thing like you wouldn't want to go there every day, because that sort of language seeps into your life. And I don't really want him to say that." Letty's ambivalence is apparent in her language—"And I'm sort of interested in having exposure to the range"—even as she adopts the strategy of exposed childhoods for her own son.[29]

Andrea shared this ambivalence:

> When they come home I'm like, "It's not, 'I ain't gonna do blah-blah!'" You know what I mean? It's almost funny. I don't get angry. I used to get angry. But there is a part of me where I kind of appreciate that. Because they can mix. And I want them to be able to do that. So it's okay, as long as you know when to mix and when not to mix.

It is as important for these parents that their children know when to use their newfound cultural fluency as that they acquire it in the first place. Parents want their children to be able to don a certain demeanor when necessary, but to shed it just as ably.

"SOMEONE SAYING I COULDN'T DO
SOMETHING MADE ME WANT TO DO IT"

Part of what makes Deborah Lamont and other affluent African-American parents unusual among the other groups of families is their stance toward social difference. As we have seen, the negative prospect of their children being singled out as different in their social milieu—be it on the basis of what they owned or what they had experienced—motivated the commodity consumption of many parents, low-income and affluent, white and nonwhite. The specter of difference evoked images of their children being teased, bullied, beaten up, ignored, bored, or lured into "trouble." In addition, upper-income families sometimes seemed to fear that racialized class diversity in schooling would pollute high academic standards. Low-income families of color worried that their children would get labeled, blamed, and shunted aside. These fears constrained and focused parents' pathway consumption for their children, making them choose sameness.

At the same time, affluent parents worked hard to frame their children as individuals, ferreting out and naming their particular idiosyncrasies. But these efforts were aimed at diagnosing their children's personal differences, with particular bundles of skills and needs, which they could then best nurture with a good match in context. In Oakland, elite parents often used such diagnoses to justify sending their children to private school, where their children's particular individuality would be protected from the uniformity they feared was required in the mass experience of the public schools. The luxury of difference was part of the ideology funneling the children of those families who could choose into contexts that segregated them by racialized class.

Not for Deborah Lamont, however. She took steps to control her children's exposure to difference, and she had her limits, but she was not afraid. Difference didn't have to threaten the children's safety when her sons played baseball—especially when she walked them to the East Oakland restroom, and when their father and uncle were the coaches.

"See, you kind of keep a certain amount of control by making sure there's an adult that you trust," she explained. Difference didn't have to threaten their future by instilling in them the wrong skills or values—especially when she made sure they left their new walk and talk back in East Oakland. Difference didn't even have to threaten their dignity by exposing them to racialized hostility, labeling, or bullying, because they got a boost by learning how to handle themselves in diverse environments—although my classroom observations of Vernon and others living exposed childhoods suggest there may be more faith than hard evidence behind such improved social skills.

In part, Deborah Lamont's fearlessness stems from her own background in what she called a "racially volatile environment." Once a guidance counselor at her Catholic high school in Philadelphia told her she should be a teacher or a nurse because girls don't do well in math. As mentioned in chapter 4, Deborah became a mathematician in response to that conversation. "I don't even remember the counselor's name, but just thinking of someone saying I couldn't do something made me want to get out there and do it." Undoubtedly, her own experience in majority-white environments has given her the same confidence about handling herself in diverse contexts that she hopes to seed in her children. As Deborah might say, it worked for her.

SKILLS, EXPOSURE, AND EMPATHY

It is important that, unlike other groups of parents, some affluent African-Americans seek out the experience of difference for their children. The persistent segregation along race and class lines that many parents of diverse backgrounds and identities actively pursue contributes to the inequality of opportunity in these settings. These experiences of difference can be challenging cultural exchanges that, because of widespread de facto segregation and their own resources, elite families do not have to elect to undertake.

Nonetheless, some of these families appeared to pursue these cross-class experiences for their children as opportunities for edification—developing the skills to survive teenage parties later on, for example—rather than for connection. When Caleb calls across the other mothers to ask whether or not the team is playing among thieves, he is revealing the way in which Deborah framed this activity for him: as an opportunity to study the Other, rather than to find the Other within.

To be sure, other families did not evince quite so strategic an approach. Scholars have emphasized the emotional benefits that affluent African-Americans derive from forging relationships with other African-Americans. In this vein, some families said they hoped for *both* exposure *and* relationship.

For others, however, there may be a hidden cost to empathy in consuming pathways that offer difference framed as a learning experience. These are exposed childhoods, and most of the time not, say, integrated childhoods, classless childhoods, or revolutionary childhoods. To the extent that for some affluent families, low-income people become sources of lessons learned and not relationships, then the likelihood for affluent children is that they will derive code-switching competence, and not compassion, from their experience.

THE IMPLICATIONS
OF EXPOSED CHILDHOODS

The affluent African-Americans in my sample live in an urban context in which they are faced with great inequality that is mapped onto the geography of racialized class. Their only options for good schools with children and parents with similar "values" and backgrounds were majority-white, because in this urban field, as in the United States generally, middle-class families and the good schools that serve them are disproportionately white. Thus these parents perceived they had little choice about inserting their children in environments of difference at school.[30]

But my affluent African-American informants also attested to beliefs about the importance of difference for their children's lives, and unlike most other parents in this study, they actively sought out experiences of difference for their children outside of school. For these parents, their children's future—diverse, challenging, unpredictable—depended on their ability to traverse social boundaries with comparative ease. They bought contexts to engender the skills they saw as necessary for success in that future, and along the way served to traverse lines of class and race that other families are not generally crossing.

Vernon Lamont absorbed the emotional cost of social marginality in his classroom, and, as we saw in chapter 3, his brother Caleb negotiated his own dignity based on the lingua franca of consumer goods like the Game Boy. Even children of privilege live with the consequences of their caregivers' particular configuration of risk and caution, difference and homogeneity. Parents constructed exposed childhoods by consuming copious amounts of object goods on the premise that equipping the child for a local economy of dignity, smoothing out interactional differences, would help lighten the experience of social difference.

For other children, the economy of dignity occupied their energy and passion, even defined their horizons. But affluent African-American children knew about class and racialized Others in intimate ways that other children did not. They experienced economies of dignity not as a wholly consuming "serious game," but rather as a series of different cultural games that may share certain universals across contexts, such as the Game Boy, but that could vary from one place to the next. In an exposed childhood, then, commodities served not to mystify other hierarchies external to the classroom or the camp, but rather to make dignity in a variety of settings. The process of sampling different economies of dignity, meanwhile, threw that hierarchy into relief, as affluent children were exposed to lives sharply distinct from their own very privileged ones.

CONCLUSION

As we have seen, child-rearing consumption involves not just equipping children with the stuff of childhood, but also arranging for the settings where they will spend time, such as neighborhoods, schools, after-school and before-school care, camps, lessons, babysitting, and other venues. I have called this pathway consumption, given that even if the children attend public school, the family arranges to rent or buy a home in a particular neighborhood or school district, which involves a host of other decisions related to purchasing—such as proportions of income spent on housing, transportation arrangements, or work-family configurations. This is consumption writ broadly, within a structured environment that shapes the parameters of what is possible.

We do not usually think about hope (as embedded in contexts) and dignity (as signaled through commodities) at the same time. These ideas are separated by more than the semantics of the economist's distinction between "investment" and "consumption"; yet these separations hide important linkages between them. The invisibility of these links surely has deep roots, in fundamental and deep contradictions in American society, such as the simultaneously oligarchic distribution of opportunity in America and democratic availability of commodities.

Many differences divide the two concepts. Most important, spending on one is not seen to be related to spending on the other, partly because compared to $13,000 in tuition, $90 for a Game Boy seems insignificant. But other differences can also be found, such as in the experience of inequality—the momentary, shallower inequality of who has what, a social reckoning that may be, and often is, different tomorrow, versus the deep, abiding inequality of the contexts in which children live and go to school over time. Different kinds of knowledge lead to the successful accumulation of dignity or hope: navigating popular culture and its meanings can lead to acquiring the right commodities, while hope requires navigating the sometimes mystifying terrain of children's contexts. These concepts also differ in their moral cast, as some adults see it—commodities simply reward desire, while contexts do the important work of developing the child. The time horizons for each are distinct, in that dignity challenges need to be solved yesterday, while hope involves long-term aspirations. Finally, the emotions behind these concepts differ—dignity has a raw, urgent cast to its ache, while hope is a deeper, more profound sort of yearning—as does the identity of those who feel them most intensely: children face the emergency of dignity, while parents are most often the ones attending to hope.

If these ideas are so different, then, why is it worthwhile to try to bring them together? Contexts and commodities are linked in several important ways that we do not normally apprehend, but that wield significant impact on families' spending on children. They affect each other both directly (in the framing of what goods matter and how much in which location) and indirectly (in the determination of what kind of commodities or what contexts are possible, given limited resources, discrepant information, and different horizons). Together the two ideas shape family budgets, as we saw in the extreme case of Simon Deng and his family; despite their often sharp difference in price, commodity consumption does limit to some unknown degree the pathway consumption of families, and vice versa. The lingua franca of childhood, commodities can also often serve to smooth the transitions across contexts as well. Lastly, contexts are inhabited by particular economies of dignity—cold or warm, exclusive or welcoming—that affect the way children are able to take advantage of whatever opportunities are offered there.

The relationship of the economy of dignity to inequality is paradoxical. On the one hand, such an economy can work to convert momentary, local inequalities into social honor, much as Veblen described for adults more than a hundred years ago. Many claims to dignity rest upon goods—from sneakers to lunches—whose distribution is at least temporarily unequal, even among relatively homogeneous groups. On the other hand, the economy of dignity can be powerfully distracting, and thus can serve to obfuscate another, more potent form of inequality—that of the contexts of childhood that separate children like those of

Danielle and Angela, the two mothers whose pathway consumption dilemmas opened this chapter, into unequal pools with different resources and opportunities. The economy of dignity reflects children's intense focus on their social world, but by focusing on dignity, and not, say, opportunity or hope, it reflects children's structured myopia about the larger hierarchies that govern their world. Children navigate the economy of dignity with what they are given, making cultural meaning through processes of contestation and interpretation that thus create local sources of social honor, which sort children into mutable, momentary hierarchies bounded by their very limited horizons. But within the increasing class segregation of American childhoods, by the time children are in their contained universe of mostly similar peers, sorting on a grander level has already taken place.

CHAPTER EIGHT

Conclusion

Beyond the Tyranny of Sameness

The buying we do for children is grounded in a central contradiction: the simultaneity of a striving for independence and a longing to belong. Part of the human condition, this contradiction is written into American cultural history. On the one hand, individualism is what one scholar called "the language of American 'common sense,' the folklore of the American middle class." On the other hand, as a long history of social analysis has maintained, Americans hunt for sameness, with a fever that hints at a widespread loneliness and a deep anxiety about what other people are thinking and doing.[1]

More than 150 years ago, Alexis de Tocqueville identified individualism as a core characteristic of the American cultural landscape and cautioned that "each man is forever thrown back on himself alone, and there is danger that he may be shut up in the solitude of his own heart." More recently, in their popular elegy for the American community, *Habits of the Heart*, Robert Bellah and his colleagues warned that Americans were adrift in a cult of the self, that they had lost a common moral vision that could justify mutual commitments—in essence, that individualism had triumphed over its uneasy subjects. The celebration of autonomy and independence is what legal scholar Martha Fineman called a "foundational myth" of the U.S. body politic. The individual, free to be different as long as he or she is not causing harm, is surely no less than a cultural icon.[2]

Yet for most of the families in this study, difference often posed fundamental challenges to children's perceived well-being. Families viewed interactional differences—arising out of who had what on a particular day—as threatening to children's sense of belonging. Most viewed social differences—such as those of race, gender, or class—as potentially menacing their children's comfort, achievement, or safety. Only personal differences—talents, skills, and deficits ferreted out almost exclusively by the affluent—sometimes came with more positive valences, although they often resulted in diagnoses of particular needs. Parents seemed to view most differences—those residing either in their own children or in other children—as potential hazards to children's experience of community. Most of all, and with few exceptions, parents and children prioritized children's participation in their social world, an essential component of which was, they agreed, reliant on having the same goods and experiences as others, those deemed meaningful within their economy of dignity.

The contradiction of rugged individualism and the appeal of connection through similarity gives rise to an ambivalence that saturates human experience, as the sociologist Neil Smelser maintained. "Neither freedom nor dependence can be realized in a full or exclusive form, because one is part of the other," Smelser contended. "Human beings long and strive for both, but, when they achieve a measure of either, the other reasserts itself. As in the nature of ambivalence itself, we want both sides at once, but cannot fully satisfy either side."[3]

For the parents and children in this study, the strain produced by such a paradox animated their consumption. The market promised to "deliver a state of unambivalence," as Arlie Hochschild wrote, noting that "the very act of fleeing ambivalence also expresses ambivalence." Parents who otherwise looked at peers askance or who cultivated their children's unique qualities nonetheless worried about their children's alienation from others, finding solace in buying commodities and events that could serve as cultural bridges into children's peer communities.

Affluent parents used symbolic deprivation to express and codify their ambivalence about spending. Low-income parents used symbolic indulgence to resolve the tensions of not having enough in a market economy in the face of overweening personal and social pressure to "make them feel normal." Their specific cultural practices of consumption allowed most parents to have it both ways. Yet what University of Texas sociologist Christine Williams called "the fantasy of the perfect commodity" promised what it cannot deliver, "that human ambivalence can be resolved once and for all."[4]

Only a few families seemed unfazed by the prospect of difference. First, certain immigrant families eschewed child-rearing consumption—those who hearkened back to their cultures of origin for a more centripetal version of family in which individuals, and particularly children, did not have as much of a voice. Second, many affluent African-Americans continually exposed their children to situations in which they were different from others on the basis of their race or class—a strategy of pathway consumption that embraced social difference as a means of cultivating in their children a certain cultural competence. These exceptions served to highlight the practices of the surrounding families, for whom children's desires were loud, children's belonging was paramount, and ambivalence reigned.

THE REAL STORY ABOUT CHILDREN'S CONSUMPTION

Writers have often framed consumption as a capitulation to the insidious forces of corporate marketing or an act of resistance and cultural creativity. My research provides evidence for a third way of viewing consumption, as part of children's meaning-making that borrows from but does not replicate corporate-made culture. In this effort, I join other scholars' recent efforts to reframe the debate. We have seen that children sometimes call upon global commodity icons to fill their locally engendered dignity needs, icons like Pokémon or the Game Boy that they hear about through advertising, older siblings, and other venues of information. Consumption, then, is neither capitulation, since children actively reinterpret and contest store-bought meanings, nor resistance, in that children quickly turn to global commodities to do their cultural work. Children invent and rely on many symbolic tokens to vie for dignity, and from their perspective, corporate marketing acts as a powerful mint, always churning out shinier coinage, but not always dictating whether or how those tokens are used.[5]

At the same time, we must not forget that a nation's mint has a civic mandate of trust and neutrality, a mandate not shared by these corporations, dedicated as they are to making a profit off of children's desires. So while consumption may not be capitulation, as children turn to commercial products for their own uses in their economies of dignity, an honest reckoning must view the purveyors of children's commodified goals and experiences more critically.

Children are of course influenced by marketing efforts; in many ways, advertising provides the common vocabulary of goods and destinations that children then use in their interactions. Yet, in tandem with the extensive scholarship on the effects of marketing, this research can be viewed as the story of what happens after children hear the corporate message, a glimpse into the rich social world that suffuses certain marketized items and experiences with a personal emotional valence for children, often amplifying and even sometimes drowning out the corporate pitch. The underlying concerns that animate the critical scholarship on corporate advertising center on children's materialism and its detrimental psychological and social effects; this work does not deny these worries. But I argue that there are crises of consumption we have yet to recognize. As the children in this study exemplify, children's desires for things stem less from individual vice, a lack of self-control, or a particular vulnerability to persuasion than from the emotional connections that possession has come to promise. The hidden crisis of consumption emanates from the social conditions that imbue commercialized goods with powerful meanings like belonging and care, harnessing them to the market.

I have also argued for a new approach to assessing the interactions of inequality and children's consumer culture, in part by bringing pathway consumption into the analysis. Most scholars have failed to take into account contexts as another form of consumption, falling prey to the move by economists to cordon off contexts as a form of "investment." In so doing, we have missed the opportunity to analyze commodities and contexts together, their interweaving in children's lives through the concept of dignity, and the practical impact they have on the ability of parents to spend in one realm or the other. The perceived ability of commodities to smooth over the transition to a new context; the idea that a context may feature a cold economy of dignity indifferent to the child's particular strengths, or worse, threatening to a child's vulnerability; the notion that certain contexts highlight the lack of a certain commodity—these are all examples of how the two concepts are intertwined in children's lives, and of ideas that motivate parents' consumption.

Thinking about context and commodity consumption as a part of the processes of child rearing has five important effects: (1) it highlights the impact and cost of public disinvestment and posits links between "collective consumption" and "private consumption"; (2) it brings to the fore the structuring of opportunity, the racial/class stratification of gateways to mobility in the United States; (3) it reveals the opportunities and the dignity the affluent are buying for their children; (4) it frames the terrible "choices" American society offers low-income caregivers, who can't afford both; and (5) it emphasizes what is at stake for children—both in their presents and in their futures.

Consumption scholars have argued that consumption practices serve to make and remake social inequality through the tastes they instill in childhood. Following Bourdieu's generative work in the field, these scholars contend that people have particular habits and preferences stemming from their backgrounds—predilections that constrain social mobility and limit the universe of potential actions from which people might choose. Often inadvertently, caregivers remake their own socioeconomic status with their child-rearing efforts, so that children's "cultural repertoires" reflect the lifestyle in which they were raised. People of all classes may consume the same things, but they sort themselves into hierarchies of taste and distinction in *how* they consume those things. While the families in this study corroborate these insights—witness how Game Boys were at once nearly universal and yet handled very differently in households of varying income levels—at the same time, they also demonstrate that the process of socialization is far from seamless. Parents and children, particularly those in affluent families, routinely disagreed about what children should have, and much of parents' chagrin stemmed from these conflicting desires; children often cared more about signaling age, gender, or access to popular culture than they did about showing the taste that parents considered appropriate to their class. Still, the experiences and memories of class and other forms of inequality proved formative for parents' stance toward their children's belonging and were often a catalyst for buying.[6]

THE IMPLICATIONS OF CHILD-REARING
CONSUMPTION: PROTECTING DIFFERENCE

Analysts convinced of corporate culpability in these issues often conclude with a call for tighter regulation of television advertising, improved ethical standards for market research, and other solutions aimed at restricting corporate behavior. It is important to recognize that my research does not suggest that corporate actors have no role in seeding children's consumer desires; rather, it acknowledges that the important preliminary role of advertising in providing the ingredients from which local notions of dignity are often made can be limited and controlled by such regulations. This study suggests, however, that these efforts will be less effective without programs that also address children's economies of dignity, including the emotional landscape that makes difference more or less fraught, the meanings of standing out, and the social importance of facework.

Schools and other contexts for childhood have an important role to play in providing a safe environment for children's difference. One means toward this end is to eliminate particular vestiges of difference, as school uniform policies attempt with varying success. Mandatory school lunches, reduced vacation time, or even field-trip vacations might be other ways of tackling some of the more charged nodes of difference in children's groups, although such practices are certainly less acceptable to upper-income parents. Clearly, however, these policies cannot actually eradicate difference; they can only limit to some degree its salience in the school yard.

Another approach, however, is to acknowledge that differences are there and help children understand and manage their feelings and interactions about these differences. Smaller schools, an explicit curriculum aimed at teaching tolerance, and alert teachers who are encouraged to respond to classroom culture, rather than ignoring conflicts until they explicitly interfere with academic learning—these, according to research, are some of the components of warm, diverse learning communities. A national education policy that bases rewards and penalties on students' performance on standardized tests discourages many educators from taking the time needed to teach children to resolve conflicts and handle differences constructively. Research shows that children's peer cultures respond to efforts by caring leaders to model positive behaviors; the laissez-faire model operating instead in most public and some private schools is an invitation for children to penalize difference, with consumer culture gleefully jumping in as the arbiter of belonging.[7]

Nonetheless, the Arrowhead example offers a cautionary note, as well as a prescription for future research. Arrowhead had a safe, caring, and warm emotional climate; children were taught to honor and welcome most forms of social difference. Yet despite the school's assiduous efforts to cultivate a celebration of difference, the children's economy of dignity there still valued commodities, still exerted pressure on children to participate through the use of various forms of scrip, and still enacted

inequality on a daily basis. As we saw, the school had not yet implemented an explicit curriculum about class difference, as they had about
gender, race, and other kinds. It is possible that the continued salience
of class was due to this omission, although the school's very identity as a
private institution charging tuition also heightened the relevance of
economic inequality among student families. Still, commodities and
class were among the only themes of difference left largely untreated
there; Arrowhead students responded to that vacuum by making both
commodities and class central pieces of their economy of dignity. The
notion that policies encouraging children to welcome difference can
serve as a blanket antidote to shame, exclusion, and indignity does not
appear to apply with regard to commodities, which might need their
own, direct campaign. Future research involving schools where children
do not make much hay out of interactional differences can help to adju-
dicate among these hypotheses.[8]

Some of the factors this study identified as leading to the commodification of difference, care, and belonging in children's lives—including the
elevation of children's presence in the home and the high stakes of social
exclusion, against a backdrop of aggressive corporate marketing and pervasive inequality—can be found in other advanced industrialized nations.
Still, there is more acute inequality in the United States than in Scandinavian countries, less emphasis on a common classroom culture than in
France, and weaker peer pressure than in Japan, according to scholars.
Cross-cultural comparisons with these and other countries would be particularly interesting in testing how some of the relationships that this
research has demonstrated change under different circumstances.[9]

While this study of children and parents has focused on children's
economies of dignity, how they vary across contexts, and how they influence consumption for children, undoubtedly adults also experience
economies of dignity in their social worlds. How do they differ—in
processes, tokens of value, and other features? How do contexts shape
adults' quests for dignity, given their status as legally autonomous people not subject to the same developmental ideology as children? Future

research investigating adults' economies of dignity could be valuable for filling out the portrait of consumer culture at all levels.

This study also has implications for parents, now seemingly trapped in a bind between coldheartedness and profligacy. As individuals confronting their children's urgent desires, parents have little recourse but to choose one of those two difficult paths. If parents reach out to others with children in the same communities, however, they can share information and practices that can drain much of the power from consumer sources of dignity. Recall what happened when Sarah told her classmates she had seen the movie *Crouching Tiger, Hidden Dragon*, some six years before her father Kevin actually planned to allow her to do so. After other parents then agreed to let their children to see it, the movie's adult images and themes took some of them aback, and they called up Kevin in frustration. Imagine if they had called up beforehand, to discuss setting a classroom-wide policy on popular movies, sneakers, or electronic gaming systems; their children would thus have less material to work with in setting the boundaries of who could join the conversation at school. We have seen how the economy of dignity presents parents with the unenviable choice between their child's social participation and their own budgetary needs and preferences. If caregivers were to approach children's consumer culture collectively, they could chart a third way for themselves and their children.

Some communities have tried, with varying success, to bar the door against the commodification of difference, care, and belonging. A team of parents and educators in St. Paul, Minnesota, has established the Birthdays Without Pressure project, involving a Web site collecting testimonials and offering tips on how to avoid birthday-party mania. An online group in England calling themselves "village mums with babies" has agreed collectively to abolish party bags. Increasing numbers of individual parents have been successful at turning birthday gifts into opportunities for charitable donations. Some schools, most of them small, private institutions filled with middle-class families, have been able to establish community-wide limits on television and other forms of popular culture. There are also many sources of help for parents and communities interested in addressing the meaning of difference; these include the Teaching Tolerance project of the Southern Poverty Law Center, which features grants, a curriculum, and age-graded activities ranging from a personalized storybook about a new kid in the classroom to "Mix It Up at Lunch Day," a day on which teens sit with a new group of people at lunch. Though small compared to the planetary scale of corporate marketing, these efforts represent the work of communities trying to regain control of the social choices facing children. It perhaps matters less that they are small than that they are collective; this book has shown that consumer culture is not something that individual parents can easily fight on their own. It is thus crucial that these campaigns are communal, that they extend beyond individual parents and children, or else we will continue to see that the only families who can hold back the flood of consumption will be the few who are impervious to cultural equations of buying and care, owning and belonging.[10]

THE COSTS OF CONSUMPTION

The economy of dignity works magic on children's consumer desires, turning them into psychological needs that both parents and children view as essential for their social citizenship, their basic humanity among their peers. Children's contexts vary in the economy of dignity that prevails, and children's dignity often forms part of the decision calculus for parents choosing one context over another. Belonging is a central focus in child rearing, a theme that shapes and is shaped by—sometimes in surprising ways—social inequalities such as race, class, and immigration.

There is a strand of current social discourse that decries the spending habits of low-income families, suggesting that they are enacting the wrong priorities and sacrificing their children to their own unfettered desires. And surely, the story of Simon—gamely, desperately, making his own dignity through gambits to redefine what might bring social honor, while his immigrant parents buy a home—is a shining example of what

some low-income families could do if perhaps they made the same sacrifices. But historical shifts have led to the empowerment of American
children inside the home, inviting peer culture inside as well, and in the
study sample, few native-born parents of any socioeconomic status were
able to consign their children to such indignity risks.

In this research, children's commercial culture traversed socioeconomic, racial/ethnic, and institutional boundaries. But how it *felt* to
partake in that culture—anxious, urgent, playful, or powerful—was influenced by the emotional landscape of the institution the children inhabited. Part of the intensity of children's consumer longings, then, stemmed
not just from their exposure to the marketer, but from the social jeopardy
involved in their ultimate campaign to belong. Children will use consumer goods to signify dignity as long as what signifies dignity is sold,
indeed, but they will also do so as long as dignity is scarce and important.

Those who study inequality have largely focused on material
inequity—of resources in the present or of opportunities for the future.
Yet children in different contexts are exposed to different emotional
regimes in their economies of dignity, regimes that map closely but not
exactly onto income disparities. The stories we've heard of these parents
and children provide evidence that the way we are encouraged to feel is
distributed unevenly as well, with implications that go beyond children's
daily lives to the emotional connections to others that underlie the
social compact. If children are not encouraged to feel for others, and are
instead taught to fear and even repulse difference, will they be able to
see the basic humanity in different Others when they are adults?

The most important cost to the economy of dignity, of course, is that a
sense of belonging that depends on sharing consumer goods and experiences is likely to be more fleeting than that based on other common characteristics. This is not to say that intimate relations are somehow
automatically corrupted by economic activity—two "hostile worlds"
incompatible with each other. Rather, because of the lightning-quick
transitions of consumer culture, in which fads and fashions change from
week to week, dignity achieved one day can be gone the next. As one

scholar observed, "while the 'peer culture' may establish norms for dress and behavior, it is not necessarily one that satisfies students' need for belongingness." Indeed, the commodified object or experience mediates human connection through the market, researchers report, and can actually serve to distance people rather than bring them together. As Sharon Zukin mused, "I wonder whether the masters of market research have really helped us. Using one method after another, they have torn apart the double helix of body and soul—selling us more things than ever without ever finding out what we 'really want.'" If what children really want is to belong, then surely buying a Game Boy is like treating not the cause of their yearning but the "referred pain" of their consumer desires.[11]

Yet what parent can resist, who has been acculturated to a prevailing model of family making, in which children's perceived social needs are overriding? None but a few of those in this study. Neither rich nor poor families could produce more than a handful of parents who could or would turn their back on their children's entreaties to spend in order to belong. For low-income families, the costs are particularly daunting, for these families are trapped in an endless cycle of consumption in which standards of dignity are constantly being reset by those for whom the burden of provisioning is, for the moment, less onerous. Thus while parents at all income levels participate in consumption for children, low-income parents have no escape from an acquisition treadmill that strains their scarce resources relentlessly. Spending on children's dignity ensnares even middle-class families in a "work-and-spend cycle"; research has found that consumption for children is part of the engine driving the commitment of American parents to their workplaces and, in particular, to their long work hours. Furthermore, parents bemoan an emotional crisis of intimacy and connection and lament the focus on material goods over meaningful interaction.[12]

Ultimately much of the cost is borne by children themselves, however. No matter what kind of an approach adults adopt, children's lives are shaped by the distortions of interpreting belonging and care through commodities and commodified events. If adults capitulate to the demands of dignity, they are offering support to the equation of possessions with meaningful connection, merely staving off for another day the problems of exclusion and alienation. If adults do the "right" thing and eschew consumption (as few were able to), they subject children to the necessary paroxysms of facework or the depressing prospect of social invisibility and exclusion.

Through the economy of dignity, children's emotional lives become suffused with constant reminders of the commodification of care and the pressures of corporate efficiency and rationalism. What adults sometimes understand at the level of abstract concepts becomes for children their daily experience, at the level of powerfully visceral, at times unconscious, feeling. Children live at the convergence of the tectonic plates of social inequality, their daily negotiations part of the small earthquakes of conflict through which such inequality finds expression and release. The costs of consuming for dignity are to be found in its savage intolerance of difference, even the helpless difference born of social inequality, and the terrible allegiance it requires to the tyranny of commodified sameness for all.

NOTES

NOTES TO THE PREFACE

1. For worries about consumer debt and adequacy of income, see Massachusetts Mutual Life Insurance Company, *Family Life Survey* (Springfield, Mass., 1994), Polling the Nations, www.poll.ors.pub.com (accessed February 20, 2006); also see Consumer Federation of America, as cited in Elizabeth Warren, "The Growing Threat to Middle-Class Families" (lecture, National Association of Consumer Bankruptcy Attorneys, 2003), http://www.nacba.org/files/new_in_debate/GrowingThreatMiddleClassFamilies.pdf (accessed November 4, 2007). For concern about values, see Robert Wuthnow, "Pious Materialism: How Americans View Faith and Money," *The Christian Century*, March 3, 1992, 239–42.

2. The survey reporting lamentations about "over-commercialized children" was conducted by the Center for a New American Dream; see Center for a New American Dream, *The New American Dream Poll* (Takoma Park, Md., 2005), http://www.newdream.org/about/poll.php (accessed March 30, 2006).

NOTES TO CHAPTER ONE

1. All names of people and institutions, including some of their identifying details, have been changed to preserve their confidentiality.

2. McNeal, a marketing expert and publisher of many books on children and consumption, is the most common source of estimates of spending related to

children. The 2004 estimate is from his research, reported in Juliet Schor, *Born to Buy: The Commercialized Child and the New Consumer Culture* (New York: Scribner, 2004), 23. McNeal's triumphant assessment is found in his 2007 book, *On Becoming a Consumer: Development of Consumer Behavior Patterns in Childhood* (Burlington, Mass.: Butterworth-Heinemann), 5. U.S. government estimates of child-rearing costs are annually furnished by Mark Lino of the U.S. Department of Agriculture, based on extrapolations from 1990 Consumer Expenditure Survey data; this estimate was reported in Mark Lino, "USDA's Expenditures on Children by Families Project: Uses and Changes over Time," *Family Economics and Nutrition Review* 13, no. 1 (Winter 2001): 81–86. The *Wall Street Journal*, while focused on elite spending, was able to update the USDA numbers with data on more contemporary purchases for children, such as cell phones, iTunes, and $900 strollers, none of which existed in 1990; see Eileen Daspin and Ellen Gamerman, "The Million-Dollar Kid," *Wall Street Journal*, March 3, 2007, http://online.wsj.com/public/article-print/SB117288281789725533.html (accessed June 14, 2007). For the "commodity frontier," see Arlie Hochschild, *The Commercialization of Intimate Life* (Berkeley: University of California Press, 2003), 35–36.

3. I define consumer culture, following Slater, as a "social arrangement . . . by which meaningful ways of life and the resources upon which they depend" take place in and through the market; see Don Slater, *Consumer Culture and Modernity* (Cambridge and Malden, Mass.: Polity Press, 1997), 8. Throughout this work I use the terms *consumer culture* and *commercial culture* interchangeably to mean this system of meanings and exchange; I also use the terms *commodification, commercialization*, and *marketization* to mean the same transformative process by which consumer culture is increasingly implicated in experiences such as childhood. The psychological and physical problems of commercialized children are reported in Schor, *Born to Buy*. See also Susan Linn, *Consuming Kids: The Hostile Takeover of Childhood* (New York and London: The New Press, 2004); *San Francisco Chronicle*, "Reclaiming Childhood," editorial, March 30, 2003; Pamela Paul, *Parenting, Inc.* (New York: Times Books, 2008).

4. Ellen Seiter argued that middle-class discomfort with children's taste was behind parents' anticommercial sentiment; see Ellen Seiter, *Sold Separately: Children and Parents in Consumer Culture* (New Brunswick, N.J.: Rutgers University Press, 1993). See also David Buckingham, *After the Death of Childhood* (Cambridge and Malden, Mass.: Polity Press, 2000); Dan Cook, *The Commodification of Childhood: The Children's Clothing Industry and the Rise of the Child Consumer* (Durham, N.C.: Duke University Press, 2004); and Gary Cross, *Kids'*

Stuff: Toys and the Changing World of American Childhood (Cambridge, Mass.: Harvard University Press, 1997).

5. For "divorce culture," see Karla Hackstaff, *Marriage in a Divorce Culture* (Philadelphia: Temple University Press, 1999).

6. For the "economy of gratitude," see Arlie Hochschild, with Anne Machung, *The Second Shift* (New York: Avon Books, 1989).

7. The idea that people are motivated by the urge to belong is grounded in the Durkheimian notion of the sacredness of communal feeling. Yet "interest theory," with its emphasis on competitive individualism, has been far more influential for contemporary scholars looking for a "rational actor" model. While I sketch the outlines of belonging as motivation here, elsewhere I expound upon the model as a possible compromise between a psychologizing that feels presumptive to many contemporary social scientists, and a view of the person as a rather sterile collection of interests, which is "clearly far too narrow," in Sherry Ortner's phrase, in its exclusion of a whole range of emotional terms. In addition, there is a developing consensus among psychologists that the need to belong is a universal human need, and a trove of educational research on how students' sense of belonging leads to a host of positive outcomes. In her extensive review of the literature, Karen Osterman concluded: "Findings are strong and consistent: Students who experience acceptance are more highly motivated and engaged in learning and more committed to school." See Allison Pugh, "The Economy of Dignity: Children's Culture and Consumer Desires" (under review). Sherry Ortner's critique of interest theory is found in her seminal article: "Theory in Anthropology since the Sixties," *Society for Contemporary Study of Society and History* 26 (1984): 126–66. See also Karen Osterman, "Students' Need for Belonging in the School Community," *Review of Educational Research*, 70, no. 3 (2000): 359. For the definition "the quality or state of being worthy," see *The Merriam-Webster Online Dictionary*, s.v. "dignity," http://www.merriam-webster.com/dictionary/dignity (accessed June 7, 2007). Amartya Sen, "The Possibility of Social Choice," *The American Economic Review* 89, no. 3 (1999): 361–62.

8. Words other than "dignity," I think, simply do not work as well to capture this fundamental humanity. "Honor," for example, evokes a more rarefied pleasure, one involving earned elevation above the rest. "Respect," in Richard Sennett's sense of "taking the needs of others seriously," is nearer the mark, but it falls short by attending more to the social interaction of providing and getting respect than to a particular state of worthiness that children seek (and such a state is oddly shrunken by the term "respectable"). And while "status" as it is

conventionally understood conveys the competitive ranking children (and other consumers) surely do sometimes seek, it ignores what I found prevalent: children's longing simply to engage each other, to be a full member, to belong in their social world. Randall Collins turns to "status" to convey the experience of belonging or not belonging but takes care to emphasize that his more restrictive definition differs from the "general term for hierarchical differences of all kinds." In *Interaction Ritual Chains,* Collins usefully explores the capacity of interaction rituals to forge group membership. Murray Milner applied a theory of status relations to teenagers and consumer culture, arguing that teenagers are intensely preoccupied with status because "they are excluded from meaningful forms of economic and political power." While this powerlessness is true as well of the children I studied, we might not expect elementary students to have much in the way of real economic or political efficacy. Yet perhaps because they, too, lacked other means of evaluating each other, they were also preoccupied by the ephemera of consumer culture and its capacity to determine who belonged. See Richard Sennett, *Respect in a World of Inequality* (New York: W. W. Norton, 2003), 52; Randall Collins, *Interaction Ritual Chains* (Princeton, N.J.: Princeton University Press, 2004), 115; and Murray Milner, Jr., *Freaks, Geeks, and Cool Kids: American Teenagers, Schools, and the Culture of Consumption* (New York: Routledge, 2004), 184. For "gain the esteem and envy," see Thorstein Veblen, *The Theory of the Leisure Class* (1899; repr., New York: Dover Publications, 1994), 21. For an excellent essay about honor, see Hans Speier, "Honor and Social Structure," *Social Research* 2 (1935): 74–97.

9. Erving Goffman coined the term "facework" to mean particular conversational rituals—such as apologies, as well as displays of deference and poise—that people employ to patch over the mutual embarrassment from an interactional stumble. Always intrigued by the seemingly orderly flow of everyday affairs, Goffman sought to document the backstage action, to reveal the active but thoughtless way in which people managed normalcy. He was less interested in the people inhabiting these interactions. My use of "facework" borrows from Goffman but shifts our focus to the selves doing the feeling. As I develop further in chapter 2, facework, then, is the effort people make not to preserve the conversational flow, but rather to achieve and preserve their own standing in entering that flow in the first place. See Erving Goffman, *Interaction Ritual: Essays on Face-to-Face Behavior* (New York: Anchor Books, 1967) .

10. Knowing what counts as a token of value is half of the battle. As the British writer Don Slater observed, "by knowing and using the codes of consumption of my own culture, I reproduce and demonstrate my membership of a

particular social order." Slater, *Consumer Culture and Modernity*, 132. Facework demands that children do more than just *identify* the symbolic scrip, however; as we see in chapter 3, to achieve dignity they must be able to enact that knowledge at the very least through strategies such as Simon's and Marco's.

11. Still relevant nearly ninety years later, Sinclair Lewis's *Babbitt* (New York: Harcourt Brace Jovanovich, 1922) is a study of conformity and the social anxiety it simultaneously arouses and soothes; see p. 186 for Babbitt's concern for his son Ted. The national survey of 1,000 parents found a smaller proportion than I did of what I call responsive parents, who nonetheless included the majority of care-givers in the sample (the proportion increased to 58 percent of parents with chil-dren thirteen–seventeen years old). My small, qualitative sample is not designed to measure the breadth of a particular trend, but rather to excavate the meanings and processes at work. Nonetheless, I would argue that requiring responsive par-ents to tell a stranger they agreed with a statement beginning "Against my better judgment" in all likelihood yields results that underrepresent their numbers among the rest of the population. See Massachusetts Mutual Life Insurance Company, *Family Life Survey* (Springfield, Mass., 1995), Polling the Nations, www.poll.ors.pub.com (accessed November 7, 2007).

12. Goffman is once again relevant here—his intense and creative focus on interaction is compelling, although he paid only scattered attention to issues of consumption. See Erving Goffman, *Stigma: Notes on the Management of Spoiled Identity* (New York: Simon and Schuster, 1963). Goffman outlined three kinds of stigma—body stigma, character stigma, and tribal stigma; my three kinds of dif-ference are related to, but not the same as, his typology. First, I prefer to remain in the realm of "difference" rather than stigma, because while some differences do carry a polluting charge, inspiring parents to shield their children from them or to treat them so that they might be cured, other differences have a positive valence, although one that still leads parents to spend. Second, I conflate the notion of embodied stigma and character stigma in "personal" differences because these animate consumption in the same way, as enduring individual problems or gifts that generate their own consumer responses, particularly among the affluent. Third, my notion of interactional differences seeks to capture the fleeting, momentary character of difference and commonality established in children's everyday conversations, conversations that are themselves shaped, but not wholly determined, by longer-lasting personal and social differences. Affluent children, for example, sometimes felt the surprise of not having the item that other children were discussing; their affluence did not always protect them from the shock of dif-ference. Goffman was deeply interested in interaction, of course; his study of

stigma attended to how personal and social differences are handled in everyday discourse. A principal focus of this study, however, are those momentary differences of possession and experience that interaction throws into relief.

13. Michel Maffesoli analyzed how consumers want not to conform but actually to be "different from the Joneses." See Michel Maffesoli, *The Time of the Tribes: The Decline of Individualism in Mass Society* (London: Sage, 1995). While his argument may certainly apply to adults, particularly upper-income ones, my research provides evidence that some children, even upper-income ones, want first to belong. Randall Collins's work *Interaction Ritual Chains* suggests some reasons, beyond developmental psychology, why this might be the case (see chapter 3, note 7).

14. For a thorough accounting of low-income caregivers' attempts to provide, see Kathryn Edin and Laura Lein, *Making Ends Meet: How Single Mothers Survive Welfare and Low-Wage Work* (New York: Russell Sage Foundation, 1997). Several scholars have documented the powerful, painful draw of the panoply of American consumer goods for low-income children and their families; see especially Elizabeth Chin, *Purchasing Power: Black Kids and American Consumer Culture* (Minneapolis: University of Minnesota Press, 2001); and Carl Nightingale, *On The Edge: A History of Poor Black Children and Their American Dreams* (New York: Basic Books, 1993).

15. For "agents of materialism," see Robert Wuthnow, "Pious Materialism: How Americans View Faith and Money," *The Christian Century*, March 3, 1992, 239–42. Regarding bloggers, Google blog searches on June 12, 2007, found 8,955 blogs for the search "children video games addicted," 1,633 for "children materialism consumer," and 19,167 for "kids consumerism." Writers on the psychological costs of materialism include Schor, *Born to Buy*; Linn, *Consuming Kids*; and Tim Kasser, "Frugality, Generosity, and Materialism in Children and Adolescents," in *What Do Children Need to Flourish? Conceptualizing and Measuring Indicators of Positive Development*, ed. K. A. Moore and L. H. Lippman, 357–74 (New York: Springer Science, 2005). For the transformation of childhood into "consumerhood," see *San Francisco Chronicle*, "Reclaiming Childhood."

16. Buckingham, *After the Death of Childhood*, 165. One study depicting materialistic parents who buy too much for their children is Joanna Higginson, "Competitive Parenting: The Culture of Teen Mothers," *Journal of Marriage and the Family* 60, no. 1 (1998): 135–49. Scholars who argue that consumerist childhoods reflect consumerist adulthoods include Christine Williams, *Inside Toyland: Working, Shopping, and Social Inequality* (Berkeley: University of California Press, 2005); Cook, *Commodification of Childhood*; and Lizabeth Cohen, *A*

Consumer's Republic: The Politics of Mass Consumption in Postwar America (New York: Knopf, 2003). See Cook, *Commodification of Childhood*, 6.

17. See Cate Doty and Rachel Thorner, "18 Shopping Bags and 3 Empty Wallets," *New York Times*, November 27, 2004. For the emerging trend of giving babies brand names, see BBC World News, "U.S. Babies Get Global Brand Names," 2003, http://news.bbc.co.uk/2/hi/americas/3268161.stm (accessed November 9, 2007).

18. Elizabeth Chin coined the term "combat consumers" in her ethnography *Purchasing Power*. Stories of the largest yacht are from Robert Frank, *Luxury Fever: Why Money Fails to Satisfy in an Era of Excess* (New York, Free Press, 1999). Frank also quotes a profile of two brothers building a fantasy castle in East Hampton; see "Alan Wilzig," *New York Times Magazine*, August 17, 1997.

19. Benjamin Barber suggested poverty insulated poor families in his book *Consumed: How Markets Corrupt Children, Infantilize Adults, and Swallow Citizens Whole* (New York: W. W. Norton, 2007), 9. An important 1988 study by Lazear and Michael reported that children's proportion of household spending actually *declined* as household income increased, and a team of London researchers recently concurred. Researcher Thierry Kochuyt confirmed this insight with a Belgian sample, arguing that low-income parents created "artificial affluence" for their children, restricting, delaying, or minimizing some parental needs so as to satisfy the desires of their children. "What people consume is not the family income divided by the number of relatives," Kochuyt wrote, arguing that child-rearing consumption should be thought of as a gift that cements family ties. He also cites Dutch research demonstrating that "the giving of goods and money to the children is relatively more important among lower income categories. They give almost 84% of what the higher incomes give, which comes down to a much higher portion of their revenues." See Thierry Kochuyt, "Giving Away One's Poverty: On the Consumption of Scarce Resources within the Family," *The Sociological Review* 52, no. 2 (2004): 139–61; see pp. 145 and 149 for the quotes. Also see Edward P. Lazear and Robert T. Michael, *Allocation of Income within the Household* (Chicago: University of Chicago Press, 1988); Robin Douthitt, "An Evaluation of the Relationship between the Percentage-of-Income Standard and Family Expenditures for Children," (discussion paper, Institute for Research on Poverty, University of Wisconsin-Madison, 1990), 921–90, as cited in Ingrid Rothe, Judith Cassetty, and Elizabeth Boehnen, "Estimates of Family Expenditures for Children: A Review Of The Literature," *Institute for Research on Poverty*, April 2001, http://www.irp.wisc.edu/research/childsup/cspolicy/csprpubs.htm (accessed November 9, 2007); and M. Brewer, A. Goodman, and

A. Leicester, "Household Spending in Britain: What Can It Teach Us about Poverty?" *Institute for Fiscal Studies Report,* http://www.ifs.org.uk/publications .php?publication_id = 3620 (accessed November 9, 2007). Recently, however, Plassmann and Norton found that while low- and middle-income families spent about the same proportion of income on children, upper-income families spend about 15 percent more. They found wide variations by ethnicity, so that for some families on the edge of poverty that are Hispanic or white, the children are poor and the adults are not, while for some that are African- or Asian-American, the adults are poor, but the children are not. Further research is needed to parse out these racial/ethnic differences. See Vandana Plassmann and Marjorie Norton, "Child-Adult Expenditure Allocation by Ethnicity," *Family and Consumer Sciences Research Journal* 33, no. 1 (2004): 475–97. For the "bulletproof" market, see Michael McDermott, "Kid's Market Is a Small World with Franchise Opportunities," *The Franchise Handbook,* Summer 2006, http://www.franchise .com/articles/Kid's Market_Is_a_Small_World_with_Franchise_Opportunities _149.asp (accessed June 23, 2008).

20. Adam Smith, *The Wealth of Nations* (1776; repr., New York: Bantam Dell, 2003), 1103.

21. The term "strange situation" refers to studies of mother-child attachment, in which psychologists would watch what would happen when babies were left and rejoined by their mothers. I use it here to point out how similarly staged are many experimental research designs, which often exclude any measure of the social world in their assessment of children's susceptibility to ads. Other scholars depict children as active, resistant, and creative in their reinterpretations of corporate messages. Children are not passive consumers of advertising, these scholars argue, but healthy cynics, regarding corporate efforts to persuade them askance, mocking or modifying claims for their own purposes. While this research offers a fuller view of the child, it remains focused, like an interrogation spotlight, on the individual child and his or her stance toward advertising. The discovery of the child as "wise consumer" is but the flip side of the discovery of the child as particularly malleable; both are animated by the central question of how TV advertising affects children, and mostly reliant on the same expose-then-ask sort of methodology. See Buckingham, *After the Death of Childhood,* 150–55, for a cogent discussion of the debate about pure children versus wise consumers. For an excellent review of research on children and advertising, see Deborah Roedder John, "Consumer Socialization of Children: A Retrospective Look at Twenty-five Years of Research," *Journal of Consumer Research* 26, no. 3 (1999): 183–213. See also Schor, *Born to Buy;* Chin,

Purchasing Power; Cross, *Kids' Stuff;* Michael Schudson, *Advertising: The Uneasy Persuasion* (New York: Basic Books, 1984); Sharon Zukin, *Point of Purchase: How Shopping Changed American Culture* (New York: Routledge, 2004); Laurel Graham, "Beyond Manipulation: Lillian Gilbreth's Industrial Psychology and the Governmentality of Women Consumers," *The Sociological Quarterly* 38, no. 4 (1997): 539–65; Linn, *Consuming Kids;* Barber, *Consumed;* Stephen Kline, *Out of the Garden: Toys, TV, and Children's Culture in the Age of Marketing* (New York: Verso, 1993); and Cook, *Commodification of Childhood.*

22. Children's time spent with media was examined in a national study by the Kaiser Family Foundation. See Victoria Rideout, Donald Roberts, and Ulla Foehr, "Generation M: Media in the Lives of 8–18 Year-Olds," http://www.kff .org/entmedia/entmedia030905pkg.cfm (accessed November 9, 2007). See also E. A. Vandewater, D. S. Bickham, and J. H. Lee, "Time Well Spent? Relating Television Use to Children's Free Time Activities," *Pediatrics* 117 (2006): 181–90. E. B. White's observation is found in his 1950 science-fiction story "The Morning of the Day They Did It," reprinted in *The Second Tree from the Corner* (New York: Harper and Row, 1978), 69.

23. This view echoes the premise behind *Babbit*, in which Sinclair Lewis wrote: "So did the large national advertisers fix the surface of his life, fix what he believed to be his individuality. These standard advertised wares—toothpastes, socks, tires, cameras, instantaneous hot-water heaters—were his symbols and proofs of excellence; at first the signs, then the substitutes, for joy and passion and wisdom." *Babbit*, 80–81. Advertisers know, of course, that it is not so easy. As Milner noted in his study of teenage cultures of consumption, "most people were not influenced by impersonal messages, but by the opinions of people they knew and interacted with." See Milner, *Freaks, Geeks, and Cool Kids*, 167. Similarly, Martens urges us to look beyond the market for how children learn about consumption; she suggests parents' influence has been underestimated, but also recommends that we consider "the broader networks of social relationships that envelop a child who grows up in a consumer world." See Lydia Martens, "Learning to Consume—Consuming to Learn: Children at the Interface between Consumption and Education," *British Journal of Sociology of Education* 26, no. 3 (2005): 343–57; see p. 350 for the quote.

24. For thousands of years, ever since sumptuary laws attempted to regulate consumption so as to weed out those pretenders to the elite, we have understood consumption as a sort of stratifying practice, a means of distinguishing ourselves from others, most often from others below. Pierre Bourdieu argued that early consumption shapes tastes, which are ranked hierarchically as a form of "symbolic

violence." See Pierre Bourdieu, *Distinction: A Social Critique of the Judgement of Taste*, trans. Richard Nice (Cambridge, Mass.: Harvard University Press, 1984). Bourdieu's ideas updated the important work of Veblen and Mauss, who demonstrated the display work consumption performed for spenders in advanced countries as well as more primitive societies; see Veblen, *Theory of the Leisure Class*; Marcel Mauss, *The Gift: Forms and Functions of Exchange in Archaic Societies*, trans. Ian Cunnison (New York: Norton, 1967). Zelizer's "connected lives" argument is presented in Viviana Zelizer, *The Purchase of Intimacy* (Princeton, N.J.: Princeton University Press, 2004). For "the material culture of love," see Daniel Miller, *A Theory of Shopping* (Ithaca, N.Y.: Cornell University Press, 1998). For Zukin's observation about "the things we need to buy," see Zukin, *Point of Purchase*, 30. For parent buying due to increasing work hours, see Arlie Hochschild, *The Time Bind* (New York: Metropolitan Books, 1997); and Craig Thompson, "Caring Consumers: Gendered Consumption Meanings and the Juggling Lifestyle," *Journal of Consumer Research* 22, no. 4 (1996): 388–407; due to children's defiance, see Theodore Caplow, "Christmas Gifts and Kin Networks," *American Sociological Review* 47, no. 3 (June 1982): 383–92; due to divorce, see Allison Pugh, "From Compensation to Childhood Wonder: Why Parents Buy" (Working Paper No. 39, Center for Working Families, University of California, Berkeley, 2002); due to the strains of poverty, see Edin and Lein, *Making Ends Meet*; and Elaine Power, "Freedom and Belonging through Consumption: The Disciplining of Desire in Single Mothers on Welfare" (paper presented to the British Sociological Association Annual Conference, University of York, 2003).

25. Other research into the ways in which consumption can be sharply divisive due to income includes Juliet Schor, *The Overspent American: Upscaling, Downshifting, and the New Consumer* (New York: Basic Books, 1998); Williams, *Inside Toyland*; Zygmunt Bauman, *Work, Consumerism, and the New Poor* (Buckingham and Philadelphia: Open University Press, 1998); Gary Cross, *An All-Consuming Century: Why Commercialism Won in Modern America* (New York: Columbia University Press, 2000); and Cohen, *Consumer's Republic*. For research on how consumption connects and separates, see Zelizer, *Purchase of Intimacy*; Thompson, "Caring Consumers"; David Cheal, *The Gift Economy* London and New York: Routledge, 1998); and Allison Pugh, "Selling Compromise: Toys, Motherhood, and the Cultural Deal," *Gender & Society* 19, no. 6 (2005): 729–49. See Eva Illouz, *Cold Intimacies: The Making of Emotional Capitalism* (Malden, Mass.: Polity Press, 2007), 91.

26. Three books by Hochschild examine these themes: for the impact of women's twin responsibilities of working and caring on family life, see

Hochschild, *Second Shift;* for outsourcing as an outgrowth of overwork, see Hochschild, *Time Bind;* and for the intersections of economic and family life, see essays in Hochschild, *Commercialization of Intimate Life.* Quotes in this paragraph are from the latter book:p. 143 of the essay "From the Frying Pan into the Fire"; p. 209 of the essay "Emotional Geography and Capitalism."

27. Viviana Zelizer, "Culture and Consumption," in *The Handbook of Economic Sociology,* ed. Neil Smelser and Richard Swedberg, 349 (Princeton, N.J.: Princeton University Press; New York: Russell Sage Foundation, 2005).

28. Nina Eliasoph and Paul Lichterman's work on culture-in-interaction is a compelling rendition of culture as group norms and expectations, made concrete through daily interaction; see Nina Eliasoph and Paul Lichterman, "Culture in Interaction," *American Journal of Sociology* 108, no. 4 (2003): 735–94. For "tastes," see Douglas B. Holt, "Does Cultural Capital Structure American Consumption?" *Journal of Consumer Research* 25 (June 1998): 1–25; see p. 19 for the quote. See Bourdieu, *Distinction;* and Seiter, *Sold Separately.* Annette Lareau's work explored the implications of class differences in child rearing: see Annette Lareau, *Unequal Childhoods* (Berkeley: University of California Press, 2003).

29. Patricia Adler and Peter Adler, *Peer Power* (New Brunswick, N.J.: Rutgers University Press, 1998), 206; John, "Consumer Socialization of Children," 206; Lydia Martens, Dale Southerton, and Sue Scott, "Bringing Children (and Parents) into the Sociology of Consumption: Towards a Theoretical and Empirical Agenda," *Journal of Consumer Culture* 4 (2004): 155–82; see pp. 158 and 175 for the quotes.

30. For examples of research on adolescents, see Randi Waerdahl, "Learning by Consuming: Consumer Culture as a Condition for Socialization and Everyday Life at the Age of 12" (diss., Department of Sociology and Human Geography, University of Oslo, 2003); Milner, *Freaks, Geeks, and Cool Kids;* Rosaleen Croghan, Christine Griffin, Janeen Hunter, and Ann Phoenix, "Style Failure: Consumption, Identity, and Social Exclusion." *Journal of Youth Studies* 9, no. 4 (2006): 463–78. For work uncovering the crucial sense of belonging, see Bernadine Chee, "Eating Snacks, Biting Pressure: Only Children in Beijing," in *Feeding China's Little Emperors: Food, Children, and Social Change,* ed. Jun Jing (Stanford, Calif.: Stanford University Press, 2000); David J. Jamison, "Idols of the Tribe: Brand Veneration and Group Identity among Pre-Adolescent Consumers" (working paper, Department of Marketing, University of Florida, Gainesville, 1996), as cited in John, "Consumer Socialization of Children," 194; and Sue Middleton, Karl Ashworth, and Robert Walker, *Family Fortunes: Pressures on Parents and Children in the 1990s* (London: Child Poverty Action Group,

1994). The British study is reported in Mark Ritson and Richard Elliott, "The Social Uses of Advertising: An Ethnographic Study of Adolescent Advertising Audiences," *Journal of Consumer Research* 26 (December 1999): 260–77; see pp. 265–66 for the quote. For "I have to try new things," see Chee, "Eating Snacks, Biting Pressure," 34.

31. Steven Mintz, *Huck's Raft: A History of American Childhood* (Cambridge, Mass.: Harvard University Press, Belknap Press, 2004), 381; Barrie Thorne, "The Crisis of Care," in *Work-Family Challenges for Low-Income Parents and Their Children*, ed. Nan Crouter and Alan Booth, 165–78 (Hillsdale, N.J.: Lawrence Erlbaum Publishers, 2004).

32. John Gillis, *A World of Their Own Making: Myth, Ritual, and the Quest for Family Values* (New York: Basic Books, 1996). A fulsome study of the withering of community bonds can be found in Robert D. Putnam, *Bowling Alone: The Collapse and Revival of American Community* (New York: Simon & Schuster, 2001). A veritable industry of social science catalogs the rates of single parenthood and the movement of women into the paid workforce; for the effects of these trends on children, see Sara McLanahan, "Diverging Destinies: How Children Fare under the Second Demographic Transition," *Demography* 41, no. 4 (2004): 607–27.

33. Children's increasing shopping participation is documented by McNeal, *On Becoming a Consumer*; and Barrie Gunter and Adrian Furnham, *Children as Consumers* (New York and London: Routledge, 1998). For "the romance of your child's childhood," see Adam Gopnik, *Paris to the Moon* (New York: Random House, 2001), 167.

34. Lareau's work *Unequal Childhoods* contributed to and inspired my own research, particularly in its compelling demonstration of how something as abstract, even theoretical, as social structure can exert powerful force in children's daily lives. Her research design molded her findings in important ways, however. For example, because she studied individual families chosen for their particular demographic features rather than a group of families within a community, she finds that class trumps race, rather than investigating its overlapping features, and she downplays the social nature of childhood and parenthood, the comparing, networking, and research tasks families conduct within their communities. Her student Patricia Berhau analyzed the consumption behavior of the same set of families, with the intriguing finding that *how* families bought things differed by class even when *what* they were buying did not; her work similarly steers clear of the social world, children's peer culture, and how parents come to decide what to buy, however. See Lareau, *Unequal Childhoods*; Sharon Hays, *The Cultural Contradictions of Motherhood* (New Haven, Conn.: Yale Uni-

versity Press, 1996); and Patricia Berhau, "Class and the Experience of Consumers: A Study of Practices of Acquisition" (diss., Temple University, 2000). For the wider impact of middle-class parenting trends, see, in addition to Lareau's work, Sara Ruddick, "Care as Labor and Relationship," in *Norms and Values: Essays in Honor of Virginia Held*, ed. Joram G. Haber and Mark S. Halfon, 3–25 (Oxford: Rowman and Littlefield, 1998). Viviana Zelizer documented children's historical transition from economically useful to emotionally priceless in *Pricing the Priceless Child* (New York: Basic Books, 1985).

35. U.S. Department of Health and Human Services, "Trends in the Well-Being of Children and Youth," 2003, http://aspe.hhs.gov/HSP/03trends/ (accessed February 23, 2008); Suzanne Bianchi, "Feminization and Juvenilization of Poverty: Trends, Relative Risks, Causes and Consequences," *Annual Review of Sociology* 25 (1999): 324.

36. For state spending, see Paul W. Newacheck and A. E. Benjamin, "Intergenerational Equity and Public Spending," *Health Affairs* 23, no. 5 (2004): 142–47; see p. 2 for the quote. For federal spending, see Susmita Pati, Ron Keren, Evaline A. Alessandrini, and Donald F. Schwartz, "Generational Differences in U.S. Public Spending, 1980–2000," *Health Affairs* S23, no. 5 (2004): 131–42.

37. Tellingly, urban theorists call this public provisioning a form of "collective consumption." For Katz's observation, see Cindi Katz, "Vagabond Capitalism and the Necessity of Social Reproduction," *Antipode* 33, no. 4 (2001): 725.

38. On inequality in net worth, earnings, and resources, see Michael Hout, "Money and Morale: What Growing Inequality Is Doing to Americans' View of Themselves and Others," (working paper, Survey Research Center, University of California, Berkeley, 2003), http://ucdata.berkeley.edu/rsfcensus/papers/ Morale_Working_Paper.pdf; Claude Fischer and Michael Hout, "Differences among Americans in Living Standards across the Twentieth Century" (working paper, Survey Research Center, University of California, Berkeley, 2002), http://ucdata.berkeley.edu/rsfcensus/papers/livingstandards.pdf (cited with permission); Daniel Lichter, "Poverty and Inequality among Children," *Annual Review of Sociology* 23 (1997): 121–45; Susan Mayer, "How Did the Increase in Economic Inequality Affect Educational Attainment?" *American Journal of Sociology* 107, no. 1 (2001):1–32; and Robert Haveman, Gary Sandefur, Barbara Wolfe, and Andrea Voyer, "Inequality of Family and Community Characteristics in Relation to Children's Attainments" (working paper, Russell Sage Foundation, 2001), http://www.russellsage.org/programs/proj_reviews/si/revhaveman01 .pdf. For the disparity in children's economic resources, see Gregory Acs and

Megan Gallagher, "Income Inequality among America's Children," Urban Institute, Washington, D.C., 2000, http://www.urban.org/url.cfm?ID=309307; and Daniel Lichter and D. J. Eggebeen, "Rich Kids, Poor Kids: Changing Income Inequality among American Children," *Social Forces* 71 (1993): 761–80.

39. Sharon Hays, "Structure, Agency, and the Sticky Problem of Culture," *Sociological Theory* 12 (1994): 57–72; see p. 65 for the quote. Scholars who emphasize the process behind making meaning—at once creating anew and reproducing modes of acting—include Sherry Ortner, William Sewell, and Ann Swidler. See Sherry Ortner, *High Religion: A Cultural and Political History of Sherpa Buddhism* (Princeton, N.J.: Princeton University Press, 1989); William Sewell, "A Theory of Structure—Duality, Agency, and Transformation." *American Journal Of Sociology* 98, no. 1 (July 1992): 1–29; and Ann Swidler, "Culture in Action: Symbols and Strategies," *American Sociological Review* 51 (April 1986): 273–86.

40. A tradition of psychoanalytic social science investigates that bridge between the personal and the social; see Nancy Chodorow, *The Power of Feelings: Personal Meaning in Psychoanalysis, Gender, and Culture* (New Haven, Conn.: Yale University Press, 1999); and Jean L. Briggs, *Inuit Morality Play: The Emotional Education of a Three-Year-Old* (New Haven, Conn.: Yale University Press, 1998). Sociologists often juxtapose "culture" and "structure," with the former representing the softer world of beliefs, values, and rituals, while the latter comprises the institutions (such as education, religion, family, the state) and social categories (such as race, class, gender, sexuality) that shape the choices and trajectories of individuals. As Sharon Hays has argued compellingly, however, collective ideas of social meaning can shape our sense of what is possible and desirable just as forcefully as the rules and regulations of schools or the political system. See Hays, "Structure, Agency, and the Sticky Problem of Culture." See also Collins, *Interaction Ritual Chains*.

41. For the phrase "organization of human existence," see Sherry Ortner, *Making Gender: The Politics and Erotics of Culture* (Boston: Beacon Press, 1996), 12. The notion that people of widely varying socioeconomic status share cultural values but diverge in the structured pathways available to them echoes a theme explored in Robert Merton's famous 1949 essay "Social Structure and Anomie," in *Social Theory and Social Structure*, 185–214 (1949; repr., New York: Free Press, 1968). Thanks to an anonymous reviewer for the reference.

42. For the increasing work hours of families with children, see Michael Hout and Caroline Hanley, "Working Hours and Inequality, 1968–2001: A Family Perspective on Recent Controversies." (working paper, Survey Research Center, University of California, Berkeley, 2003), http://www.russellsage.org/

publications/workingpapers/workinghrsineq/document(accessed November 4, 2007). For the debt load of married families with children, see Elizabeth Warren and Amelia Warren Tyagi, *The Two-Income Trap* (New York: Basic Books, 2003). See Kochuyt, "Giving Away One's Poverty"; Edin and Lein, *Making Ends Meet;* and Power, "Freedom and Belonging through Consumption."

43. See Marianne Cooper, "Made-to-Order Lives: Upper-Income Families in the New Economy" (Presentation at American Sociological Association, Montreal, 2006).

44. Similarly, in her study of how working couples sort out the second shift, Hochschild argues that the "saddest cost" for women is that they had to implement the speed-up of their own families, and thus bear the emotional fallout—"Mom is always rushing us"—from a system in which they were also the primary victims. See Hochschild, *Second Shift.*

NOTES TO CHAPTER TWO

1. For income inequality in Oakland, see Edward P. Lazear and Angie Rodgers, "Income Inequality in the District of Columbia Is Wider Than in Any Major U.S. City," DC Fiscal Policy Institute, July 23, 2004; and Neena Murgai, "Oakland Health Profile 2004," Alameda County Public Health Department, Oakland, 2005, http://www.acphd.org. For wages data, see Howard Greenwhich and Christopher Niedt, "Decade of Divide: Working, Wages, and Inequality in the East Bay," East Bay Alliance for a Sustainable Economy, Oakland, 2001, http://www.workingeastbay.org/pdf/decade.pdf.

2. Robert O. Self, *American Babylon: Race and the Struggle for Postwar Oakland* (Princeton, N.J.: Princeton University Press, 2003), 21.

3. For Oakland poverty rates for children, see Murgai, "Oakland Health Profile 2004." For school data on Oakland's children, see Ed-Data, "Education Data Partnership: California Public School Enrollment in 2004–2005," http://www.ed-data.k12.ca.us (accessed February 20, 2006). The Annie E. Casey Foundation ranks the nation's fifty largest cities on several different indicators of children's problems, including child poverty, teen dropouts, children without a vehicle in the home, and so on. While Oakland ranked in the bottom half for all of these, other cities ranked far worse for such measures as rates of single parenthood, whether or not the child had a telephone in the home, and percentage of teenagers not working or attending school. For these measures as well as data on adult employment in children's homes, see Annie E. Casey Foundation, *City and Rural Kids Count*

Data Book (Baltimore, 2005), http://www.aecf.org/publications/data/city_rural
_databook.pdf.

4. For "apartheid schools," see Erica Frankenberg and Chungmei Lee, *Race in American Public Schools: Rapidly Resegregating School Districts* (Cambridge, Mass.: The Civil Rights Project, Harvard University, 2002). For an excellent discussion of the dilemmas of Oakland public schools, see Pedro Noguera, "Racial Isolation, Poverty, and the Limits of Local Control in Oakland," *Teachers College Record* 106 no. 11 (2004): 2146–70.

5. Juliet Schor, *Born to Buy: The Commercialized Child and the New Consumer Culture* (New York: Scribner, 2004); Allison James and Alan Prout, "Strategies and Structures: A New Perspective on Children's Experiences of Family Life," in *Children in Families: Research and Policy*, ed. Julia Brannen and Margaret O'Brien, 41–52 (London and Washington, D.C.: Falmer Press). For "unrelated talking heads," see Sherry Ortner, *New Jersey Dreaming: Capital, Culture, and the Class of '58.* (Durham, N.C., and London: Duke University Press, 2003), 15.

6. For the quote about treating school truancy "as a criminal case," see Alex Katz, "D.A. Takes on Truant's Parents," *Oakland Tribune*, March 26, 2004.

7. See California Budget Project 2005, "Making Ends Meet: How Much Does It Cost to Raise a Family in California?" Sacramento, November 2005, http://www.cbp.org/pdfs/2005/0509mem.pdf (accessed August 16, 2007).

8. On serving as "a playmate and toy," see Debra Van Ausdale and Joe Feagin, *The First R: How Children Learn Race and Racism* (Lanham, Md.: Rowman and Littlefield, 2001), 40.

9. For exuberance as a demeanor celebrated in African-American culture, see Shirley Hill, *Black Intimacies: A Gender Perspective on Families and Relationship.* (Walnut Creek, Calif.: AltaMira Press, 2005).

10. For the "the least adult role," see Nancy Mandell, "The Least-Adult Role in Studying Children," *Contemporary Ethnography* 16, no. 4 (1988): 433–67. For a careful rendition of how an adult researcher can cultivate a position more on a par with children, see William Corsaro, *Friendship and Peer Culture in the Early Years* (Norwood, N.J.: Ablex Publishing, 1985).

11. The nail polish idea actually came from Illinois sociologist Laurie Schaffner, who used it to help her interviewees, who were teenage runaways, relax. It was not appropriate for my sample, and I abandoned it quickly, because nail polish carried a symbolic charge for some parents—of sexuality, perhaps, or precocious adulthood—that I was not trying to evoke.

12. The lack of any real middle class in my community-based samples is testimony to the extreme housing prices and other cost-of-living pressures, which

served to chase out many people of moderate incomes who were ineligible for state subsidies but unable to afford living in the area without them.

13. See Elizabeth Chin, *Purchasing Power: Black Kids and American Consumer Culture* (Minneapolis: University of Minnesota Press, 2001). For "devotional love," see Daniel Miller, *A Theory of Shopping* (Ithaca, N.Y.: Cornell University Press, 1998).

14. See Robert M. Emerson, Rachel I. Fretz, and Linda L. Shaw, *Writing Ethnographic Fieldnotes* (Chicago: University of Chicago Press, 1995).

15. An intriguing compilation of essays on fieldwork and its ethical, epistemological, and other conundrums is Diane Wolf's *Feminist Dilemmas in Fieldwork* (Boulder, Colo.: Westview Press, 1996). For "the colonizing aspect" of ethnography, see Julie Bettie, *Women without Class* (Berkeley: University of California Press, 2003), 27.

16. Sherry Ortner, "Theory in Anthropology since the Sixties," *Comparative Studies in Society and History* 26 (1984): 143.

NOTES TO CHAPTER THREE

1. Randall Collins, *Interaction Ritual Chains* (Princeton, N.J.: Princeton University Press, 2004), 297.

2. Sharon Zukin and George Ritzer have analyzed the commodified wonder offered by the market, which both deflates and builds enchantment. See Sharon Zukin, *Landscapes of Power: From Detroit to Disney World.* (Berkeley: University of California Press, 1991); and George Ritzer, *Enchanting a Disenchanted World: Revolutionizing the Means of Consumption* (Thousand Oaks, Calif.: Pine Forge Press, 1999).

3. Charles Derber argues that attention is "a fundamental human need" that prevents "the problem of invisibility," which is corrosive for self-esteem, respect, and belonging. What distinguishes societies is "the intensity of the hunger for attention, the ways people compete or cooperate to satisfy it," and how egalitarian or unequal the distribution of attention becomes. See Charles Derber, *The Pursuit of Attention: Power and Ego in Everyday Life* (Oxford: Oxford University Press, 2000), xxiv. Baudrillard contended people buy things to engage in an "active manipulation of signs," in which objects are bought as much for their use as for what they communicate about the owner, or their "sign value." For Veblen, leisure consumption communicated elite standing for the affluent, while Bourdieu postulated that consumption habits are learned so early

as to feel natural, part of one's individual personality, but that they ultimately communicate group membership with important social ramifications. See Jean Baudrillard, *For a Critique of the Political Economy of the Sign*, trans. Charles Levin (St. Louis: Telos, 1972, 1981), 5; Thorstein Veblen, *The Theory of the Leisure Class* (1899; repr., New York: Dover Publications, 1994); Pierre Bourdieu, *Distinction: A Social Critique of the Judgement of Taste*, trans. Richard Nice (Cambridge, Mass.; Harvard University Press, 1984). For consumption as "a criterion for cultural membership," see Michele Lamont, *The Dignity of Working Men* (New York and Cambridge, Mass.: Russell Sage Foundation and Harvard University Press, 2000), 76. Writing of adults, Lamont notes on the same page: "Today, work gives access to consumption, that is, to external signals that one is 'in,' (a bike, new shoes, and later, a car, a house).'"

4. One study found that Israeli children shared treats and other commodified foodstuffs to confer mutual social visibility upon a quite diffuse group membership. "Ritualized sharing signals the social recognition of the party deferred to as included with the domain of one's social world, as having a social identity," wrote author Tamar Katriel. Tamar Katriel, "Bexibudim! Ritualized Sharing among Israeli Children," *Language in Society* 16 (1987): 319. Thanks to an anonymous reviewer for the reference.

5. Many of the quotes and observations in this paragraph come from analysis of Goffman's essay "On Facework" in Erving Goffman, *Interaction Ritual: Essays on Face-to-Face Behavior* (New York: Anchor Books, 1967); see p. 43 for "social life [as] an uncluttered, orderly thing," p. 3 for Goffman's famous line about "moments and their men," and p. 5 for the "line" as people's own "view of the situation." For Sherry Ortner's contention that these are "serious games," see Sherry Ortner, *Making Gender: The Politics and Erotics of Culture* (Boston: Beacon Press, 1996), 12.

6. Goffman, "On Facework," in Goffman, *Interaction Ritual*, 43.

7. Randall Collins's work on "interaction ritual chains" offers some useful insights related to the economy of dignity. Collins would consider the birthday party conversation as a "status ritual," defining status as he does in the particularly restricted sense of inclusion, much as I mean dignity here (see chapter 1, note 8). According to his typology, children's schools generally involve high density and little "diversity," or, as he means the term, little changeover in the cast of characters. These traits encourage situations of high conformity, as well as strong attachment to "reified symbols," in this case, to established forms of scrip such as GameBoys. Thus Collins enables us to understand why children might be more concerned with "keeping up with the Joneses" rather than being

"different from the Joneses"—due to the specific characteristics of schools, which are dense social worlds featuring the same people day after day (see chapter 1, note 13). Like Goffman, Collins emphasizes the situation rather than the actors within it, and he views rituals through the lens of what they contribute to a group—a "successful" ritual generates social solidarity, he contends. His confessedly diffuse central concept also makes it hard to imagine what would not qualify as a "ritual." Still, his theory is complex and powerful, allowing us to explain and perhaps even predict certain characteristics of economies of dignity. See Collins, *Interaction Ritual Chains*, esp. 115–18.

8. In his study of different Little League teams, Gary Alan Fine documents how small groups generate their own forms of scrip, or what he terms "idioculture." Fine argues that cultural forms must have five characteristics: they must be commonly known, usable (not in violation of sacred taboos), functional for group goals, appropriate (in supporting the existing status hierarchy), and triggered by particular events in order for them to form part of a particular group's idioculture. The contestation between Marco and Loretta over what to be thankful for depicts a rather more conflictual process at work than Fine's typology suggests, but in his discussion Fine does emphasize the contested nature of culture creation: "Groups negotiate meanings, and this ongoing negotiation structures the culture of groups." Gary Alan Fine, "Small Groups and Culture Creation: The Idioculture of Little League Baseball Teams," *American Sociological Review* 44, no. 5 (1979): 733–45; see p. 737 for the quote.

9. This emphasis on the popular, the fashionable, is widespread. In Bernadine Chee's report on Beijing children's culture, one girl described a scenario in which the token of value was ice cream. "Once a classmate brought a package of New Continent ice cream to school. I said 'I have not seen this kind before.' She said that the [commercial] market had been selling them for a long time; New Continent was the most famous—how could I not know? After school I went and bought one. It was winter and although it tasted good, I was so cold that my teeth were sore." Bernadine Chee, "Eating Snacks, Biting Pressure: Only Children in Beijing," in *Feeding China's Little Emperors: Food, Children, and Social Change*, ed. Jun Jing, 33 (Stanford, Calif.: Stanford University Press, 2000), 33.

10. The historian Gary Cross has written about how children interpret their social anxieties through consumer culture. See Gary Cross, *The Cute and the Cool: Wondrous Innocence and Modern American Children's Culture* (Oxford: Oxford University Press, 2004).

11. Dignity was at stake in the public high school where Julie Bettie did her fieldwork. She reported that consumption was highly relevant in the

performative dance of class subtexts that she witnessed. The use of light versus dark nail polish, for example, formed part of a "symbolic economy of style" that the working-class Latina and white "prep" girls deployed as part of their identity performances. Observing working-class girls across racial/ethnic lines, Bettie noted: "Through these commodities they created styles and practices that worked as alternative badges of dignity." Julie Bettie, *Women without Class* (Berkeley: University of California Press, 2003), 167.

12. Zygmunt Bauman introduced the concept of the castigation of the poor as "flawed consumers," in Zygmunt Bauman, *Work, Consumerism, and the New Poor* (Buckingham and Philadelphia: Open University Press, 1998).

13. Annette Lareau, *Unequal Childhoods* (Berkeley: University of California Press, 2003), 39.

14. Bernadine Chee's Beijing study offered another example of claiming, in the story of a low-income Chinese boy who had told classmates that he had already tried some popular ice cream. One day, Chee relates, the boy begged his father to go to Wall's Ice Cream, which at 3.50 yuan was a considerable expense for a family that made 100 yuan a month. But the boy had really wanted it, and it was unusual for him to say so. Apparently, "his classmates had asked him [if he had tried Wall's, and the boy has said yes and that it had tasted very good.] The father remarked 'Actually the child had never tried it before. [He was] afraid others would laugh at him. In light of this I had to buy it for the child to taste.'" See Chee, "Eating Snacks, Biting Pressure," 54. For "wanting an item and not just possessing it," see Elizabeth Chin, *Purchasing Power: Black Kids and American Consumer Culture* (Minneapolis: University of Minnesota Press, 2001), 6. For the active role of fantasy in consumption, see Colin Campbell, *The Romantic Ethic and the Spirit of Modern Consumerism* (Oxford and New York: Blackwell, 1987).

15. See Barrie Thorne, "'The Chinese Girls' and 'The Pokémon Kids': Children Negotiating Differences in Urban California" (Paper presented at the conference Global Comings of Age: Youth and the Crisis of Reproduction, School for American Research, Santa Fe, N. Mex, 2005). For "threats to the social bond," see Thomas Scheff, "Shame in Self and Society," *Symbolic Interaction* 26, no. 2 (2003): 239–62; see also Jack Katz, *How Emotions Work* (Chicago: University of Chicago Press, 1999); and Arlene Stein, *Shameless: Sexual Dissidence in American Culture* (New York, New York University Press, 2006). Thorne observed how "free lunch" was the source of some stigma, although she also noted the ways in which children reinterpreted such badges of inequality. See Barrie Thorne, "Unpacking School Lunchtime: Structure, Practice, and the Negotiation of Difference," in *Developmental Pathways through Middle Childhood:*

Rethinking Contexts and Diversity as Resources, ed. Catherine Cooper, Cynthia Garcia Coll, W. Todd Bartko, Helen M. Davis, and Celina Chatman, 63–88 (Hillsdale, N.J.: Lawrence Erlbaum Associates, 2005). Free lunch may also increasingly risk shame as children get older; Elaine Bell Kaplan found middle schoolers disparaged free lunch as signifying poverty: "You're not trying to have people look at you like that," one African-American girl told her. Elaine Bell Kaplan, "Using Food as a Metaphor for Care: Middle-School Kids Talk about Family, School, and Class Relationships," *Journal of Contemporary Ethnography* 29, no. 4 (August 2000): 474–509; see p. 498 for the quote.

16. See Nina Eliasoph and Paul Lichterman, "Culture in Interaction," *American Journal of Sociology* 108, no. 4 (2003): 735–94; see p. 775 for the quote.

17. For "windfall childrearing," see Allison Pugh, "Windfall Childrearing," *Journal of Consumer Culture* 4, no. 2 (July 2004): 229–49.

18. For a discussion of "othermothers," see Patricia Hill Collins, "Shifting the Center: Race, Class, and Feminist Theorizing about Motherhood," In *Mothering: Ideology, Experience, and Agency*, ed. Evelyn Nakano Glenn, Grace Change, and Linda Rennie Forcey, 45–66 (New York: Routledge, 1994).

19. William Corsaro has written on the oppositional group style in African-American children's settings, comparing it to group norms in white middle-class American and Italian contexts. William Corsaro, *We're Friends, Right? Inside Kids' Culture* (Washington, D.C.: Joseph Henry Press, 2003).

20. See George Orwell, "Such, Such Were the Joys," in *The Collected Essays, Journalism, and Letters*, vol. 4, *In Front of Your Nose, 1946–1950*, ed. Sonia Orwell and Ian Argus, 330–68 (Boston: Nonpareil Books, David R. Godine, 2000).

21. Ellen Seiter, *Sold Separately: Children and Parents in Consumer Culture* (New Brunswick, N.J.: Rutgers University Press, 1993).

22. Eleanor Estes, *The Hundred Dresses* (1944; repr., New York: Scholastic, 1973), 29–30.

23. Judith Harris, *The Nurture Assumption* (New York: Simon and Schuster, 1998).

24. Milner argues that teenagers' very inefficacy fuels the inflated importance of consumer culture for them. See Murray Milner, Jr., *Freaks, Geeks, and Cool Kids: American Teenagers, Schools, and the Culture of Consumption* (New York: Routledge, 2004). For children's efforts to make their own meaning from cultural schemas shaped by adults, see especially Chin, *Purchasing Power;* William Corsaro, *Friendship and Peer Culture in the Early Years* (Norwood, N.J.: Ablex Publishing, 1985); William Corsaro and Donna Eder, "Children's Peer Cultures," *Annual Review of Sociology* 16 (1990): 197–220; Thorne, "Unpacking School

Lunchtime"; Barrie Thorne, *Gender Play* (New Brunswick, N.J.: Rutgers University Press, 1993); and Debra Van Ausdale and Joe R. Feagin, *The First R: How Children Learn Race and Racism* (Lanham, Md.: Rowman and Littlefield, 2001).

25. Jeffrey Eugenides, *Middlesex* (New York: Farrar, Straus and Giroux, 2002), 217.

NOTES TO CHAPTER FOUR

1. Culture organizes action. Because culture is not a unified, coherent program, however, but rather a skein of multiple, overlapping, and contradictory schemas, people can be trapped by cultural ideas that oppose each other in the kind of action they organize. Some scholars argue that such are the necessary conditions of some forms of social change: when people with high status in one cultural schema are disempowered by another, they can effect change in the latter using the power they have accumulated elsewhere. This is the story Sahlins tells about native Hawaiian taboos and Ortner tells about elite women nunneries in Nepal, for example. The testimony of the high-status people in this chapter, however, suggests they still feel caught in a vise between spending and not spending. Marshall Sahlins, *Historical Metaphors and Mythical Realities* (Ann Arbor: University of Michigan Press, 1981); and Sherry Ortner, *High Religion: A Cultural and Political History of Sherpa Buddhism* (Princeton, N.J.: Princeton University Press, 1989). The historian Gary Cross remarks on the rise and fall and rise again of "jeremiads" against consumption in Gary Cross, *An All-Consuming Century: Why Commercialism Won in Modern America* (New York: Columbia University Press, 2000). For middle-class parenting styles, see Annette Lareau, *Unequal Childhoods: Class, Race, and Family Life* (Berkeley: University of California Press, 2003). The poll was carried out by *Working Mother* magazine and reported in Ellen Seiter, *Sold Separately: Children and Parents in Consumer Culture* (New Brunswick, N.J.: Rutgers University Press, 1993); for the quote from Seiter, see p. 8.

2. John Gillis, *A World of Their Own Making: Myth, Ritual, and the Quest for Family Values* (New York: Basic Books, 1996).

3. We can excavate culture from the discrepancies between what people do and what people say they want to do, analyzing their efforts to present themselves as honorable people to themselves as well as to others. Hochschild's own work demonstrates how this insight works: harassed flight attendants told cynical jokes that conveyed the distance they maintained from customers demanding that they "smile," so as not to be totally estranged from their authentic

selves. Working mothers reinterpreted the oppressive household division of labor ("He cooks all of the pies we eat") so they would not have to face the fact that they were settling for inequity. Busy executives collected equipment like canoes for vacations they never took, and assured themselves that they were there for their children because they attended their graduations or performances. In this case, symbolic deprivation is how affluent parents reconcile themselves to their consumption compromises. For harassed flight attendants, see Arlie Hochschild, *The Managed Heart: The Commercialization of Human Feeling* (Berkeley: University of California Press, 1983); for working mothers, see Arlie Hochschild, *The Second Shift* (New York: Avon Books, 1989); for busy executives, see Arlie Hochschild, *The Time Bind* (New York: Metropolitan Books, 1997).

4. Seiter, *Sold Separately*; Pierre Bourdieu, *Distinction: A Social Critique of the Judgement of Taste*, trans. Richard Nice (Cambridge, Mass.: Harvard University Press, 1984); Michelle Lamont and Annette Lareau, "Cultural Capital: Allusions, Gaps, and Glissandos in Recent Theoretical Developments," *Sociological Theory* 6, no. 2 (Autumn 1988): 153–68.

5. While scholars have found significant discrepancies in how much mothers and fathers spend on their children, my sample of parent informants did not yield the same divergence by gender, possibly because they were all self-identified primary caregivers. With only a handful of men, the sample size is too small to draw definitive conclusions, however.

6. Winnicott described the good-enough mother; in much the same way we might use the notion of the good-enough childhood to convey a sense not of perfectability but of reasonably good effort and outcome. See D. W. Winnicott, *Playing and Reality* (London and New York: Tavistock Publications, 1971).

7. Gregory Bateson, *Mind and Nature: A Necessary Unity* (New York: Dutton, 1979). The question of when a difference makes a difference was later reprised in Barrie Thorne, "Children's Experiences of Race and Ethnicity in California Public Schools" (Presentation at the conference *Diversities in the Classroom: New Findings to Foster Children's Development*, Berkeley, Calif., November 2, 2002).

8. One report on the upward mobility of Mexican immigrants quoted one woman as saying: "I had nothing once. Now I can't bear to see them have nothing." See Julia Preston, "Making a Life in the U.S., But Feeling Mexico's Tug," *New York Times*, December 19, 2006. Carolyn Kay Steedman, *Landscape for a Good Woman: A Story of Two Lives* (New Brunswick, N.J.: Rutgers University Press, 1986), 2. Karen Lacy, *Blue-Chip Black: Race, Class, and Status in the New Black Middle Class* (Berkeley: University of California Press, 2007), 146.

9. For a report suggesting that African-Americans do best when attending majority-white schools, see Carl Bankston and Stephen Caldas, "The American School Dilemma: Race and Scholastic Performance," *The Sociological Quarterly* 38, no. 3 (1999): 423–29. For Oakland schools, see Gwynne Coburn and Pamela Riley, "Failing Grade: Crisis and Reform in the Oakland Unified School District," Pacific Research Institute for Public Policy, San Francisco, 2000, www.pacificresearch.org; Allison Pugh, "The Social Context of Childrearing: Public Spending in Oakland 1970–2000" (working paper, Institute for the Study of Social Change, University of California, Berkeley, 2005); Jill Tucker and Robert Gammon, "Separate and Unequal: Fundraisers Give Schools an Edge," *Oakland Tribune*, June 18, 2003, http://www.oaklandtribune.com (accessed April 20, 2004). For schools nationally, see C. Boger, *The Socioeconomic Composition of the Public Schools: A Crucial Consideration in Student Assignment Policy* (Chapel Hill, N.C.: Center for Civil Rights, 2005); Anthony Carnevale and Donna Desrochers, *School Satisfaction: A Statistical Profile of Cities and Suburbs* (Princeton, N.J.: Educational Testing Service, 1999); Dennis J. Condron and Vincent J. Roscigno, "Disparities Within: Unequal Spending and Achievement in an Urban School District," *Sociology of Education* 76, no. 1 (2003): 18–36; Erica Frankenberg and Chungmei Lee, *Race in American Public Schools: Rapidly Resegregating School Districts* (Cambridge, Mass.: The Civil Rights Project, Harvard University, 2002); Erica Frankenberg, Chungmei Lee, and Gary Orfield, *A Multiracial Society with Segregated Schools: Are We Losing the Dream?* (Cambridge, Mass.: The Civil Rights Project, Harvard University, 2003).

10. Increasingly, parents are trying to support rather than change children with unusual gender identities, according to a *New York Times* report. But the report quoted one mother, who, incidentally, lived in Oakland, on the difficulties of protecting your child from others: "It's hard to convey the relentlessness of it. Every social encounter, every time you go out to eat, every day feeling like a balance between your kid's self-esteem and protecting him from the hostile outside world." The article also quoted the child psychologist Dr. Herbert Schreier about parents' worries about "how to protect [their children] from the savagery of other children." See Patricia Leigh Brown, "Supporting Boys or Girls When the Line Isn't Clear," *New York Times*, December 2, 2006. See Barrie Thorne's study of how boys and girls navigate gender and teasing in elementary school. Barrie Thorne, *Gender Play* (New Brunswick, N.J.: Rutgers University Press, 1993); C. J. Pascoe's research provides ample evidence for continued bullying based on sexual identity in high school. C. J. Pascoe, *Dude You're a Fag: Masculinity and Sexuality in High School* (Berkeley: University of California Press, 2007).

11. Eva Illouz, "Suffering, Emotional Field and Emotional Capital," in *Cold Intimacies: The Making of Emotional Capitalism*, 42 (Malden, Mass.: Polity Press, 2007).

12. In this view, *noblesse oblige* is a form of cultural hegemony helping to shore up the stratification that continues under late modern capitalism. Antonio Gramsci is most influential for his work analyzing the processes by which such bourgeois values come to be seen as common sense. See Antonio Gramsci, Selections from the Prison Notebooks, trans. Quintin Hoare and Geoffrey Nowell Smith (New York: International Publishers, 1983).

13. Douglas B. Holt, "Does Cultural Capital Structure American Consumption?" *Journal of Consumer Research* 25 (June 1998): 1–25.

14. The notion of middle-class "concerted cultivation" comes from Lareau, *Unequal Childhoods*. For research into parents' quest for their children's sense of wonder, see Allison Pugh, "From Compensation to Childhood Wonder: Why Parents Buy" (Working Paper No. 39, Center for Working Families, University of California, Berkeley, 2002); Gary Cross, "Valves of Desire: A Historian's Perspective on Parents, Children, and Marketing," *Journal of Consumer Research* 29 (2002): 441–47; and Gary Cross, *The Cute and the Cool: Wondrous Innocence and Modern American Children's Culture* (New York: Oxford University Press, 2004).

15. For parents' concerns about children's desires, see Seiter, *Sold Separately*; see also David Buckingham, *After the Death of Childhood* (Cambridge and Malden, Mass.: Polity Press, 2000); Dan Cook, *The Commodification of Childhood: The Children's Clothing Industry and the Rise of the Child Consumer* (Durham, N.C.: Duke University Press, 2004); and Gary Cross, *Kids' Stuff: Toys and the Changing World of American Childhood* (Cambridge, Mass.: Harvard University Press, 1997). For concerns about delayed gratification, see Barbara Ehrenreich, *Fear of Falling: The Inner Life of the Middle Class* (New York: Pantheon Books, 1989).

16. For the national survey results, see *Time*/CNN, *Video Games*, Polling the Nations, http://poll.orspub.com/index.php (accessed November 10, 2007). In Vermont, 16 percent of eighth graders reported they played video games or on the computer three hours or more per school day. See Vermont Department of Health, *Vermont Youth Risk Behavior Survey* (Burlington, Vt., 1999), Polling the Nations, www.poll.ors.pub.com (accessed February 20, 2006).

17. See Lareau, *Unequal Childhoods*; and Patricia Berhau, "Class and the Experience of Consumers: A Study of Practices of Acquisition" (diss., Temple University, 2000).

18. Studies have linked social class to attitudes and practices having to do with children's pocket money. See Jeylan T. Mortimer, Katherine Dennehy,

Chaimun Lee, and Michael D. Finch, "Economic Socialization in the American Family: The Prevalence, Distribution, and Consequences of Allowance Arrangements," *Family Relations* 43, no. 1 (1994): 23–30; and A. Furnham and A. Thomas, "Adult Perception of the Economic Socialization of Children," *Journal of Adolescence* 7 (1984): 217–31; but see A. Furnham, "Parental Attitudes towards Pocket Money/Allowances for Their Children," *Journal of Economic Psychology* 22, no. 3 (2001): 397–422. See also the discussion of allowances in Viviana Zelizer, *Pricing the Priceless Child* (New York: Basic Books, 1985).

19. One study found that while many parents give allowances so their children will learn to save, there was no evidence that the practice worked as intended. "Neither receipt of allowance nor its duration were significantly related to students' reported savings," observed the study's authors, who suggested that allowances might still be useful because they may teach children how to consume wisely. See Mortimer et al., "Economic Socialization in the American Family."

20. For the observation about affluence, relationships, and "real life," see Cross, *All-Consuming Century*, 10. For work on American cultural views against "excessive" desire, see Peter Stearns, *American Cool: Constructing a 20th Century Emotional Style* (New York: New York University Press, 1994).

NOTES TO CHAPTER FIVE

1. In 2005, the California Budget Project computed average costs in housing, child care, food, and other necessities for a single-parent family with just two children living in Alameda County, which includes Oakland, and came up with an annual tally of $62,969. Even taking into account Sandra's housing and child-care subsidies, her annual costs would have exceeded $40,000, according to this report. See California Budget Project 2005, "Making Ends Meet: How Much Does It Cost to Raise a Family in California?" Sacramento, November 2005, http://www.cbp.org/pdfs/2005/0509mem.pdf (accessed August 16, 2007).

2. As explored in the previous chapter, the "good-enough childhood" captures the standard of reasonably good effort and outcome, as opposed to perfectability. See D. W. Winnicott, *Playing and Reality* (London and New York: Tavistock Publications, 1971).

3. The question remains of why these items and not others were valued by children's peer culture. The answer is likely a complex one beyond the scope of this study, involving the impact of corporate marketing, children's existing hier-

archies of taste that valorize goods with power to invoke identities based on age and gender as opposed to class, and adult propensities to buy that are shaped by structural constraints of space, time, and money. Chee provides some evidence that low-income parents in China make the same calculation as low-income parents in Oakland, saving their money for goods that had the greatest impact. See Bernadine Chee, "Eating Snacks, Biting Pressure: Only Children in Beijing," in *Feeding China's Little Emperors: Food, Children, and Social Change*, ed. Jun Jing, 54 (Stanford, Calif.: Stanford University Press, 2000).

4. As noted in chapter 1, Smith understood the cultural dimension behind measures of relative well-being and was also sensitive to its implications for human dignity. "Though it is in order to supply the necessities and conveniencies of the body, that the advantages of external fortune are originally recommended to us, yet we cannot live long in the world without perceiving that the respect of our equals, our credit and rank in the society we live in, depend very much upon the degree in which we possess, or are supposed to possess, those advantages," Smith wrote. "The desire of becoming the proper objects of this respect, of deserving and obtaining this credit and rank among our equals, is, perhaps, the strongest of all our desires, and our anxiety to obtain the advantages of fortune is accordingly much more excited and irritated by this desire, than by that of supplying all the necessities and conveniencies of the body, which are always very easily supplied." Adam Smith, *Theory of Moral Sentiments* (Amherst, N.Y.: Prometheus Books, 1759), pt. VI, sec. 1.

5. For examples of social science that argued that low-income people were less able to defer gratification, see Edward Banfield, *The Unheavenly City Revisited* (Boston: Little, Brown, 1974); L. Schneider and S. Lysgaard, "The Deferred Gratification Pattern: A Preliminary Study," *American Sociological Review* 18 (1953): 142–49; Pierre Martineau, "Social Classes and Spending Behavior," in *Classics in Consumer Behavior*, ed. L. E. Boone, 303–17 (Tulsa, Okla.: PPC Books, 1977); W. Mischel, Y. Shoda, and M. L. Rodriguez, "Delay of Gratification in Children," *Science* 244, no. 26 (1989): 933–37. But see M. F. Levy, "Deferred Gratification and Social Class," *Journal of Social Psychology* 100 (1976): 123–35. See M. Wood's excellent review, in which he concludes: "The available evidence for a propensity on the part of lower-status consumers for present spending vs. a contrasting deferment of gratification among the middle class is largely negative, despite the apparent continued appeal of the idea to consumer behaviorists." M. Wood, "Socio-Economic Status, Delay of Gratification, and Impulse Buying," *Journal of Economic Psychology* 19 (1998): 295–320. For bloggers, see the "motivate yourself to delay gratification" page at http://bestmotivationquotes.com

(accessed September 7, 2007), which offers the following: "Instant gratification is a habit of the poor. It is the habit of people who want to enjoy now and having no patience to wait for future benefits. They spend more than they earned. Delayed gratification is the habit of the rich." Other examples include the July 16, 2007, page at http://boringmadedull.blogspot.com, in which the writer muses: "I've often heard of class discussed as a relative time preference—the ability to delay gratification, plan, and execute for a long term future." In his 2008 campaign for president, Barack Obama folded in discussion of the poor's inability to delay gratification as part of his two-pronged call for mutual responsibility and individual responsibility. The cultural values of "educational achievement and delayed gratification and intergenerational responsibility and hard work and entrepreneurship" produce success, he said, but "if a child is raised in a disorderly environment with inadequate health care and guns going off late at night, then it's a lot harder to incorporate those values." Quoted in Eugene Robinson, "Obama: Moving Beyond Either-Or," *Seattle Times,* March 13, 2007. In the popular press and blogosphere, writers maintain that low-income parents pass down their materialistic values, as when the journalist Clarence Page wrote a column in response to Oprah Winfrey's comments decrying materialism in America's inner city. "Our kids don't know anything except that which they are taught by parents, peers, teachers and other role models," he said, in agreement with Winfrey. Clarence Page, "Oprah's Truth Does Not Hurt," *Chicago Tribune,* January 8, 2007, www.realclearpolitics.com (accessed September 10, 2007). Blog commentary sings the same refrain, as in "If the parents are bothered about brand names then the children are much more likely to be." "Panorama: The World's Longest Running Investigative TV Show: Your Comments," http://news.bbc.co.uk/2/hi/programmes/panorama/4027003.stm (accessed September 10, 2007).

6. Sharon Hays refers to the "Candy Store Syndrome," or the seeking of pleasure through consumption, in a chapter on "the least sympathetic of all welfare recipients" and their culture of poverty. "The cultures of poverty are our cultures," and the candy-store syndrome is "so widespread in American culture that it hardly requires an accounting," she concludes. The oppositional culture of some poor women was not as surprising as the fact that "women like these are in a minority among welfare recipients." See Sharon Hays, *Flat Broke with Children: Women in the Age of Welfare Reform* (New York: Oxford University Press, 2003), 210–13.

7. For undisciplined children, see Glenn Loury, "The Poverty of Reason," *Boston Review* 19, no. 1 (February/March 1994). Other studies confirm harsher

discipline practices among low-income parents, particularly those who experience more family stress. See Ellen Pinderhughes, Kenneth Dodge, John Bates, Gregory Pettit, and Arnaldo Zelli, "Discipline Responses: Influences of Parents' Socioeconomic Status, Ethnicity, Beliefs about Parenting, Stress, and Cognitive-Emotional Processes," *Journal of Family Psychology* 14 (2000): 380–400. For "a sense of emerging constraint," see Annette Lareau, *Unequal Childhoods: Class, Race, and Family Life* (Berkeley: University of California Press, 2003), 6.

8. A wide-ranging literature covers the ways in which children influence family purchases. Children's influence increases with age, and the more child-relevant an item is (for example, cereal, toys, and clothes). See Deborah Roedder John, "Consumer Socialization of Children: A Retrospective Look at Twenty-five Years of Research," *Journal of Consumer Research* 26, no. 3 (1999): 183–213; see also Sharon Boden, "'Another Day, Another Demand': How Parents and Children Negotiate Consumption Matters," *Sociological Research Online* 11, no. 2 (2006), www.socresonline.org.uk/11/2/boden.html (accessed February 10, 2007). Children's arrays of tactics were observed by Palan and Wilkes, who reported bargaining strategies, persuasion strategies (as when Darrin asked repeatedly), request strategies (as when Darrin framed his desires as part of the equipment he needed for his future goals), and emotional strategies (as when Darrin got mad at Sandra). See Kay Palan and Robert E. Wilkes, "Adolescent-Parent Interaction in Family Decision Making," *Journal of Consumer Research* 24 (September 1997): 159–69.

9. Lareau reported that low-income children were less likely to nag or cajole their parents than were middle-income children. See Lareau, *Unequal Childhood*, 238.

10. See Allison Pugh, "Windfall Childrearing," *Journal of Consumer Culture* 4, no. 2 (July 2004): 229–49.

11. See Patricia Berhau, "Class and the Experience of Consumers: A Study of Practices of Acquisition" (diss., Temple University, 2000); Lareau, *Unequal Childhoods;* and Pierre Bourdieu, *Distinction: A Social Critique of the Judgement of Taste,* trans. Richard Nice (Cambridge, Mass.: Harvard University Press, 1984).

12. According to Fischer and Hout, "whether they are rationally distributing their purchases over time or thinking wishfully about their future incomes, the poor borrow and the rich save; young families go into debt and retirees spend down their assets. Consequently, Americans differ less in what they consume than in their incomes and wealth." Claude Fischer and Michael Hout, "What Americans Had: Differences in Standards of Living" (working paper, Survey Research Center, University of California, Berkeley, 2005), http://ucdata.berkeley

.edu:7101/rsfcensus/papers/Fischer-Hout_Ch4_June05.pdf (accessed November 11, 2007), 23.

13. Kathryn Edin and Laura Lein, *Making Ends Meet: How Single Mothers Survive Welfare and Low-Wage Work* (New York: Russell Sage Foundation, 1997); and Elaine Kempson, Alex Bryson, and Karen Rowlingson, *Hard Times? How Poor Families Make Ends Meet* (London: Policy Studies Institute, 1994).

14. See Berhau, "Class and the Experience of Consumers."

15. Some of the writing in the next few paragraphs is taken from Pugh, "Windfall Childrearing."

16. Some studies have found that materialistic parents have materialistic children and that low-income children are more likely to be materialistic. See Marvin Goldberg, Gerald Gorn, Laura Peracchio, and Gary Bamossy, "Understanding Materialism among Youth," *Journal Of Consumer Psychology* 13, no. 3 (2003): 278–88. For the definition of materialism, see Douglas Holt, "How Consumers Consume: A Typology of Consumption Practices," *Journal of Consumer Research* 22, no. 1 (1995): 1–16; for the quote, see p. 13. Judith Harris argued forcefully that parents exaggerate the extent to which they can transmit their values to their children, however, and that we underestimate the impact of children's peer culture. See Judith Harris, *The Nurture Assumption: Why Children Turn Out the Way They Do* (New York: Simon and Schuster, 1998).

17. In this way, Margaret exemplified the women in Edin and Kefalas's study of poor, unmarried mothers, who held marriage in abeyance because it represented a higher moral standard than they had yet attained, but who were confident about their child rearing. See Kathryn Edin and Maria Kefalas, *Promises I Can Keep* (Berkeley: University of California Press, 2005).

18. As mentioned in chapter 3, Chin demonstrated how the poor sometimes participate in consumer culture merely by talking about an item. See Elizabeth Chin, *Purchasing Power: Black Kids and American Consumer Culture* (Minneapolis: University of Minnesota Press, 2001).

19. Blogs, America's superego unleashed, are rife with this thinking. See www.theworldofpolitics.com; www.bluelight.ru; or http://wizbangblog.com.

20. Clearly, tastes are not devoid of politics. Critics of what low-income parents buy can be found in academia and lay culture alike. Chin condemns those scholars who seem to be arguing that if low-income families would just change their preferences, they would improve their lot. Susan Mayer has argued that a low income can be considered a proxy for other traits with negative implications for child rearing, such as instability. If one gave a low-income family $1000 for their children, she argued, they might not spend it on things middle-class values

would prioritize, such as books or educational trips. See Chin, *Purchasing Power;* and Susan Mayer, *What Money Can't Buy: Family Income and Children's Life Chances* (Cambridge, Mass.: Harvard University Press, 1997).

21. Edin and Kefalas, *Promises I Can Keep*, 147.

22. See Berhau, "Class and the Experience of Consumers."

23. Elaine Power, "Freedom and Belonging through Consumption: The Disciplining of Desire in Single Mothers on Welfare" (Paper presented to the British Sociological Association Annual Conference, University of York, 2003).

24. Richard Sennett and Jonathan Cobb, *The Hidden Injuries of Class* (New York: Vintage Books, 1973), 171. Randall Collins argued that the process of meaning-making hinges on the ability of culture to invoke emotion. See Randall Collins, *Interaction Ritual Chains* (Princeton, N.J.: Princeton University Press, 2004); and Nina Eliasoph and Paul Lichterman, "Culture in Interaction," *American Journal of Sociology* 108, no. 4 (2003): 735–94.

NOTES TO CHAPTER SIX

1. Kevin's memories of boys' teasing around issues of gender, recounted in chapter 4, were far more searing for him; he used them to narrate why they sent Sarah to Arrowhead. In contrast, his memories of not knowing TV culture were milder, suggesting they were a source of continuing disappointment, even some embarrassment, but not shame or other intense feeling. We can only speculate on the reasons for the difference, but one factor could be the protective bubble of his boyhood middle-class comfort: his family station provided proof that he was not poor, while "proving" one's masculinity can be a far more personal, difficult task. See C. J. Pascoe, *Dude, You're a Fag: Masculinity and Sexuality in High School* (Berkeley: University of California Press, 2007).

2. Culture scholars argue there are two kinds of social systems that shape human action: systems of social relations and systems of meaning. Systems of social relations include social categories that position us in our contexts—from race, class and gender to education, religion, and other powerful groupings. Systems of meaning include the ideas and values, the rituals and practices, that give these groupings their particular flavor. The circumstances behind consumption-resistant parenting reflect both realms. See Sharon Hays, "Structure, Agency, and the Sticky Problem of Culture," *Sociological Theory* 12 (1994): 57–72; William Sewell, "A Theory Of Structure—Duality, Agency, and Transformation," *American Journal of Sociology* 98, no. 1 (July 1992): 1–29; Ann Swidler,

"Culture in Action: Symbols and Strategies," *American Sociological Review* 51 (April 1986): 273–86; and Anthony Giddens, *Central Problems in Social Theory: Action, Structure, and Contradiction in Social Analysis* (Berkeley: University of California Press, 1979).

3. For a discussion of how competing cultural frames, or repertoires of meaning, work to organize human action, see Ann Swidler, *Talk of Love* (Chicago: University of Chicago Press, 2001).

4. Scholars have investigated immigrants' use of "outsiderness" in their social mobility projects. See Alejandro Portes and Julia Sensenbrenner, "Embeddedness and Immigration: Notes on the Social Determinants of Economic Action," *American Journal of Sociology* 98, no. 6 (1993): 1320–50; Ruben G. Rumbaut, "The Crucible Within: Ethnic Identity, Self-Esteem, and Segmented Assimilation among Children of Immigrants," *International Migration Review* 28, no. 4 (1994): 748–94; and Min Zhou and Carl L. Bankston III, "Social Capital and the Adaptation of the Second Generation: The Case of Vietnamese Youth in New Orleans," *International Migration Review* 28, no. 4 (1994): 821–45. It is important to recall how immigrants' type, trajectory, and degree of acculturation can vary dramatically, as Katerina and Anne-Marie's examples attest. See K. Kwak and J. W. Berry, "Generational Differences in Acculturation among Asian Families in Canada: A Comparison of Vietnamese, Korean, and East-Indian Groups," *International Journal of Psychology* 36 (2001): 152–62. For Chinese immigrants' emphases on family cohesion, see W. H. Meredith, D. A. Abbott, R. Tsai, Z. F. Ming, "Healthy Family Functioning in Chinese Cultures: An Exploratory Study Using the Circumflex Model," *International Journal of Sociology of the Family* 24 (1994): 147–57.

5. For how the immigration experience structures the immigrant's use of comparative reference groups in the host or originating country, see Aida Hurtado, Patricia Gurin, and Timothy Peng, "Social Identities—A Framework for Studying the Adaptations of Immigrants and Ethnics: The Adaptations of Mexicans in the United States," *Social Problems* 41, no. 1, Special Issue on Immigration, Race, and Ethnicity in America (February 1994): 129–51. Hurtado et al. rely on an exposition of social identity theory by Henri Tajfel, specifically when particular categories (say, a parent who sets consumer limits) become part of an identity. See Henri Tajfel, *Differentiation between Social Groups: Studies in the Social Psychology of Intergroup Relations*, European Monographs in Social Psychology (London: Academic Press, 1978); and Henri Tajfel, *Human Groups and Social Categories: Studies in Social Psychology*. London: Cambridge University Press, 1981.

6. Nations are not reducible to cultures or vice versa, of course. Still, while it is important not to overstate the degree to which these values are shared across a culture, some research has focused on cultural meanings of childhood, specifically the contrast between the elevation of the individual, including individual children, common in the United States and the sense of a more unified family mission constructed by some immigrants' cultures of origin. See C. Raeff, "Individuals in Relationships: Cultural Values, Children's Social Interactions, and the Development of an American Individualistic Self," *Developmental Review* 17 (1997): 205–38. Kwak notes that "some ethnic groups, particularly those of Asian and Latin descent, are known to retain strong family values of embeddedness after migration." Kyunghwa Kwak, "Adolescents and Their Parents: A Review of Intergenerational Family Relations for Immigrant and Non-Immigrant Families," *Human Development* 46 (2003): 132. See also Kwak and Berry, "Generational Differences in Acculturation"; and A. Fuligni, V. Tseng, and M. Lam, "Attitudes towards Family Obligations among American Adolescents with Asian, Latin American, and European Backgrounds," *Child Development* 70 (1999): 1030–44. In Latino families, researchers have called this "familismo," which includes among other characteristics "the commitment to the family over individual needs and desires." Linda C. Halgunseth, Jean M. Ispa, and Duane Rudy, "Parental Control in Latino Families: An Integrated Review of the Literature," *Child Development* 77, no. 5 (2006): 1285.

7. Census data portray Africans as one of the most highly educated, if not *the* most highly educated, of all immigrant groups. See Kristin Butcher, "Black Immigrants in the United States: A Comparison with Native Blacks and Other Immigrants," *Industrial and Labor Relations Review* 47 (1994): 265–84.

8. See Christine Williams, *Inside Toyland: Working, Shopping, and Social Inequality.* Berkeley: University of California Press, 2005.

9. For "segmented assimilation," see Alejandro Portes and Min Zhou, "The New Second Generation: Segmented Assimilation and Its Variants," *Annals of the American Political and Social Sciences* 530 (1993): 74–96; and Portes and Sensenbrenner, "Embeddedness and Immigration." While Neckerman, Carter, and Lee argue for an expansion of this model to include what they term "minority cultures of mobility," the Dengs' social isolation from middle-class blacks makes that route less available to them at the time of our interviews. See Katherine Neckerman, Prudence Carter, and Jennifer Lee, "Segmented Assimilation and Minority Cultures of Mobility," *Ethnic and Racial Studies* 22, no. 6 (November 1999): 945–65.

10. My thanks to Milton Vickerman for emphasizing this point. For an analysis of consumption practices in Trinidad, see Daniel Miller, *Capitalism: An*

Ethnographic Approach (Oxford: Berg, 1997). See also F. Nii-Amoo Dodoo, "Assimilation Differences among Africans in America," *Social Forces* 76, no. 2 (December 1997): 527–46; John Arthur, *Invisible Sojourners: African Immigrant Diaspora in the United States* (Westport, Conn.: Praeger Publishers, 2000); and Yoku Shaw-Taylor and Steven Tuch, eds. *The Other African-Americans: Contemporary African and Caribbean Immigrants to the United States.* Lanham, Md.: Rowman and Littlefield, 2007.

11. Some scholars have posited a hierarchy of child-rearing goals for immigrant parents, suggesting that when they are in an unstable position economically, they strive for the second goal, beyond physical survival to be sure, but which is focused on developing the child's self-sustaining capacity for when he or she grows up. Only when economic security is established, according to the theory, can a parent reach for tertiary goals, such as the development of the child's capacities for "other cultural values, such as morality, prestige, wealth, religious piety, intellectual achievement." Mary's focus on maintaining and transmitting her cultural values to her children in the midst of her economic struggle, however, suggests that "tertiary goals" can come earlier in the immigration process. See Andrew Fuligni and Hirokazu Yoshikawa, "Investments in Children among Immigrant Families," in *Family Investments in Children's Potential: Resources and Parenting*, ed. Ariel Kalil and Thomas C. DeLeire, 143 (Mahwah, N.J.: Lawrence Erlbaum Associates, 2004).

12. See Viviana Zelizer, *Pricing the Priceless Child* (New York: Basic Books, 1985).

13. See Kwak, "Adolescents and Their Parents."

14. Steven Mintz has elegantly portrayed the changes in American childhoods as rife with contradictions, involving a more child-centered family, with "hovering parents" making it "more difficult to separate," within a nonetheless more "adult-centered society." Steven Mintz, *Huck's Raft: A History of American Childhood* (Cambridge, Mass.: Harvard University Press, Belknap Press, 2004), 383. The development of newly intensive child-rearing in the United States is also documented in Sharon Hays, *The Cultural Contradictions of Motherhood*. New Haven, Conn.: Yale University Press, 1996. For American children's larger role in shopping, see James McNeal, *On Becoming a Consumer: Development of Consumer Behavior Patterns in Childhood* (Burlington, Mass.: Butterworth-Heinemann, 2007); and Barrie Gunter and Adrian Furnham, *Children as Consumers* (New York and London: Routledge, 1998).

15. Some researchers have looked at how tensions arise within immigrant families over changing views of "autonomy," or individuality, versus "embed-

dedness," or family cohesion. See, for example, J. S. Phinney, A. Ong, and T. Madden, "Cultural Values and Intergenerational Value Discrepancies in Immigrant and Non-immigrant Families," *Child Development* 71 (2000): 528–39.

16. Simon's choice was not unusual for someone in his situation, according to Kwak, who wrote that "for recent immigrant families, which particularly emphasize family cohesion, family members may be more adept at avoiding conflict, and further, may have learned to decrease the psychological impact of family problems." Kwak, "Adolescents and Their Parents," 132.

17. While some immigrant children take Simon's tack, the strategies David adopts are common in other immigrant families, research suggests. Scholars have documented the role immigrant children play as "cultural brokers," performing work as cultural and linguistic translators between their homes and the outside world. See Marjorie Faulstich Orellana, "The Work Kids Do: Mexican and Central American Immigrant Children's Contributions to Households and Schools in California," *Harvard Educational Review* 71, no. 3 (2001): 366–89. There is some indication that the difference between the two strategies could be related to how long the family had been in the country and the age at migration (David's mother moved to the United States in high school, in the mid-nineties; the Dengs came as adults with three children, just three years before this research); other factors researchers have explored include the socioeconomic status of the families involved, the cultural "fit" between the immigrant's culture and that of the adopted country, gender and the education level of the parents. See Kwak, "Adolescents and Their Parents"; Kwak and Berry, "Generational Differences in Acculturation"; and N. Nguyen and H. Williams, "Transition from East to West: Vietnamese Adolescents and Their Parents," *Journal of the American Academy of Child and Adolescent Psychiatry* 28 (1989): 505–15.

NOTES TO CHAPTER SEVEN

1. Several hundred thousand students are defrauded each year by "scholarship scams," losing more than $100 million annually, according to the congressional testimony of a leading financial aid information provider (United States Senate Committee on the Judiciary, 2001). In 1996, the Federal Trade Commission began a crackdown called "Project Scholarscam"; four years later, the U.S. Congress ordered even more extensive monitoring of the industry as well as stiffer penalties for companies found guilty of scholarship fraud. According to the FTC, among the common indicators of fraud are claims that the company

guarantees scholarships, the use of high-pressure sales seminars, and the words "We'll do all the work." The FTC notes that legitimate companies exist that do charge a fee for their search services, but the difference is that "legitimate companies *never* guarantee or promise scholarships or grants" (Federal Trade Commission, 1999). We do not know for sure that Angela's service was a scam, and at the time of our interview, she could not remember the name of the service— "I forgot. Epic? I forgot the name of it," she said. Unfortunately, however, her recounting of how she signed up for it included all three of the above indicators.

2. For the rise of the "college premium," the divergence in income between those with and without college degrees, see Peter Gottschalk and Sheldon Danziger, "Inequality of Wage Rates, Earnings, and Family Income in the United States, 1975–2002," *Review of Income and Wealth* 51 (2005): 231–54. Some powerful ethnographic analyses of contemporary inequality in children's lives, and its impact on their later trajectories, include Jay MacLeod, *Ain't No Makin' It* (Boulder, Colo.: Westview, 1987); Annette Lareau, *Unequal Childhoods: Class, Race, and Family Life* (Berkeley: University of California Press, 2003); Alex Kotlowitz, *There Are No Children Here* (New York: Doubleday, 1991); Jonathan Kozol, *Savage Inequalities: Children in America's Schools* (New York: Crown, 1991).

3. Only 13 percent of American children over three years old went to private school in 2003, calculations from U.S. census data revealed. Educational spending goes beyond the still-unusual practice of writing a check for tuition, however. Most middle-class families pour their resources into buying a home in a neighborhood that could offer what Warren called "the new private-public commodity: a viable public school." Elizabeth Warren, "Middle Class and Broke," *The American Prospect*, April 25, 2004, www.prospect.org/cs/articles?articleid=7635 (accessed July 24, 2008). In addition, the growing consensus that preschool and college are part of a basic education for the middle class has weighted parents down with the financial burden of an additional six years of school. "The public-school system is now largely public in name only, as families bankrupt themselves to buy admission to decent public schools by purchasing expensive homes and paying tuition for a third of a basic education." Warren, "Middle Class and Broke."

4. The traditional conception of an investment versus consumption suggests that the difference lies in when the benefits are enjoyed. "Consumption goods and investment goods deliver their benefits on different schedules. The benefits of private consumption goods such as food, clothing, automobiles, television sets, and ice cream cones are used up as the goods are consumed. Private invest-

ment in plant and equipment, home building and inventory provides benefits over longer periods of time." John Winfrey, *Social Issues: The Ethics and Economics of Taxes and Public Programs* (New York: Oxford University Press, 1998), 46. Yale Professor Jacob Hacker critiqued "the over-consumption school" for its view of middle-class spending as consumption, "a simple cash outflow that straitjackets family finances. . . . Yet many of the big-ticket items . . . housing, education, even childcare—are best thought of not merely as consumption but also as investments . . . scarcely [to be] viewed as money down the drain." Jacob Hacker, "Economic Risk Has Shifted from the Government and Corporations to Workers and Their Families," *Boston Review*, September/October 2005, http://bostonreview.net/BR30.5/hacker.html (accessed November 12, 2007). For the characterization "an impure critique," see Eva Illouz, *Cold Intimacies: The Making of Emotional Capitalism* (Malden, Mass.: Polity Press, 2007), 95.

5. For a discussion of different parent preferences in school choice, see P. Teske and Mark Schneider, "What Research Can Tell Policymakers about School Choice," *Journal of Policy Analysis and Management* 20, no. 4 (Autumn 2001): 609–31. A burgeoning literature examines neighborhood effects on child outcomes, and correlations of numerous negative outcomes associated with growing up in an area of concentrated poverty are generally considered robust. See Robert Sampson, Jeffrey Morenoff, and Thomas Gannon-Rowley, "Assessing 'Neighborhood Effects': Social Processes and New Directions in Research," *Annual Review of Sociology* 28 (2002): 443–78. For a review of research on school effects, see Meredith Philips and Tiffani Chin, "School Inequality: What Do We Know?" (working paper, Russell Sage Foundation, 2003), http://www.russellsage.org/programs/main/inequality/050516.010743/ (accessed November 12, 2007); and Gary Orfield and Chungmei Lee, *Why Segregation Matters: Poverty and Educational Inequality.* (Cambridge, Mass.: The Civil Rights Project, Harvard University, 2005), http://www.civilrightsproject.harvard.edu/research/deseg/Why_Segreg_Matters.pdf (accessed February 15, 2007).

6. In earlier work, I developed the notion of concentric circles of collective consumption to try and treat theoretically the existence of PTA fund-raising that elevated one school above another in the same district. See Allison Pugh, "The Social Context of Childrearing: Public Spending in Oakland 1970–2000." (working paper, Institute for the Study of Social Change, University of California, Berkeley, 2005). For the uneven distribution of urban resources, see Dennis J. Condron and Vincent J. Roscigno, "Disparities Within: Unequal Spending and Achievement in an Urban School District," *Sociology of Education* 76, no. 1 (2003): 18–36. For the estimate of Sally Foster and other campaigns, see Steve

Hendrix, "Reading, Writing, Retailing: Fundraising for Schools Have Become Fall Fixture," *Washington Post*, Tuesday, October 9, 2007.

7. Noguera reported how school funding exacerbated inequality in the East Bay. He observed: "Even though more affluent children in neighboring school districts such as Piedmont, Moraga and Orinda arrive at school better prepared academically and generally have fewer unmet needs, significantly more money is spent on their education than is spent on children in Oakland." Pedro Noguera, "Racial Isolation, Poverty, and the Limits of Local Control in Oakland," *Teachers College Record* 106, no. 11 (2004): 2153. For a powerful portrayal of these contrasting schools, see Jill Tucker, "Our Public Schools: Separate and Unequal," *Oakland Tribune*, June 15, 2003. For differences in PTA involvement around the Bay Area, see C. W. Nevius, "Affluent Parents Cover for State School Cuts: Districts in Lower-Income Areas Not as Lucky," *San Francisco Chronicle*, March 19, 2004. For "apartheid schools," see Erica Frankenberg and Chungmei Lee, *Race in American Public Schools: Rapidly Resegregating School Districts* (Cambridge, Mass.: The Civil Rights Project, Harvard University, 2002).

8. Different types of parents systematically make different choices, wrote Teske and Schneider. "Higher-SES parents and white parents appear more likely to favor schools with fewer low-income students or minorities." Teske and Schneider, "What Research Can Tell Policymakers about School Choice," 614. For research regarding conditions in fully funded schools, see Salvatore Saporito, "Private Choices, Public Consequences: Magnet School Choice and Segregation by Race and Poverty," *Social Problems* 50, no. 2 (2003): 181–203. See also Salvatore Saporito, William Yancey, and Vincent Louis, "Quality, Race, and the Urban Market Place Reconsidered," *Urban Affairs Review* 37 (2001): 267–76.

9. I use the terms "racial/class" and "racialized class" to emphasize that the meanings and segregation at issue here involve intersections of race and class and are not thus reducible to either.

10. Noguera discusses the "captured market" for children's education that is largely poor, immigrant, and nonwhite in Oakland, noting that their constrained ability to opt out meant that the "miserable status quo" would continue. Noguera, "Racial Isolation, Poverty, and the Limits of Local Control." To be sure, those low-income families who *could* move their children from the city schools would not be in my sample. But the same argument could be made about the affluent families, and at Oceanview alone I witnessed three families move out of Oakland in the six months of my most intensive fieldwork. None of these affluent families intended to keep their children in the Oakland schools.

11. Some of the media reports, for example, included a series by Jill Tucker in the *Oakland Tribune* on the eve of the fiftieth anniversary in 2004 of the *Brown v. Board of Education* decision. See Tucker, "Our Public Schools." For a discussion of the problems of constrained choice and uneven school information for low-income and minority parents, see M. Schneider, P. Teske, and M. Marschall, *Choosing Schools: Consumer Choice and the Quality of American Schools* (Princeton, N.J.: Princeton University Press, 2000).

12. For the Vallejo story, see Steven Holmes, "A Diverse City Exists Equal but Separate," *New York Times*, May 11, 2001.

13. For a discussion of "racial safety" in child-care preferences, see Lynet Uttal, "Custodial Care, Surrogate Care, and Coordinated Care: Employed Mothers and the Meaning of Childcare," *Gender and Society* 10, no. 3 (1996): 291–311.

14. There is some evidence that African-American boys are less likely to be identified as gifted in school. See C. J. Maker, "Identification of Gifted Minority Students: A National Problem, Needed Change, and a Promising Solution," *Gifted Child Quarterly* 40 (1996): 42–50; and Hala Elhoweris, Kagendo Mutua, Negmeldin Alsheikh, and Pauline Holloway, "Effect of Children's Ethnicity on Teachers' Referral and Recommendation Decisions in Gifted and Talented Programs," *Remedial and Special Education* 26, no. 1 (2005): 25–32.

15. Ann Ferguson, *Bad Boys: Public Schools in the Making of Black Masculinity* (Ann Arbor: University of Michigan Press, 2000), 39.

16. Research has found upper-income families are more likely to spend money on their children's education, and among families who spend money, they are more likely to spend more money. See Teresa Mauldin, Yoko Mimura, and Mark Lino, "Parental Expenditures on Children's Education," *Journal of Family and Economic Issues* 22, no. 3 (2001): 221. For Warren's research on the primacy of school in family decision-making, see Warren and Tyagi, *Two-Income Trap*, 23–46.

17. For the parenting styles of the middle class, see Lareau, *Unequal Childhoods*.

18. See Saporito, "Private Choices, Public Consequences"; Saporito, Yancey, and Louis, "Quality, Race and the Urban Market Place Reconsidered"; and Teske and Schneider, "What Research Can Tell Policymakers about School Choice."

19. Heather Knight, "Agonizing over S.F. School Options: 3 Families' Paths Diverge—Public, Private, Parochial," *San Francisco Chronicle*, August 29, 2005.

20. For housing segregation, see Paul Jargowski, "Take the Money and Run: Economic Segregation in U.S. Metropolitan Areas," *American Sociological*

Review 61 (December 1996): 984–98; and P. Jargowski, *Poverty and Place: Ghettos, Barrios, and the American City* (New York: Russell Sage Foundation, 1997). For school segregation, see Frankenberg and Lee, *Race in American Public Schools;* Erica Frankenberg, Chungmei Lee, and Gary Orfield, *A Multiracial Society with Segregated Schools: Are We Losing the Dream?* (Cambridge, Mass.: The Civil Rights Project, Harvard University, 2003); and Orfield and Lee, *Why Segregation Matters.*

21. Author's calculations are from 2000 census data for West Oakland.

22. For a discussion of African-American community values, see Shirley Hill, *Black Intimacies: A Gender Perspective on Families and Relationship* (Walnut Creek, Calif.: AltaMira Press, 2005).

23. For "strategic assimilation," see Karyn Lacy, *Blue-Chip Black* (Berkeley: University of California Press, 2007), 151; see p. 152 for the other quotes.

24. This phenomenon was in contrast to the Pattillo-McCoy's findings, in which middle-class black parents expended effort (often in vain) to shield their children from the poor and working-class blacks whose neighborhoods abutted their own. It is possible that the Lamonts and their peers in this study, like the affluent black families in one of the communities Lacy studied, were more isolated from contact with lower-income blacks and thus had to go looking for them. See Mary Pattillo-McCoy, *Black Picket Fences: Privilege and Peril among the Black Middle Class* (Chicago: University of Chicago Press, 1999); Lacy, *Blue-Chip Black;* and Elijah Anderson, *Code of the Street: Decency, Violence, and the Moral Life of the Inner City* (New York: W. W. Norton, 1999).

25. While theoretically parents of diverse backgrounds could employ this strategy, in my sample it was restricted to affluent African-Americans.

26. See Lareau, *Unequal Childhoods,* for an account of black and white affluent mothers engaging in the same concerted cultivation.

27. While Vernon was less socially adroit than other children of affluent African-Americans who were experiencing exposed childhoods, his air of not-quite-belonging was actually not that unusual among the children that I observed. Lois, for example, was a smart, tough girl in the same class, but she had some mannerisms that made her stand apart—hugging herself, dancing, talking to herself. She often made sarcastic remarks at the margins of classroom goings-on. The sample is too small to generalize that children experiencing "exposure" must necessarily suffer socially, and although other affluent African-American children were popular, it is also plausible that experiences of racism contributed to any alienation. But it is also possible that one risk of exposed childhoods was to accentuate the sense of displacement the children experienced. While discomfort for the children surely waxed and waned, and varied depending on the per-

sonal resources of the children and the classroom dynamic in which they found themselves, it seemed an emotional burden at least distantly related to the project of always being different. Their experience of multiple situations of difference surely gives them insight into what others consider normal, but it is at least possible that it also leads them to feel like they do not quite belong.

28. Lacy, *Blue-Chip Black*, 153–57.

29. For humor expressing "pleasure at subversion," see Michael Billig, "Humor and Embarrassment: Limits of "Nice-Guy" Theories of Social Life," *Theory, Culture & Society* 18, no. 5 (2001): 39.

30. Frankenberg and Lee, *Race in American Public Schools.*

NOTES TO THE CONCLUSION

1. For "the language of `common sense,'" see William E. Grant, "Individualism and the Tensions in American Culture," *American Quarterly* 38, no. 2 (Summer 1986): 311–18; see p. 317 for the quote. There are many important works analyzing the simultaneity of American individualism and conformity, including Alexis de Tocqueville's *Democracy in America*, John Dewey's *Individualism, Old and New*, David Riesman et al.'s *The Lonely Crowd*, and Robert Bellah et al.'s *Habits of the Heart*. See Joshua W. Clegg, "A Phenomenological Investigation of the Experience of Not Belonging," *Journal of Phenomenological Psychology* 37, no.1 (Spring 2006): 53–83. See Alexis de Tocqueville, *Democracy in America*, trans. George Lawrence and ed. J. P. Mayer (1848; repr., Garden City, N.Y.: Anchor Books, 1969); Robert Bellah, Richard Madsen, William Sullivan, Ann Swidler, and Steven Tipton, *Habits of the Heart* (Berkeley: University of California Press, 1985); John Dewey, *Individualism, Old and New* (New York: Minton Balch & Co., 1930); and Riesman, David, with Nathan Glazer and Reuel Denney, *The Lonely Crowd: A Study of the Changing American Character* (New Haven, Conn.: Yale University Press, 1950).

2. Tocqueville, *Democracy in America*, 508. See Bellah et al., *Habits of the Heart*. Martha Fineman argues that the foundational myth of autonomy and independence has led to a willful blindness to dependency and the subversion of care in U.S. law and society. See Martha Albertson Fineman, *The Autonomy Myth: A Theory of Dependency* (New York: The New Press, 2004), xv–xvii, 7–30.

3. Neil J. Smelser, "The Rational and the Ambivalent in the Social Sciences: 1997 Presidential Address," *American Sociological Review* 63, no. 1 (February 1998): 1–16; for the quote, see p. 13.

4. Arlie Hochschild, "The Commodity Frontier," in *The Commercialization of Intimate Life* (Berkeley: University of California Press, 2003), 41. For low-income parents' use of symbolic indulgence to "make [their children] feel normal," see Kathryn Edin and Laura Lein, *Making Ends Meet: How Single Mothers Survive Welfare and Low-Wage Work* (New York: Russell Sage Foundation, 1997), 30. Christine Williams, *Inside Toyland: Working, Shopping, and Social Inequality* (Berkeley: University of California Press, 2006), 181. Hochschild contended that the promise of resolving ambivalence is part of "the hidden appeal in the marketing associated with much modern commodification" (p. 41). Yet, as Williams observed, "achieving social recognition through gifts or money may make us more insecure than before, more in need of reassurance that the recognition we get from others is authentic and not superficial or fleeting" (pp. 181–82).

5. Others charting this middle path include Daniel Cook, *The Commodification of Childhood: The Children's Clothing Industry and the Rise of the Child Consumer* (Durham, N.C.: Duke University Press, 2004); Elizabeth Chin, *Purchasing Power: Black Kids and American Consumer Culture* (Minneapolis: University of Minnesota Press, 2001); and Grant McCracken, *Culture and Consumption: New Approaches to the Symbolic Character of Consumer Goods and Services* (Bloomington: Indiana University Press, 1988).

6. See Pierre Bourdieu, *Distinction: A Social Critique of the Judgement of Taste*, trans. Richard Nice (Cambridge, Mass.: Harvard University Press, 1984); Annette Lareau, *Unequal Childhoods: Class, Race, and Family Life* (Berkeley: University of California Press, 2003); Ann Swidler, "Culture in Action: Symbols and Strategies," *American Sociological Review* 51 (April 1986): 273–86; and Douglas Holt, "Poststructuralist Lifestyle Analysis: Conceptualizing the Social Patterning of Consumption in Postmodernity," *Journal of Consumer Research* 23 (March 1997): 326–50.

7. In the era of No Child Left Behind and "high-stakes testing," many public schools have cut back on all but the core subjects to enable their students to perform well on tests that measure basic skills. See Council for Basic Education, "Academic Atrophy: The Condition of Liberal Arts in America's Schools," cited in *Educators, Nonprofits, Concerned Public Schools Neglect the Arts* (New York: The Foundation Center, 2004), http://fdncenter.org/pnd/news/story.jhtml?id= 73800033 (accessed April 21, 2006). Education researcher Karen Osterman reported that some experimental studies on establishing a sense of community at school found that adults can effectively shape the sense of belonging and relatedness among children. She observed: "By encouraging teachers to facili-

tate dialogue about democratic values, provide opportunities for supportive interaction in and out of the classroom, and support students' autonomy within and outside of the classroom, this change effort shows that it is possible to enhance students' sense of community. . . . Where design strategies were implemented, there were significant changes in students' sense of community as well as a wide range of motivational and behavioral outcomes." Karen Osterman, "Students' Need for Belonging in the School Community," *Review of Educational Research* 70, no. 3 (2000): 323–67; see p. 356 for the quote.

8. According to one of my informants, there is apparently a mixed-income school in New York where children visited each others' houses as a group, and difference is treated openly and, by teachers, as something to manage; I have not been able to track down this institution, however. Corsaro reports an Italian nursery school where the group of children paid visits to each child's home, were fed and welcomed by the parents, and inspected the host child's toys. While he does not use these episodes to talk about inequality so much as children's visible public presence in Italian streets, in contrast to the United States, such a program could arguably bring differences to the fore in a way that, if handled correctly, mitigates shame and improves mutual understanding. See William Corsaro, *We're Friends, Right? Inside Kids' Culture* (Washington, D.C.: Joseph Henry Press, 2003), 207–12.

9. For Scandinavian versus American inequality, see Rolf Aaberge, Anders Bjorklund, Markus Jantti, Marten Palme, Peder J. Pedersen, Nina Smith, and Tom Wennemo, "Income Inequality and Income Mobility in the Scandinavian Countries Compared to the United States," *Review of Income and Wealth* 48 (2002): 443–69, http://ssrn.com/abstract = 371554 (accessed November 13, 2007). With regard to French devotion to common culture, Jennings wrote that "despite an astonishing level of cultural and ethnic diversity, France has seen itself as and has sought to become a monocultural society." See Jeremy Jennings, "Citizenship, Republicanism, and Multiculturalism in Contemporary France" *British Journal of Political Science* 30 (2000): 575–98; for the quote, see p. 575. For Japanese peer pressure in schools, see Anne Allison, "Japanese Mothers and Obentos: The Lunch Box as Ideological State Apparatus," in *Permitted and Prohibited Desires: Mothers, Comics, and Censorship in Japan*, 81–104 (Berkeley: University of California Press, 2000); and Joseph J. Tobin, David Wu, and Dana Davidson, *Preschool in Three Cultures: Japan, China, and the United States* (New Haven, Conn.: Yale University Press, 1991).

10. For a report on parents encouraging charitable donations instead of birthday gifts, see Tina Kelley, "Cake, But No Presents, Please," *New York Times*, July 27, 2007.

11. For "hostile worlds," see Viviana Zelizer, *The Purchase of Intimacy* (Princeton, N.J.: Princeton University Press, 2004), 20–29. For the observation about peer culture, norms, and belonging, see Osterman, "Students' Need for Belonging," 360. Sharon Zukin, *Point Of Purchase: How Shopping Changed American Culture* (New York: Routledge, 2004), 112. The phrase "referred pain" is Hochschild's; see Hochschild, *Commercialization of Intimate Life*, 3.

12. For "work-and-spend cycle," see Juliet Schor, *The Overworked American* (New York: Basic Books, 1992), 9.

BIBLIOGRAPHY

Aaberge, Rolf, Anders Bjorklund, Markus Jantti, Marten Palme, Peder J. Pedersen, Nina Smith, and Tom Wennemo. "Income Inequality and Income
Mobility in the Scandinavian Countries Compared to the United States."
Review of Income and Wealth 48 (2002): 443–69. http://ssrn.com/abstract=
371554 (accessed November 13, 2007).

Acs, Gregory, and Megan Gallagher. "Income Inequality among America's
Children." Urban Institute, Washington, D.C., 2000. http://www.urban
.org/url.cfm?ID = 309307.

Adler, Patricia, and Peter Adler. *Peer Power.* New Brunswick, N.J.: Rutgers University Press, 1998.

Allison, Anne. *Permitted and Prohibited Desires: Mothers, Comics, and Censorship in
Japan.* Berkeley: University of California Press, 2000.

Anderson, Elijah. *Code of the Street: Decency, Violence, and the Moral Life of the
Inner City.* New York: W. W. Norton, 1999.

Annie E. Casey Foundation. *City and Rural Kids Count Data Book.* Baltimore,
2005. http://www.aecf.org/publications/data/city_rural_databook.pdf.

Arthur, John. *Invisible Sojourners: African Immigrant Diaspora in the United States.*
Westport, Conn.: Praeger Publishers, 2000.

Banfield, Edward. *The Unheavenly City Revisited.* Boston: Little, Brown, 1974.

Bankston, Carl, and Stephen Caldas. "The American School Dilemma: Race and
Scholastic Performance." *The Sociological Quarterly* 38, no. 3 (1999): 423–29.

Barber, Benjamin. *Consumed: How Markets Corrupt Children, Infantilize Adults,
and Swallow Citizens Whole.* New York: W. W. Norton, 2007.

Bateson, Gregory. *Mind and Nature: A Necessary Unity*. New York: Dutton, 1979.

Baudrillard, Jean. *For a Critique of the Political Economy of the Sign*. Translated by Charles Levin. St. Louis: Telos, 1972, 1981.

Bauman, Zygmunt. *Work, Consumerism, and the New Poor*. Buckingham and Philadelphia: Open University Press, 1998.

BBC World News. "U.S. Babies Get Global Brand Names." Thursday, November 13, 2003. http://news.bbc.co.uk/2/hi/americas/3268161.stm (accessed November 9, 2007).

Bellah, Robert, Richard Madsen, William Sullivan, Ann Swidler, and Steven Tipton. *Habits of the Heart*. Berkeley: University of California Press, 1985.

Berhau, Patricia. "Class and the Experience of Consumers: A Study of Practices of Acquisition." Diss., Temple University, 2000.

Bettie, Julie. *Women without Class*. Berkeley: University of California Press, 2003.

Bianchi, Suzanne. "Feminization and Juvenilization of Poverty: Trends, Relative Risks, Causes, and Consequences." *Annual Review of Sociology* 25 (1999): 307–33.

Billig, Michael. "Humor and Embarrassment: Limits of "Nice-Guy" Theories of Social Life." *Theory, Culture & Society* 18, no. 5 (2001): 23–43.

Boden, Sharon. "'Another Day, Another Demand': How Parents and Children Negotiate Consumption Matters." *Sociological Research Online* 11, no. 2 (2006). www.socresonline.org.uk/11/2/boden.html (accessed February 10, 2007).

Boger, C. *The Socioeconomic Composition of the Public Schools: A Crucial Consideration in Student Assignment Policy*. Chapel Hill, N.C.: Center for Civil Rights, 2005.

Bourdieu, Pierre. *Distinction: A Social Critique of the Judgement of Taste*. Translated by Richard Nice. Cambridge, Mass.: Harvard University Press, 1984.

Brewer, M., A. Goodman, and A. Leicester. "Household Spending in Britain: What Can It Teach Us about Poverty?" *Institute for Fiscal Studies Report*, 2006. http://www.ifs.org.uk/publications.php?publication_id=3620 (accessed November 9, 2007).

Briggs, Jean L. *Inuit Morality Play: The Emotional Education of a Three-Year-Old*. New Haven: Yale University Press, 1998.

Brown, Patricia Leigh. "Supporting Boys or Girls When the Line Isn't Clear." *New York Times*, December 2, 2006.

Buckingham, David. *After the Death of Childhood*. Cambridge and Malden, Mass.: Polity Press, 2000.

Butcher, Kristin. "Black Immigrants in the United States: A Comparison with Native Blacks and Other Immigrants." *Industrial and Labor Relations Review* 47 (1994): 265–84.

California Budget Project 2005. "Making Ends Meet: How Much Does It Cost to Raise a Family in California?" Sacramento, November 2005. http://www.cbp .org/pdfs/2005/0509mem.pdf (accessed August 16, 2007).

Campbell, Colin. *The Romantic Ethic and the Spirit of Modern Consumerism.* Oxford and New York: Blackwell, 1987.

Caplow, Theodore. "Christmas Gifts and Kin Networks." *American Sociological Review* 47, no. 3 (June 1982): 383–92.

Carnevale, Anthony, and Donna Desrochers. *School Satisfaction: A Statistical Profile of Cities and Suburbs.* Princeton, N.J.: Educational Testing Service, 1999.

Center for a New American Dream. *The New American Dream Poll.* Takoma Park, Md., 2005. http://www.newdream.org/about/poll.php (accessed March 30, 2006).

Cheal, David. *The Gift Economy.* London and New York: Routledge, 1998.

Chee, Bernadine. "Eating Snacks, Biting Pressure: Only Children in Beijing." In *Feeding China's Little Emperors: Food, Children, and Social Change*, edited by Jun Jing, 48–70. Stanford, Calif.: Stanford University Press, 2000.

Chin, Elizabeth. *Purchasing Power: Black Kids and American Consumer Culture.* Minneapolis: University of Minnesota Press, 2001.

Chodorow, Nancy. *The Power of Feelings: Personal Meaning in Psychoanalysis, Gender, and Culture.* New Haven, Conn.: Yale University Press, 1999.

Clegg, Joshua W. "A Phenomenological Investigation of the Experience of Not Belonging." *Journal of Phenomenological Psychology* 37, no. 1 (Spring 2006): 53–83.

Coburn, Gwynne, and Pamela Riley. "Failing Grade: Crisis and Reform in the Oakland Unified School District." Pacific Research Institute for Public Policy, San Francisco, 2000. www.pacificresearch.org.

Cohen, Lizabeth. *A Consumer's Republic: The Politics of Mass Consumption in Postwar America.* New York: Knopf, 2003.

Collins, Patricia Hill. 1994. "Shifting the Center: Race, Class, and Feminist Theorizing about Motherhood." In *Mothering: Ideology, Experience, and Agency*, edited by Evelyn Nakano Glenn, Grace Change, and Linda Rennie Forcey, 45–66. New York: Routledge, 1994.

Collins, Randall. *Interaction Ritual Chains.* Princeton, N.J.: Princeton University Press, 2004.

Condron, Dennis J., and Vincent J. Roscigno. "Disparities Within: Unequal Spending and Achievement in an Urban School District." *Sociology of Education* 76, no. 1 (2003): 18–36.

Cook, Daniel. *The Commodification of Childhood: The Children's Clothing Industry and the Rise of the Child Consumer.* Durham, N.C.: Duke University Press, 2004.

Cooper, Marianne. "Made-to-Order Lives: Upper-Income Families in the New Economy." Presentation at American Sociological Association, Montreal, 2006.

Corsaro, William. *Friendship and Peer Culture in the Early Years.* Norwood, N.J.: Ablex Publishing, 1985.

———. *We're Friends, Right? Inside Kids' Culture.* Washington, D.C.: Joseph Henry Press, 2003.

Corsaro, William, and Donna Eder. "Children's Peer Cultures." *Annual Review of Sociology* 16 (1990): 197–220.

Council for Basic Education. "Academic Atrophy: The Condition of Liberal Arts in America's Schools." Cited in *Educators, Nonprofits, Concerned Public Schools Neglect the Arts.* New York: The Foundation Center, 2004. http://fdncenter.org/pnd/news/story.jhtml?id=73800033 (accessed April 21, 2006).

Croghan, Rosaleen, Christine Griffin, Janeen Hunter, and Ann Phoenix. "Style Failure: Consumption, Identity, and Social Exclusion." *Journal of Youth Studies* 9, no. 4 (2006): 463–78.

Cross, Gary. *Kids' Stuff: Toys and the Changing World of American Childhood.* Cambridge, Mass.: Harvard University Press, 1997.

———. *An All-Consuming Century: Why Commercialism Won in Modern America.* New York: Columbia University Press, 2000.

———. "Valves of Desire: A Historian's Perspective on Parents, Children, and Marketing." *Journal of Consumer Research* 29 (2002): 441–47.

———. *The Cute and the Cool: Wondrous Innocence and Modern American Children's Culture.* Oxford: Oxford University Press, 2004.

Daspin, Eileen, and Ellen Gamerman. "The Million-Dollar Kid." *Wall Street Journal*, March 3, 2007. http://online.wsj.com/public/article-print/SB117288281789725533.html (accessed June 14, 2007).

Derber, Charles. *The Pursuit of Attention: Power and Ego in Everyday Life.* Oxford: Oxford University Press, 2000.

Dewey, John. *Individualism, Old and New.* New York: Minton Balch & Co., 1930.

Dodoo, F. Nii-Amoo. "Assimilation Differences among Africans in America." *Social Forces* 76, no. 2 (December 1997): 527–46.

Doty, Cate, and Rachel Thorner. "18 Shopping Bags and 3 Empty Wallets." *New York Times*, November 27, 2004.

Douthitt, Robin. "An Evaluation of the Relationship between the Percentage-of-Income Standard and Family Expenditures for Children." Discussion paper, Institute for Research on Poverty, University of Wisconsin-Madison, 1990 (cited in Ingrid Rothe, Judith Cassetty, and Elizabeth Boehnen, "Estimates of Family Expenditures for Children: A Review Of The Literature," *Institute for Research on Poverty* [April 2001], http://www.irp.wisc.edu/research/childsup/cspolicy/csprpubs.htm [accessed on November 9, 2007]).

Ed-Data. "Education Data Partnership: California Public School Enrollment in 2004–2005." http://www.ed-data.k12.ca.us (accessed February 20, 2006).

Edin, Kathryn, and Maria Kefalas. *Promises I Can Keep.* Berkeley: University of California Press, 2005.

Edin, Kathryn, and Laura Lein. *Making Ends Meet: How Single Mothers Survive Welfare and Low-Wage Work.* New York: Russell Sage Foundation, 1997.

Ehrenreich, Barbara. *Fear of Falling: The Inner Life of the Middle Class.* New York: Pantheon Books, 1989.

Eliasoph, Nina, and Paul Lichterman. "Culture in Interaction." *American Journal of Sociology* 108, no. 4 (2003): 735–94.

Elhoweris, Hala, Kagendo Mutua, Negmeldin Alsheikh, and Pauline Holloway. "Effect of Children's Ethnicity on Teachers' Referral and Recommendation Decisions in Gifted and Talented Programs." *Remedial and Special Education* 26, no. 1 (2005): 25–32.

Emerson, Robert M., Rachel I. Fretz, and Linda L. Shaw. *Writing Ethnographic Fieldnotes.* Chicago: University of Chicago Press, 1995.

Estes, Eleanor. *The Hundred Dresses.* 1944. Reprint, New York: Scholastic, 1973.

Eugenides, Jeffrey. *Middlesex.* New York: Farrar, Straus and Giroux, 2002.

Ferguson, Ann. *Bad Boys: Public Schools in the Making of Black Masculinity.* Ann Arbor: University of Michigan Press, 2000.

Fine, Gary Alan. "Small Groups and Culture Creation: The Idioculture of Little League Baseball Teams." *American Sociological Review* 44, no. 5 (1979): 733–45.

Fineman, Martha Albertson. *The Autonomy Myth: A Theory of Dependency.* New York: The New Press, 2004.

Fischer, Claude, and Michael Hout. "Differences among Americans in Living Standards across the Twentieth Century." Working paper, Survey Research

Center, University of California, Berkeley, 2005. http://ucdata.berkeley
.edu/rsfcensus/papers/livingstandards.pdf (cited with permission; accessed
November 11, 2007).

Frank, Robert. *Luxury Fever: Why Money Fails to Satisfy in an Era of Excess.* New
York: Free Press, 1999.

Frankenberg, Erica, and Chungmei Lee. *Race in American Public Schools: Rapidly
Resegregating School Districts.* Cambridge, Mass.: The Civil Rights Project,
Harvard University, 2002.

Frankenberg, Erica, Chungmei Lee, and Gary Orfield. *A Multiracial Society with
Segregated Schools: Are We Losing the Dream?* Cambridge, Mass.: The Civil
Rights Project, Harvard University, 2003.

Fuligni, A., V. Tseng, and M. Lam. "Attitudes towards Family Obligations
among American Adolescents with Asian, Latin American, and European
Backgrounds." *Child Development* 70 (1999): 1030–44.

Fuligni, Andrew, and Hirokazu Yoshikawa. "Investments in Children among
Immigrant Families." In *Family Investments in Children's Potential: Resources
and Parenting,* edited by Ariel Kalil and Thomas C. DeLeire, 139–62. Mahwah, N.J.: Lawrence Erlbaum Associates, 2004.

Furnham, A. "Parental Attitudes towards Pocket Money/Allowances for Their
Children." *Journal of Economic Psychology* 22, no. 3 (2001): 397–422.

Furnham, A., and A. Thomas. "Adult Perception of the Economic Socialization
of Children." *Journal of Adolescence* 7 (1984): 217–31.

Giddens, Anthony. *Central Problems in Social Theory: Action, Structure, and Contradiction in Social Analysis.* Berkeley: University of California Press, 1979.

Gillis, John. *A World of Their Own Making: Myth, Ritual, and the Quest for Family Values.* New York: Basic Books, 1996.

Goffman, Erving. *Stigma: Notes on the Management of Spoiled Identity.* New York:
Simon and Schuster, 1963.

———. *Interaction Ritual: Essays on Face-to-Face Behavior.* New York: Anchor
Books, 1967.

Goldberg, Marvin, Gerald Gorn, Laura Peracchio, and Gary Bamossy. "Understanding Materialism among Youth." *Journal Of Consumer Psychology* 13, no.
3 (2003): 278–88.

Gopnik, Adam. *Paris to the Moon.* New York: Random House, 2001.

Gottschalk, Peter, and Sheldon Danziger. "Inequality of Wage Rates, Earnings,
and Family Income in the United States, 1975–2002." *Review of Income and
Wealth* 51 (2005): 231–54.

Graham, Laurel. "Beyond Manipulation: Lillian Gilbreth's Industrial Psychology and the Governmentality of Women Consumers." *The Sociological Quarterly* 38, no. 4 (1997): 539–65.

Gramsci, Antonio. Selections from the Prison Notebooks. Translated by Quintin Hoare and Geoffrey Nowell Smith. New York: International Publishers, 1983.

Grant, William E. "Individualism and the Tensions in American Culture." *American Quarterly* 38, no. 2 (Summer 1986): 311–18.

Greenwhich, Howard, and Christopher Niedt. "Decade of Divide: Working, Wages, and Inequality in the East Bay." East Bay Alliance for a Sustainable Economy, Oakland, 2001. http://www.workingeastbay.org/pdf/decade.pdf.

Gunter, Barrie, and Adrian Furnham. *Children as Consumers*. New York and London: Routledge, 1998.

Hacker, Jacob. "Economic Risk Has Shifted from the Government and Corporations to Workers and Their Families." *Boston Review*, September/October 2005. http://bostonreview.net/BR30.5/hacker.html (accessed November 12, 2007).

Hackstaff, Karla. *Marriage in a Divorce Culture*. Philadelphia: Temple University Press, 1999.

Halgunseth, Linda C., Jean M. Ispa, and Duane Rudy. "Parental Control in Latino Families: An Integrated Review of the Literature." *Child Development* 77, no. 5 (2006): 1282–97.

Harris, Judith. *The Nurture Assumption: Why Children Turn Out the Way They Do*. New York: Simon and Schuster, 1998.

Haveman, Robert, Gary Sandefur, Barbara Wolfe, and Andrea Voyer. "Inequality of Family and Community Characteristics in Relation to Children's Attainments." Working paper, Russell Sage Foundation, 2001. http://www.russellsage.org/programs/proj_reviews/si/revhaveman01.pdf.

Hays, Sharon. "Structure, Agency, and the Sticky Problem of Culture." *Sociological Theory* 12 (1994): 57–72.

———. *The Cultural Contradictions of Motherhood*. New Haven, Conn.: Yale University Press, 1996.

———. *Flat Broke with Children: Women in the Age of Welfare Reform*. New York: Oxford University Press, 2003.

Hendrix, Steve. "Reading, Writing, Retailing: Fundraising for Schools Have Become Fall Fixture." *Washington Post*, Tuesday, October 9, 2007.

Higginson, Joanna. "Competitive Parenting: The Culture of Teen Mothers." *Journal of Marriage and the Family* 60, no. 1 (1998): 135–49.

Hill, Shirley. *Black Intimacies: A Gender Perspective on Families and Relationship.* Walnut Creek, Calif.: AltaMira Press, 2005.

Hochschild, Arlie. *The Managed Heart: The Commercialization of Human Feeling.* Berkeley: University of California Press, 1983.

———. *The Time Bind.* New York: Metropolitan Books, 1997.

———. *The Commercialization of Intimate Life.* Berkeley: University of California Press, 2003.

Hochschild, Arlie, with Anne Machung. *The Second Shift.* New York: Avon Books, 1989.

Holmes, Steven. "A Diverse City Exists Equal but Separate." *New York Times,* May 11, 2001.

Holt, Douglas B. "How Consumers Consume: A Typology of Consumption Practices." *Journal of Consumer Research* 22, no. 1 (1995): 1–16.

———. "Poststructuralist Lifestyle Analysis: Conceptualizing the Social Patterning of Consumption in Postmodernity." *Journal of Consumer Research* 23 (March 1997): 326–50.

———. "Does Cultural Capital Structure American Consumption?" *Journal of Consumer Research* 25 (June 1998): 1–25.

Hout, Michael. "Money and Morale: What Growing Inequality Is Doing to Americans' View of Themselves and Others." Working paper, Survey Research Center, University of California, Berkeley, 2003. http://ucdata .berkeley.edu/rsfcensus/papers/Morale_Working_Paper.pdf.

Hout, Michael, and Caroline Hanley. "Working Hours and Inequality, 1968–2001: A Family Perspective on Recent Controversies." Working paper, Survey Research Center, University of California, Berkeley, 2003. http:// www.russellsage.org/publications/workingpapers/workinghrsineq/ document(accessed November 4, 2007).

Hurtado, Aida, Patricia Gurin, and Timothy Peng. "Social Identities—A Framework for Studying the Adaptations of Immigrants and Ethnics: The Adaptations of Mexicans in the United States." *Social Problems* 41, no. 1, Special Issue on Immigration, Race, and Ethnicity in America (1994): 129–51.

Illouz, Eva. *Cold Intimacies: The Making of Emotional Capitalism.* Malden, Mass.: Polity Press, 2007.

James, Allison, and Alan Prout. "Strategies and Structures: A New Perspective on Children's Experiences of Family Life." In *Children in Families: Research and Policy,* edited by Julia Brannen and Margaret O'Brien, 41–52. London and Washington, D.C.: Falmer Press.

Jamison, David J. "Idols of the Tribe: Brand Veneration and Group Identity among Pre-Adolescent Consumers." Working paper, Department of Marketing, University of Florida, Gainesville, 1996.

Jennings, Jeremy. "Citizenship, Republicanism, and Multiculturalism in Contemporary France." *British Journal of Political Science* 30 (2000): 575–98.

John, Deborah Roedder. "Consumer Socialization of Children: A Retrospective Look at Twenty-five Years of Research." *Journal of Consumer Research* 26, no. 3 (1999): 183–213.

Kaplan, Elaine Bell. "Using Food as a Metaphor for Care: Middle-School Kids Talk about Family, School, and Class Relationships." *Journal of Contemporary Ethnography* 29, no. 4 (August 2000): 474–509.

Kasser, Tim. "Frugality, Generosity, and Materialism in Children and Adolescents." In *What Do Children Need to Flourish? Conceptualizing and Measuring Indicators of Positive Development*, edited by K. A. Moore and L. H. Lippman, 357–74. New York: Springer Science, 2005.

Katriel, Tamar. "Bexibudim! Ritualized Sharing among Israeli Children." *Language in Society* 16 (1987): 305–20.

Katz, Alex. "D.A. Takes on Truant's Parents." *Oakland Tribune*, March 26, 2004.

Katz, Cindi. "Vagabond Capitalism and the Necessity of Social Reproduction." *Antipode* 33, no. 4 (2001): 709–28.

Katz, Jack. *How Emotions Work*. Chicago: University of Chicago Press, 1999.

Kelley, Tina. "Cake, But No Presents, Please." *New York Times*, July 27, 2007.

Kempson, Elaine, Alex Bryson, and Karen Rowlingson. *Hard Times? How Poor Families Make Ends Meet*. London: Policy Studies Institute, 1994.

Kline, Stephen. *Out of the Garden: Toys, TV, and Children's Culture in the Age of Marketing*. New York: Verso, 1993.

Knight, Heather. "Agonizing over S.F. School Options: 3 Families' Paths Diverge—Public, Private, Parochial." *San Francisco Chronicle*, August 29, 2005.

Kochuyt, Thierry. "Giving Away One's Poverty: On the Consumption of Scarce Resources within the Family." *The Sociological Review* 52, no. 2 (2004): 139–61.

Kotlowitz, Alex. *There Are No Children Here*. New York: Doubleday, 1991.

Kozol, Jonathan. *Savage Inequalities: Children in America's Schools*. New York: Crown, 1991.

Kwak, K., and J. W. Berry. "Generational Differences in Acculturation among Asian Families in Canada: A Comparison of Vietnamese, Korean, and East-Indian Groups." *International Journal of Psychology* 36 (2001): 152–62.

Kwak, Kyunghwa. "Adolescents and Their Parents: A Review of Intergenerational Family Relations for Immigrant and Non-Immigrant Families." *Human Development* 46 (2003): 115–36.

Lacy, Karen. *Blue-Chip Black: Race, Class, and Status in the New Black Middle Class.* Berkeley: University of California Press, 2007.

Lamont, Michele. *The Dignity of Working Men.* New York and Cambridge, Mass.: Russell Sage Foundation and Harvard University Press, 2000.

Lamont, Michele, and Annette Lareau. "Cultural Capital: Allusions, Gaps, and Glissandos in Recent Theoretical Developments." *Sociological Theory* 6, no. 2 (Autumn 1988): 153–68.

Lareau, Annette. *Unequal Childhoods: Class, Race, and Family Life.* Berkeley: University of California Press, 2003.

Lazear, Edward P., and Robert T Michael. *Allocation of Income within the Household.* Chicago: University of Chicago Press, 1988.

Lazear, Edward P., and Angie Rodgers. "Income Inequality in the District of Columbia Is Wider Than in Any Major U.S. City." DC Fiscal Policy Institute, July 23, 2004.

Levy, M. F. "Deferred Gratification and Social Class." *Journal of Social Psychology* 100 (1976): 123–35.

Lewis, Sinclair. *Babbitt.* New York: Harcourt Brace Jovanovich, 1922.

Lichter, Daniel. "Poverty and Inequality among Children." *Annual Review of Sociology* 23 (1997): 121–45.

Lichter, Daniel, and D. J. Eggebeen. "Rich Kids, Poor Kids: Changing Income Inequality among American Children." *Social Forces* 71 (1993): 761–80.

Linn, Susan. *Consuming Kids: The Hostile Takeover of Childhood.* New York and London: The New Press, 2004.

Lino, Mark. "USDA's Expenditures on Children by Families Project: Uses and Changes over Time." *Family Economics and Nutrition Review* 13, no. 1 (Winter 2001): 81–86.

Loury, Glenn. "The Poverty of Reason." *Boston Review* 19, no. 1 (February/March 1994). http://bostonreview.net/BR19.1/loury.html (accessed June 23, 2008).

MacLeod, Jay. *Ain't No Makin' It.* Boulder, Colo.: Westview, 1987.

Maffesoli, Michel. *The Time of the Tribes: The Decline of Individualism in Mass Society.* London: Sage, 1995.

Maker, C. J. "Identification of Gifted Minority Students: A National Problem, Needed Change, and a Promising Solution." *Gifted Child Quarterly* 40 (1996): 42–50.

Martens, Lydia. "Learning to Consume—Consuming to Learn: Children at the Interface between Consumption and Education." *British Journal of Sociology of Education* 26, no. 3 (2005): 343–57.

Martens, Lydia, Dale Southerton, and Sue Scott. "Bringing Children (and Parents) into the Sociology of Consumption: Towards a Theoretical and Empirical Agenda." *Journal of Consumer Culture* 4 (2004): 155–82.

Martineau, Pierre. "Social Classes and Spending Behavior." In *Classics in Consumer Behavior*, edited by L. E. Boone, 303–17. Tulsa, Okla.: PPC Books, 1977.

Massachusetts Mutual Life Insurance Company. *Family Life Survey*. Springfield, Mass., 1994. Polling the Nations. www.poll.ors.pub.com (accessed February 20, 2006).

———. *Family Life Survey*. Springfield, Mass., 1995. Polling the Nations. www.poll.ors.pub.com (accessed November 7, 2007).

Mauldin, Teresa, Yoko Mimura, and Mark Lino. "Parental Expenditures on Children's Education." *Journal of Family and Economic Issues* 22, no. 3 (2001): 221–41.

Mauss, Marcel. *The Gift: Forms and Functions of Exchange in Archaic Societies*. Translated by Ian Cunnison. New York: Norton, 1967.

Mayer, Susan. *What Money Can't Buy: Family Income and Children's Life Chances*. Cambridge, Mass.: Harvard University Press, 1997.

———. "How Did the Increase in Economic Inequality Affect Educational Attainment?" *American Journal of Sociology* 107, no. 1 (2001): 1–32.

McCracken, Grant. *Culture and Consumption: New Approaches to the Symbolic Character of Consumer Goods and Services*. Bloomington: Indiana University Press, 1988.

McDermott, Michael. "Kid's Market Is a Small World with Franchise Opportunities." *The Franchise Handbook*, Summer 2006. http://www.franchise.com/articles/Kid'sMarket_Is_a_Small_World_with_Franchise_Opportunities_149.asp (accessed June 23, 2008).

McLanahan, Sara. "Diverging Destinies: How Children Fare under the Second Demographic Transition." *Demography* 41, no. 4 (2004): 607–27.

McNeal, James. *On Becoming a Consumer: Development of Consumer Behavior Patterns in Childhood*. Burlington, Mass.: Butterworth-Heinemann, 2007.

Meredith, W. H, D. A. Abbott, R. Tsai, Z. F. Ming. "Healthy Family Functioning in Chinese Cultures: An Exploratory Study Using the Circumflex Model." *International Journal of Sociology of the Family* 24 (1994): 147–57.

Merton, Robert. *Social Theory and Social Structure*. 1949. Reprint, New York: Free Press, 1968.

Middleton, Sue, Karl Ashworth, and Robert Walker. *Family Fortunes: Pressures on Parents and Children in the 1990s.* London: Child Poverty Action Group, 1994.

Miller, Daniel. *Capitalism: An Ethnographic Approach.* Oxford: Berg, 1997.

———. *A Theory of Shopping.* Ithaca, N.Y.: Cornell University Press, 1998.

Milner, Murray, Jr. *Freaks, Geeks, and Cool Kids: American Teenagers, Schools, and the Culture of Consumption.* New York: Routledge, 2004.

Mintz, Steven. *Huck's Raft: A History of American Childhood.* Cambridge, Mass.: Harvard University Press, Belknap Press, 2004.

Mischel, W., Y. Shoda, and M. L. Rodriguez. "Delay of Gratification in Children." *Science* 244, no. 26 (1989): 933–37.

Mortimer, Jeylan T, Katherine Dennehy, Chaimun Lee, and Michael D. Finch. "Economic Socialization in the American Family: The Prevalence, Distribution, and Consequences of Allowance Arrangements." *Family Relations* 43, no. 1 (1994): 23–30.

Murgai, Neena. "Oakland Health Profile 2004." Alameda County Public Health Department, Oakland, 2005. http://www.acphd.org.

Neckerman, Katherine, Prudence Carter, and Jennifer Lee. "Segmented Assimilation and Minority Cultures of Mobility." *Ethnic and Racial Studies* 22, no. 6 (November 1999): 945–65.

Nevius, C. W. "Affluent Parents Cover for State School Cuts: Districts in Lower-Income Areas Not as Lucky." *San Francisco Chronicle,* March 19, 2004.

Newacheck, Paul W., and A. E. Benjamin. "Intergenerational Equity and Public Spending." *Health Affairs* 23, no. 5 (2004): 142–47.

New York Times Magazine, "Alan Wilzig," August 17, 1997.

Nguyen, N., and H. Williams. "Transition from East to West: Vietnamese Adolescents and Their Parents." *Journal of the American Academy of Child and Adolescent Psychiatry* 28 (1989): 505–15.

Nightingale, Carl. *On The Edge: A History of Poor Black Children and Their American Dreams.* New York: Basic Books, 1993.

Noguera, Pedro. "Racial Isolation, Poverty, and the Limits of Local Control in Oakland." *Teachers College Record* 106, no. 11 (2004): 2146–70.

Orellana, Marjorie Faulstich. "The Work Kids Do: Mexican and Central American Immigrant Children's Contributions to Households and Schools in California." *Harvard Educational Review* 71, no. 3 (2001): 366–89.

Orfield, Gary, and Chungmei Lee. *Why Segregation Matters: Poverty and Educational Inequality.* Cambridge, Mass.: The Civil Rights Project, Harvard University, 2005. http://www.civilrightsproject.harvard.edu/research/deseg/Why_Segreg_Matters.pdf (accessed February 15, 2007).

Ortner, Sherry. "Theory in Anthropology since the Sixties." *Comparative Studies in Society and History* 26 (1984): 126–66.

———. *High Religion: A Cultural and Political History of Sherpa Buddhism.* Princeton, N.J.: Princeton University Press, 1989.

———. *Making Gender: The Politics and Erotics of Culture.* Boston: Beacon Press, 1996.

———. *New Jersey Dreaming: Capital, Culture, and the Class of '58.* Durham, N.C., and London: Duke University Press, 2003.

Orwell, George. *The Collected Essays, Journalism, and Letters.* Vol. 4, *In Front of Your Nose, 1946–1950.* Edited by Sonia Orwell and Ian Argus. Boston: Nonpareil Books, David R. Godine, 2000.

Osterman, Karen. "Students' Need for Belonging in the School Community." *Review of Educational Research* 70, no. 3 (2000): 323–67.

Page, Clarence. "Oprah's Truth Does Not Hurt." *Chicago Tribune*, January 8, 2007. www.realclearpolitics.com (accessed September 10, 2007).

Palan, Kay, and Robert E. Wilkes. "Adolescent-Parent Interaction in Family Decision Making." *Journal of Consumer Research* 24 (September 1997): 159–69.

"Panorama: The World's Longest Running Investigative TV Show: Your Comments." http://news.bbc.co.uk/2/hi/programmes/panorama/4027003.stm (accessed September 10, 2007).

Pascoe, C. J. *Dude, You're a Fag: Masculinity and Sexuality in High School.* Berkeley: University of California Press, 2007.

Pati, Susmita, Ron Keren, Evaline A. Alessandrini, and Donald F. Schwartz. "Generational Differences in U.S. Public Spending, 1980–2000." *Health Affairs* S23, no. 5 (2004): 131–42.

Pattillo-McCoy, Mary. *Black Picket Fences: Privilege and Peril among the Black Middle Class.* Chicago: University of Chicago Press, 1999.

Paul, Pamela. *Parenting, Inc.* New York: Times Books, 2008.

Philips, Meredith, and Tiffani Chin, "School Inequality: What Do We Know?" Working paper, Russell Sage Foundation, 2003. http://www.russellsage.org/programs/main/inequality/050516.010743/ (accessed November 12, 2007).

Phinney, J. S., A. Ong, and T. Madden. "Cultural Values and Intergenerational Value Discrepancies in Immigrant and Non-immigrant Families." *Child Development* 71 (2000): 528–39.

Pinderhughes, Ellen, Kenneth Dodge, John Bates, Gregory Pettit, and Arnaldo Zelli. "Discipline Responses: Influences of Parents' Socioeconomic Status, Ethnicity, Beliefs about Parenting, Stress, and Cognitive-Emotional Processes." *Journal of Family Psychology* 14 (2000): 380–400.

Plassmann, Vandana, and Marjorie Norton. "Child-Adult Expenditure Allocation by Ethnicity." *Family and Consumer Sciences Research Journal* 33, no. 1 (2004): 475–97.

Portes, Alejandro, and Julia Sensenbrenner. "Embeddedness and Immigration: Notes on the Social Determinants of Economic Action." *American Journal of Sociology* 98, no. 6 (1993): 1320–50.

Portes, Alejandro, and Min Zhou. "The New Second Generation: Segmented Assimilation and Its Variants." *Annals of the American Political and Social Sciences* 530 (1993): 74–96.

Power, Elaine. "Freedom and Belonging through Consumption: The Disciplining of Desire in Single Mothers on Welfare." Paper presented to the British Sociological Association Annual Conference, University of York, 2003.

Preston, Julia. "Making a Life in the U.S., But Feeling Mexico's Tug." *New York Times*, December 19, 2006.

Pugh, Allison. "From Compensation to Childhood Wonder: Why Parents Buy." Working Paper No. 39, Center for Working Families, University of California, Berkeley, 2002.

———. "Windfall Childrearing." *Journal of Consumer Culture* 4, no. 2 (July 2004): 229–49.

———. "Selling Compromise: Toys, Motherhood, and the Cultural Deal." *Gender & Society* 19, no. 6 (2005): 729–49.

———. "The Social Context of Childrearing: Public Spending in Oakland 1970–2000." Working paper, Institute for the Study of Social Change, University of California, Berkeley, 2005.

———. "The Economy of Dignity: Children's Culture and Consumer Desires." Under review.

Putnam, Robert D. *Bowling Alone: The Collapse and Revival of American Community*. New York: Simon & Schuster, 2001.

Raeff, C. "Individuals In Relationships: Cultural Values, Children's Social Interactions, and the Development of an American Individualistic Self." *Developmental Review* 17 (1997): 205–38.

Rideout, Victoria, Donald Roberts, and Ulla Foehr. "Generation M: Media in the Lives of 8–18 Year-Olds." http://www.kff.org/entmedia/entmedia030905 pkg.cfm (accessed November 9, 2007).

Riesman, David, with Nathan Glazer and Reuel Denney. *The Lonely Crowd: A Study of the Changing American Character*. New Haven, Conn.: Yale University Press, 1950.

Ritson, Mark, and Richard Elliott. "The Social Uses of Advertising: An Ethnographic Study of Adolescent Advertising Audiences." *Journal of Consumer Research* 26 (December 1999): 260–77.

Ritzer, George. *Enchanting a Disenchanted World: Revolutionizing the Means of Consumption.* Thousand Oaks, Calif.: Pine Forge Press, 1999.

Robinson, Eugene. "Obama: Moving Beyond Either-Or." *Seattle Times,* March 13, 2007.

Ruddick, Sara. "Care as Labor and Relationship." In *Norms and Values: Essays in Honor of Virginia Held,* edited by Joram G. Haber and Mark S. Halfon, 3–25. Oxford: Rowman and Littlefield, 1998.

Rumbaut, Ruben G. "The Crucible Within: Ethnic Identity, Self-Esteem, and Segmented Assimilation among Children of Immigrants." *International Migration Review* 28, no. 4 (1994): 748–94.

Sahlins, Marshall. *Historical Metaphors and Mythical Realities.* Ann Arbor: University of Michigan Press, 1981.

Sampson, Robert, Jeffrey Morenoff, and Thomas Gannon-Rowley. "Assessing 'Neighborhood Effects': Social Processes and New Directions in Research." *Annual Review of Sociology* 28 (2002): 443–78.

San Francisco Chronicle, "Reclaiming Childhood," editorial, March 30, 2003.

Saporito, Salvatore. "Private Choices, Public Consequences: Magnet School Choice and Segregation by Race and Poverty." *Social Problems* 50, no. 2 (2003): 181–203.

Saporito, Salvatore, William Yancey, and Vincent Louis. "Quality, Race, and the Urban Market Place Reconsidered." *Urban Affairs Review* 37 (2001): 267–76.

Scheff, Thomas. "Shame in Self and Society," *Symbolic Interaction* 26, no. 2 (2003): 239–62.

Schneider, L., and S. Lysgaard. "The Deferred Gratification Pattern: A Preliminary Study." *American Sociological Review* 18 (1953): 142–49.

Schneider, M., P. Teske, and M. Marschall. *Choosing Schools: Consumer Choice and the Quality of American Schools.* Princeton, N.J.: Princeton University Press, 2000.

Schor, Juliet. *The Overworked American.* New York: Basic Books, 1992.

———. *The Overspent American: Upscaling, Downshifting, and the New Consumer.* New York: Basic Books, 1998.

———. *Born to Buy: The Commercialized Child and the New Consumer Culture.* New York: Scribner, 2004.

Schudson, Michael. *Advertising: The Uneasy Persuasion.* New York: Basic Books, 1984.

Self, Robert O. *American Babylon: Race and the Struggle for Postwar Oakland.* Princeton, N.J.: Princeton University Press, 2003.

Seiter, Ellen. *Sold Separately: Children and Parents in Consumer Culture.* New Brunswick, N.J.: Rutgers University Press, 1993.

Sen, Amartya. "The Possibility of Social Choice." *The American Economic Review* 89, no. 3 (1999): 349–78.

Sennett, Richard. *Respect in a World of Inequality.* New York: W. W. Norton, 2003.

Sennett, Richard, and Jonathan Cobb. *The Hidden Injuries of Class.* New York: Vintage Books, 1973.

Sewell, William. "A Theory of Structure—Duality, Agency, and Transformation." *American Journal of Sociology* 98, no. 1 (July 1992): 1–29.

Shaw-Taylor, Yoku, and Steven Tuch, eds. *The Other African-Americans: Contemporary African and Caribbean Immigrants to the United States.* Lanham, Md.: Rowman and Littlefield, 2007.

Slater, Don. *Consumer Culture and Modernity.* Cambridge and Malden, Mass.: Polity Press, 1997.

Smelser, Neil J. "The Rational and the Ambivalent in the Social Sciences: 1997 Presidential Address." *American Sociological Review* 63, no. 1 (February 1998): 1–16.

Smith, Adam. *Theory of Moral Sentiments.* 1759. Reprint, Amherst, N.Y.: Prometheus Books, 2000.

———. *The Wealth of Nations.* 1776. Reprint, New York: Bantam Dell, 2003.

Speier, Hans. "Honor and Social Structure." *Social Research* 2 (1935): 74–97.

Stearns, Peter. *American Cool: Constructing a 20th Century Emotional Style.* New York: New York University Press, 1994.

Steedman, Carolyn Kay. *Landscape for a Good Woman: A Story of Two Lives.* New Brunswick, N.J.: Rutgers University Press, 1986.

Stein, Arlene. *Shameless: Sexual Dissidence in American Culture.* New York: New York University Press, 2006.

Swidler, Ann. "Culture in Action: Symbols and Strategies." *American Sociological Review* 51 (April 1986): 273–86.

———. *Talk of Love.* Chicago: University of Chicago Press, 2001.

Tajfel, Henri. *Differentiation between Social Groups: Studies in the Social Psychology of Intergroup Relations.* European Monographs in Social Psychology. London: Academic Press, 1978.

———. *Human Groups and Social Categories: Studies in Social Psychology.* London: Cambridge University Press, 1981.

Teske, P., and Mark Schneider. "What Research Can Tell Policymakers about School Choice." *Journal of Policy Analysis and Management* 20, no. 4 (Autumn 2001): 609–31.

Thompson, Craig. "Caring Consumers: Gendered Consumption Meanings and the Juggling Lifestyle." *Journal of Consumer Research* 22, no. 4 (1996): 388–407.

Thorne, Barrie. *Gender Play.* New Brunswick, N.J.: Rutgers University Press, 1993.

———. "Children's Experiences of Race and Ethnicity in California Public Schools." Presentation at the conference *Diversities in the Classroom: New Findings to Foster Children's Development*, Berkeley, Calif., November 2, 2002.

———. "The Crisis of Care." In *Work-Family Challenges for Low-Income Parents and Their Children*, edited by Nan Crouter and Alan Booth, 165–78. Hillsdale, N.J.: Lawrence Erlbaum Publishers, 2004.

———. "'The Chinese Girls' and 'The Pokémon Kids': Children Negotiating Differences in Urban California." Paper presented at the conference *Global Comings of Age: Youth and the Crisis of Reproduction*, School for American Research, Santa Fe, N.Mex., 2005.

———. "Unpacking School Lunchtime: Structure, Practice, and the Negotiation of Difference." In *Developmental Pathways through Middle Childhood: Rethinking Contexts and Diversity as Resources*, edited by Catherine Cooper, Cynthia Garcia Coll, W. Todd Bartko, Helen M. Davis, and Celina Chatman, 63–88. Hillsdale, N.J.: Lawrence Erlbaum Associates, 2005.

Time/CNN. Video Games. Polling the Nations. http://poll.orspub.com/index .php (accessed November 10, 2007).

Tobin, Joseph J., David Wu, and Dana Davidson. *Preschool in Three Cultures: Japan, China, and the United States.* New Haven, Conn.: Yale University Press, 1991.

Tocqueville, Alexis de. *Democracy in America.* Translated by George Lawrence and edited by J. P. Mayer. 1848. Reprint, Garden City, N.Y.: Anchor Books, 1969.

Tucker, Jill. "Our Public Schools: Separate and Unequal." *Oakland Tribune*, June 15, 2003.

Tucker, Jill, and Robert Gammon. "Separate and Unequal: Fundraisers Give Schools an Edge." *Oakland Tribune*, June 18, 2003. http://www.oaklandtri bune.com (accessed April 20, 2004).

U.S. Department of Health and Human Services. "Trends in the Well-Being of Children and Youth." http://aspe.hhs.gov/HSP/03trends/ (accessed February 23, 2008).

Uttal, Lynet. "Custodial Care, Surrogate Care, and Coordinated Care: Employed Mothers and the Meaning of Childcare." *Gender and Society* 10, no. 3 (1996): 291–311.

Van Ausdale, Debra, and Joe R. Feagin. *The First R: How Children Learn Race and Racism.* Lanham, Md.: Rowman and Littlefield, 2001.

Vandewater, E. A., D. S. Bickham, and J. H. Lee. "Time Well Spent? Relating Television Use to Children's Free Time Activities." *Pediatrics* 117 (2006): 181–90.

Veblen, Thorstein. *The Theory of the Leisure Class.* 1899. Reprint, New York: Dover Publications, 1994.

Vermont Department of Health. *Vermont Youth Risk Behavior Survey.* Burlington, Vt., 1999. Polling the Nations. www.poll.ors.pub.com (accessed February 20, 2006).

Waerdahl, Randi. "Learning by Consuming: Consumer Culture as a Condition for Socialization and Everyday Life at the Age of 12." Diss., Department of Sociology and Human Geography, University of Oslo, 2003.

Warren, Elizabeth. "The Growing Threat to Middle-Class Families." Lecture, National Association of Consumer Bankruptcy Attorneys, 2003. http://www.nacba.org/files/new_in_debate/GrowingThreatMiddleClass Families.pdf (accessed November 4, 2007).

Warren, Elizabeth, and Amelia Warren Tyagi. *The Two-Income Trap.* New York: Basic Books, 2003.

White, E. B. "The Morning of the Day They Did It." In *The Second Tree from the Corner.* New York: Harper and Row, 1978.

Williams, Christine. *Inside Toyland: Working, Shopping, and Social Inequality.* Berkeley: University of California Press, 2005.

Winfrey, John. *Social Issues: The Ethics and Economics of Taxes and Public Programs.* New York: Oxford University Press, 1998.

Winnicott, D. W. *Playing and Reality.* London and New York: Tavistock Publications, 1971.

Wolf, Diane. *Feminist Dilemmas in Fieldwork.* Boulder, Colo.: Westview Press, 1996.

Wood, M. "Socio-Economic Status, Delay of Gratification, and Impulse Buying." *Journal of Economic Psychology* 19 (1998): 295–320.

Wuthnow, Robert. "Pious Materialism: How Americans View Faith and Money." *The Christian Century*, March 3, 1992, 239–42.

Zelizer, Viviana. *Pricing the Priceless Child.* New York: Basic Books, 1985.

————. *The Purchase of Intimacy.* Princeton, N.J.: Princeton University Press, 2004.

————. "Culture and Consumption." In *The Handbook of Economic Sociology,* edited by N. Smelser and R. Swedberg, 331–54. Princeton, N.J.: Princeton University Press; New York: Russell Sage Foundation, 2005.

Zhou, Min, and Carl L. Bankston III. "Social Capital and the Adaptation of the Second Generation: The Case of Vietnamese Youth in New Orleans." *International Migration Review* 28, no. 4 (1994): 821–45.

Zukin, Sharon. *Landscapes of Power: From Detroit to Disney World.* Berkeley: University of California Press, 1991.

————. *Point of Purchase: How Shopping Changed American Culture.* New York: Routledge, 2004.

INDEX

Text:	10/15 Janson
Display:	Janson
Compositor:	BookComp, Inc.
Indexer:	Twin Oaks Indexing
Printer & Binder:	Sheridan